THE
International Money Game

THE
International Money Game

Robert Z. Aliber

SECOND AND EXPANDED EDITION

Basic Books, Inc., Publishers

NEW YORK

Library of Congress Cataloging in Publication Data

Aliber, Robert Z.
  The international money game.

  Includes index.
  1. International finance. I. Title.
HG3881.A44   1976   332.4'5   75-36768
ISBN 0-465-03371-7
ISBN 0-465-03372-5 pbk.

CONTENTS

v

Contents

PART III

Epilogue

PREFACE

International finance is frequently viewed as esoteric, understood only by a few skilled arbitragers and central bankers. In part, the mystery results from the specialized use of everyday language—"gliding parities" and "sliding bands," "support limits" and "counterspeculation," "SDRs" and "Eurodollars," "cross-rates" and "intervention limits," "tax havens" and "transfer pricing." The words are common enough, the meanings elusive. The nonspecialist is deterred from approaching the issues because of the effort which learning the special language requires.

Even if the language problem is surmounted, a second problem appears—recognized experts in the field are in open disagreement. Some experts favor floating exchange rates; others favor pegged rates. Some propose an increase in the monetary gold price; others propose that gold be eliminated as an international money. Some want to abandon national monies in favor of a worldwide currency; others only want to eliminate the use of the dollar and of gold as international monies. The nonspecialist is bewildered, for in few other areas is the disagreement so extensive.

One objective of this book is to break the language barrier. Technical issues are presented in a straightforward manner with minimal use of specialized terms. Concepts are clarified by use of common metaphor. A second objective is to explain why the experts differ.

The first edition of this book was completed as the pegged-rate system was about to break down. Since then, the international economy has experienced a peacetime inflation that has no good historical parallel; the move to floating exchange rates was thus inevitable. Then came the shock of the quadrupling of oil price, which was followed by a worldwide recession more severe than any since World War II. At times the analogies with certain aspects of the period before the Great Depression seemed uncomfortably close.

The financial world appeared increasingly unstable. Countries worried about financing their oil imports. A number of big banks suffered massive losses from speculation in the foreign exchange market; a few banks failed.

The financial crises underline the several themes of this book. Changes in exchange rates are inevitable because national economic policies diverge and national economic interests conflict. The successive devaluations of the dollar are part of the transition of the international monetary system from its U.S.-centered, dollar-oriented phase. The efforts of other industrialized countries to devise rules to limit the external impact of U.S. economic policies and to lessen the dominant U.S. international role will intensify, for monetary reform is a political process accommodating economic relationships. As long as national interests diverge, crises are predictable. Only their timing and form are uncertain.

Two individuals have been important in the writing of this book. Martin Kessler provided the necessary condition, for he suggested the concept—that serious economic concepts could be discussed in a relatively light manner. And Fran Miller provided the sufficient condition; she cheerfully typed the N drafts of the first edition. Without her encouraging feedback, the project would have stalled with the $N - (N - 1)$ draft. Patti Pazera continued the practice of converting illegible script into type.

PART I

The International Money System: Politics and Economics

The Name of the Game Is Money

International finance is a game with two sets of players: the politicians and bureaucrats in national governments, and the presidents and treasurers of giant, large, medium, and small firms. The government officials want to win elections and secure a firm niche in the history of their countries. The corporate presidents and treasurers want to profit—or at least avoid losses—from changes in exchange rates that are inevitable in a world with more than 100 national currencies.

Opportunities for profit occur because national monetary and fiscal policies are inconsistent with each other, making changes in national currency values inevitable. Under the pegged-rate system, the authorities in different countries disagreed over which country should take the initiative in changing the national currency price, so that the necessary change was frequently long delayed. From 1970 on, for example, it was obvious that the yen was too cheap in terms of the dollar; either the Japanese would have to reduce the yen price of the dollar, or the Americans would have to raise the dollar price of the yen. As it turned out, the U.S. government took the initiative and forced a revaluation of the yen, so that Japanese autos would cost more in the United States—and fewer U.S. workers in autos, steel, and textiles would lose their jobs because of Japanese imports. Three times in ten years (in 1961, 1969, and 1971) Germany raised the price of the mark in terms of the dollar to reduce its balance-of-payments surplus, at the same time reducing the likelihood that substantial numbers of U.S. troops would be withdrawn from Europe to reduce the U.S. payments deficit. In the 1960s, French President Charles de Gaulle bought $2 billion worth of gold from the U.S. Treasury to force a U.S. initiative to double the gold price, a move that would have benefited his domestic supporters, restored the prestige of France as a country with monetary stability, and demonstrated that the dollar was a weak currency. The change in the dollar price of gold that he anticipated was delayed—but one step in that direction occurred in 1971 (under Georges Pompidou, his successor), when the gold price was raised to $38, a second step in 1973 when the price was increased to $42. Private parties pushed the price to nearly $200 in 1974, a price that could have been viable only with central bank support.

From March 1973 the major industrial countries abandoned the system of pegged exchange rates that they had relied on for most of the twentieth century; thereafter, the foreign exchange value of their currencies would be determined by market forces. Over the next two years, the price of the dollar in terms of the European currencies varied by nearly 20 percent every six months.

Business fortunes are made on the ability to forecast such changes in the values of national currencies, while political futures become frayed as a result of these changes. Under a pegged-rate system, the direction of the change (and, frequently, the approximate amount) are predictable. What is less readily predictable is the precise date of the change. At one time, periodic cycles could be discerned. The pound sterling was devalued in 1913, 1931, 1949, and 1967, an evident eighteen-year cycle. Similarly, the French franc has generally been devalued every ten years—in 1919, 1939, 1949, 1959, and 1969 (not, however, in 1929).

Devaluations and revaluations came much more frequently in the late 1960s and early 1970s than in previous decades. Exchange rate crises occurred in November 1967 (sterling),

May 1968 (French franc), September-October 1969 (German mark), June 1970 (Canadian dollar), May 1971 (German mark, Dutch guilder, and Swiss franc), August 1971 (U.S. dollar, Japanese yen, and all major European currencies), and June 1972 (sterling and Italian lira). The increased frequency of such changes in exchange rates was closely associated with inflationary financial policies, and the inability of countries to agree on an acceptable rate of inflation.

The relations among governments and the positions of political leaders in their respective countries are affected by the various measures employed to reduce payments imbalances. During the 1960s Germany had large payments surpluses while the United States had large deficits. U.S. pressure on the German government to take measures to offset the foreign exchange costs of U.S. troops in Germany forced the downfall of Ludwig Erhard as German prime minister. And the 10 percent import surcharge adopted by the U.S. government in August 1971, followed by the 17 percent revaluation of the yen, advanced the date of Prime Minister Sato's resignation in Japan.

British governments—especially Labor governments—have resisted devaluing sterling because of the perceived costs in domestic support. The inevitable devaluation of sterling that should have occurred in 1964 was delayed until November 1967. In 1974, the British continued to support sterling rather than allow it to depreciate; eventually, as their ability to maintain the value of sterling diminished, they permitted it to depreciate in the exchange market.

Similarly, the U.S. government refused for years to recognize that a change in the dollar price of gold was necessary. When the change was finally made, it was done reluctantly, and the government continued to urge that gold be phased out of the monetary system. Such a posture was necessary; otherwise, investors would have speculated on the increase in the gold price.

Finance ministers everywhere are continually concerned with

changes in the price of their currencies relative to the dollar; they are also concerned with the price relationship between the dollar and gold. This is what being a finance minister is all about.

Whether the dollar price of gold should be raised or lowered is much more than a U.S. problem. All countries with large gold holdings are involved, for the change redistributes wealth among countries. Similarly, whether the yen price of the dollar should be raised is a question that involves not only the United States and Japan but also the many other countries which are customers of or competitors with Japan. Volkswagen's profits vary directly with the foreign exchange value of the yen, even though few Volkswagens are sold in Japan.

Changes in exchange rates redistribute payments surpluses and deficits and, therefore, jobs and business profits. The immediate consequence of revaluing the yen was to lower profits and wages (or at least the increase of wages) in Japanese export industries and to raise profits and permit a more rapid increase in wages in competitive U.S. industries. In 1974, Volkswagen reported a loss of $350 million, partly because the appreciation of the mark meant a sharp rise in the dollar prices of Volkswagens, which in turn reduced VW's share of the U.S. market for imported cars from 70 percent to 25 percent.

Exporting national problems is a classic form of international behavior. Foreign votes do not count in national elections. The political costs of domestic measures that might solve an unemployment problem, an inflation problem, or a "depressed industry" problem are usually higher than the political costs of exporting the problem. Nevertheless, no country can export its problems unless some other countries import them. In the Great Depression of the 1930s, nations sought to export their unemployment by "beggar thy neighbor" policies, such as raising import tariffs and devaluing their currencies. Not surprisingly, few countries were eager or willing to import unemployment.

The Politics and Technology of Money

The politics of international money is decentralized. Each of the 100 national producers of money has its own interests and objectives. Each central bank wants to control the rate at which its money supply grows so as to achieve its own (national) objectives. Because the objectives and economic structures of countries differ, so do their preferred rates of monetary growth.

International financial institutions such as the International Monetary Fund in Washington and the Bank for International Settlements in Basel, Switzerland, provide a coordinating mechanism for national monetary policies. The forms of international financial coordination vary: central banks borrow from each other when their holdings of foreign currencies decline, ministers of finance meet annually at the International Monetary Fund, and some steps have been taken to develop paper substitutes for gold. Such coordination, while useful as a counter to the decentralized decisions of national governments, is not an effective substitute for centralized decision making.

The international system must somehow accommodate the divergent national policies. The "rules of the game" seek to ensure that the conflicts among national authorities occur within an established framework. These rules are a set of commitments that countries have accepted. When the rules seem too confining, countries sometimes ignore the rules unilaterally and search for the legal justification later, as did President Nixon when he suspended the U.S. Treasury's gold transactions in August 1971.

Firms and individuals play their own game against the background of changing national currency values. They borrow currencies which they expect to fall in price, and lend currencies which they expect to rise. Some sharp foreign exchange traders and corporate treasurers earned millions of dollars—and

German marks and Swiss francs—for their companies in the late 1960s and early 1970s by correctly anticipating changes in exchange rates. Between 1967 and 1972, profits from exchange speculation probably reached $5 billion. But not all corporate treasurers participated in these profits. Some believed the statements of the authorities that parities would not be changed, invested accordingly, and lost their jobs—and others deserved to. The corporate treasurer of an international firm is supposed to know all about profiting from the differences in interest rates in various countries, from changes in exchange rates, and from other misfortunes of the ministers of finance.

Many foreign exchange traders developed great confidence in their ability to predict changes in exchange rates during the pegged-rate period. Their confidence led them to speculate on a large scale during the period of floating exchange rates. Some did well. Some did not—Banque du Bruxelles reported losses of $60 million; Franklin National, $42 million; Herstatt, $400 million.

Part of the drama of international finance involves circumventing national regulations. Indian peasants hoard gold because they believe the government's financial policies will lead to higher prices; they believe gold is a better store of value than the rupee. American banks establish branches in London and Nassau to avoid the regulations of the U.S. monetary authorities. Italian investors smuggle lira notes into Switzerland because they want to reduce the tax bite of the Italian government. All these moves are designed to increase personal income.

Bernie Cornfeld took the U.S. mutual fund industry to Europe and sold shares in firms to Europeans and, for a brief period, beat the European financial establishment at its own game. U.S. companies compete aggressively in Canada, Europe, and Latin America, buying out some of their host-country competitors and forcing others into insolvency. Machine Bull, the last independent French-owned computer firm, could not survive in the competitive international league because the world price level for computers, set by IBM, was too low relative to French costs. Nor could Rolls Royce continue to compete in jet aircraft engines, for the prices set by its U.S. competitors—General Electric and United Aircraft—were too low relative to British costs. British Leyland, the largest auto firm in Great Britain, was forced into bankruptcy because British costs and prices were rising much more rapidly than foreign prices.

One view about the game plan—a view reinforced by the daily newspaper columns—is that the changes in currency values and international business competition are independent of each other. A competing view—the view of this book—is that these events are related, for developing international patterns in the growth of industry and banking reflect the competitive forces in world finance.

The drama of international finance reflects the contrast between the politics and the technology of money. All the financial assets in the world—currency notes, bank deposits, government bonds, mortgages—must be denominated in one national currency or another. The advantages of having a national money are rarely questioned, for they seem intuitively obvious. A national money, like a national airline, a steel mill, and a branch of the Playboy Club, brings prestige. Control of the production of a national money also brings profit. Kings and presidents finance wars in Algeria and Vietnam and build monuments to themselves with newly produced money. Debasement of the money, reducing its purchasing power, occurs worldwide as an indirect or backdoor form of taxation. Taxation through the printing press and inflation is easier and less messy than raising tax rates. Sovereigns manipulate monetary policy because they want to secure full employment, speed growth and development, or accomplish some other worthy objective that will win the approval of their constituents.

Central bankers and finance ministers in each country can only make their economic policies effective if they can isolate their national market for money and credit from the international market. The U.S. military draft offered an analogy: if too many potential draftees had moved to Canada, the draft would not have been effective. Similarly, if too many holders of dollar assets or sterling assets or franc assets anticipate the actions of the authorities and move their money abroad, their transactions frustrate the government's policies.

Changes in technology have introduced a new factor in the relationship among national monies. As the cost of transportation and communication across national borders continues to diminish, the effectiveness of national monopolies in the production of money has declined. As knowledge about foreign investment opportunities grows and the cost of taking advantage of these opportunities declines, differences in national monetary systems become increasingly important.

In an isolated world, kings had monopoly power over their subjects, who had no other place to send their wealth and no other currency in which they might hold their assets to escape the sovereign's tax. So the politics of money was largely national.

But the monopoly power of kings and presidents is declining, and the constituents of various governments are adjusting to this new world more rapidly than the governments themselves. Governments frequently need international agreements to revise established institutions, and negotiating these agreements takes years. International conferences are becoming larger and more frequent. Meanwhile, established agreements fall into disuse before new agreements can be made.

Today, because of instantaneous and low-cost transportation and communication, the national markets for monies, bonds, deposits, and shares denominated in the various currencies are more nearly parts of one international market. At any given moment, the price of IBM shares in Amsterdam and the price of IBM shares in London—and in the other foreign centers where IBM shares are traded—differ only by pennies from the New York price. Specialized stockbrokers buy these shares where they are cheap and sell them where they are dear to profit from the differential, thus keeping the prices in line. The technology of money is international.

The Plan of This Book

The first part of this book examines the structure of national monies, with the focus on the tension between the economic pressures toward integration of national monetary policies and the political pressures toward decentralization. The concern throughout is with the basic components of the international financial system—gold, the dollar, the foreign exchange market —and with the problems encountered in modifying the framework to lessen this conflict.

The second part of the book examines some of the direct and indirect consequences of segmenting the world into 100 currency areas. Each chapter focuses on a particular issue. Thus, the chapter on taxation focuses on the impact of differences in national taxes on the competitive position of firms based in various countries. The chapter on commercial banking asks whether, as the technology of the banking industry changes so that the distance between banks and their customers becomes unimportant, banks in the United States, Europe, or Japan will have a competitive advantage in the international marketplace. The rise and fall of Bernie Cornfeld is generally seen as a tale of a swashbuckling entrepreneur; Chapter 14 shows that the setting for his success and failure reflected the echo effect in Europe of U.S. financial events.

During the last 100 years, changes in technology have led to a widening of the marketplace for goods, services, and securities. For generations, the market had been smaller than the nation-state. The expansion of the boundaries of the market beyond the fixed boundaries of the state has threatened the viability of both national economic independence and of national firms in many industries.

Adjustments are inevitable, but the form of the adjustment is in doubt. One adjustment involves harmonization of national policies to reduce the competitive advantage or disadvantage encountered by firms in various countries as a result of policy differences. Then firms in various countries would be equally able to compete—and to fail. The scope for independent national financial policies would be narrowed. The alternative adjustment involves protection of national firms against more successful foreign competitors through a variety of discriminatory barriers to the movement of goods and capital, thus protecting the efficacy of national policies.

A System Is How the Pieces Fit

The goal of every science is a conceptual model which shows how the pieces of its universe are related. An economist who seeks to become the Copernicus of the international financial system finds the task complicated by the fact that this system has changed substantially in the last 100 years. And in the last decade the pace of change has quickened.

Before World War I the system was described as the "gold standard." Then a change in concept led to a change in name, and "gold exchange standard" became the applicable term for the interwar arrangement; between 1946 to 1971, the international financial order was known as the Bretton Woods System. Since 1971, the system has become a mixed set of arrangements to which no name has yet been attached.

These changes have been more than cosmetic, for the systemic relationships among the key components—the mechanisms for setting exchange rates and for supplying the money to use in payments between central banks in different countries—were also revamped.

Changes in the system have usually been precipitated by a crisis over the relative values of different national monies, when the established arrangements for financing payments imbalances are about to break down. Thus, the move to the gold exchange standard reflected a prospective shortage of gold. The gold exchange standard failed in the Great Depression of the 1930s because of too frequent changes in exchange rates. And the

13

Bretton Woods System collapsed in 1971 because it was unable to cope with the large payments imbalances generated by U.S. inflation. The pattern is one of crisis, breakdown, and innovation.

The Copernicus of the international financial system must resolve two issues. First he must develop a model of the relationships among the major components of the system: the monetary policies of various countries, the foreign exchange market in which these national monies are traded, and the international monies like gold. Then he must explain why the relationships change over time, and whether these changes follow a pattern or are random. This chapter discusses the relationships among these components, while the next chapter reviews the changes in the system over the last 100 years.

Fitting the Pieces: The Foreign Exchange Market

International transactions have one common element that makes them uniquely different from domestic transactions—one of the participants must deal in a foreign currency. When an American buys a new Volkswagen, he pays in either dollars or marks. If he pays in dollars, the Volkswagen company must convert the dollars into marks. If the Volkswagen company receives payment in marks, the buyer must first exchange his dollars for marks. At some stage in the chain of transactions between the American buyer and the German seller, dollars must be converted into marks. This transaction is inevitable, since Volkswagen pays its labor force and its supplier in marks, while the American buyer receives his salary in dollars. Either the American buyer or the Volkswagen seller takes the dollars to the foreign exchange market to buy marks.

The foreign exchange market is a market in national monies; the exchange rate is the price. There are two basic types of exchange rate systems—two basic ways of organizing the market. One involves floating exchange rates; the price of foreign monies in terms of domestic money rises and falls in response to changes in the supply and demand, much as the prices of shares on the stock market or of wheat on the commodity market rise and fall. If U.S. residents must pay for their Volkswagens in marks, the increase in their demand for marks leads to a fall in the mark price of the dollar—one mark buys more dollars. If Mexican companies buy more U.S.-produced computers, the price of the U.S. dollar rises in terms of the peso as Mexican importers sell more pesos to acquire more dollars.

The concept of the floating-rate system is simple: the exchange rate or price moves freely in response to market forces. National governments may participate in the exchange market to raise or lower the price of their money; they might seek to dampen daily or weekly movements in the exchange rate.

Despite the simplicity and neatness of the concept, few countries have adopted a floating system for more than a year or two. Among developed countries, Canada has the longevity record for using a floating rate (1950–1962 and 1970 to the present). Lebanon holds the record for developing countries (1950 to the present). On three occasions, a substantial number of countries have used the floating-rate system at the same time. The first time came after World War I, between 1919 and 1925, when most European countries were adjusting to the inflationary impact of World War I. The second time, August-December 1971, most Western European countries and Japan briefly permitted their currencies to float as an interim measure; they anticipated that the prices of their currencies would rise in terms of the U.S. dollar. (In June 1972, sterling was again floated in anticipation of British entry into the Common Market in January 1973.) The currencies of the major industrialized countries have been floating since mid-February 1973, but the extent of central bank participation has been much greater than in the two previous periods. The Bank of Japan has intervened extensively in the exchange market to ensure smooth rate movements. Large external loans have enabled the Bank of England to support sterling at substantially higher levels than the transactions of private parties might have established.

The alternative to a floating exchange rate is a pegged-rate system. This system has two main features. First the government authority, usually the central bank, limits variations in the prices of foreign monies in terms of the national money within a more or less narrow range. The price at the center of this range is the parity or peg for the currency, a reference point by which its value is stated. At one time, most currencies were pegged to gold. For more than 100 years the historic peg for the U.S. dollar was $20.67 per fine ounce of gold; the $35 price was adopted in 1934. Alternatively, some countries use the currency of another country as the peg; the Mexican peso is pegged to the U.S. dollar. After 1945 most foreign countries pegged their currencies to the U.S. dollar.

The second feature of a pegged-rate system is that on occasion—perhaps once a generation, or a decade, or a year, or a month—the government may change the peg for its currency, as the British did when they altered the dollar price of sterling from $2.80 to $2.40 in November 1967 and to $2.60 in December 1971.

Pegged-rate systems are more complex than floating-rate systems, for the authorities must limit variations in the price of their currency in the foreign exchange market. Usually the central bank buys its own currency to prevent the price from falling substantially below the peg, and sells its own currency to prevent the price from rising substantially above the peg. Such purchases and sales prevent any significant deviation of the market exchange rate from the official parity. The boundaries of the range within which the price of the currency may vary before the central bank is obliged to intervene are known as the support limits or margins. For example, the Bank of England bought sterling in exchange for dollars when the demand for sterling was weak, thus limiting the decline in the price of sterling in terms of the dollar. And the Bank of England sold sterling when the demand was strong to limit the increase in the price of sterling. In the 1960s, when sterling was pegged at $2.80, the support limits were about $2.78 and $2.82, or nearly 0.75 percent on either side of the parity. When sterling was pegged at $2.60 at the end of 1971, these limits were widened to 2.25 percent, or about $2.54 and $2.66.

Under pegged-rate systems, countries incur payments imbalances—surpluses and deficits—which are measured by the central bank's transactions in the exchange market. A payments surplus occurs when the central bank sells its currency in the exchange market and buys gold or other international monies (the concept of international money is discussed later in this chapter). Conversely, a payments deficit occurs when the central bank buys its currency and sells international money.

From time to time, the authorities must change the exchange rate peg to reduce payments deficits or surpluses. A country with a payments deficit devalues its currency by increasing the price at which it buys and sells foreign money in terms of its own money. Conversely, a country with a surplus revalues by reducing the price at which it buys and sells foreign monies.

Most countries are reluctant to change their parities (the basis of their concern is discussed in Chapter 4) despite large payments imbalances; thus, the pegs tend to become somewhat frozen. Still, measures must be taken to limit deficits. So governments raise taxes and impose controls on foreign payments, and they also subsidize exports. Some importers find that they must pay more for foreign exchange than they would if the currency had been devalued. In effect, such controls devalue the currency by the "back door." Conversely, countries with large payments surpluses may reduce controls on foreign payments rather than revalue.

In the last twenty-five years, exchange rate pegs have been

changed more than 100 times, an average of slightly more than one change per country. But this average covers a wide range of behavior. Some countries have maintained the same peg throughout this period, while a few have changed their peg every six or eight weeks for a year or two.

Central bank transactions in the foreign exchange market under pegged-rate systems are the counterpart of changes in the exchange rate under a floating-rate system—they match demand and supply. If a central bank does not participate in the exchange market under a floating-rate system, payments surpluses and deficits do not occur; the exchange rate changes to balance supply and demand. The floating-rate system's equivalent of a payments deficit is an increase in the price of foreign monies in terms of domestic money.

Although the two exchange systems are by no means identical, the distinction between them can become fuzzy, for the more frequently the exchange rate pegs are changed, the more nearly the pegged-rate system resembles a floating-rate system. Conversely, the more frequently authorities in countries with floating exchange rates intervene in the exchange market to dampen the movements in the foreign exchange price of their currency, the more nearly the floating-rate system resembles the pegged system. The differences between the two systems are smaller in the long run than in the short run.

Changes in the exchange rate pegs and variations in the price of foreign exchange under the floating system are not economic accidents. Such changes result from differences in the monetary and fiscal policies of various countries.

Fitting the Pieces: National Financial Policies

One approach toward the formulation of national monetary and fiscal policies involves gearing these policies to the maintenance of the existing exchange rate peg. A competing approach is to direct these policies to the attainment of full employment, price stability, rapid economic growth, or financing government expenditures. If the second approach is followed, then changes in the exchange rate are necessary; the authorities may either opt for a floating rate or alter their exchange rate peg as frequently as necessary.

The monetary policies of the central bank and the fiscal policies of the national treasury have a major impact on each country's international financial position, affecting, for example, whether a country with pegged rates will be in deficit or surplus or whether a country with floating rates will find the price of its currency rising or falling.

Monetary policy changes the amount of money held by the public. Central banks increase or reduce the money supply to induce changes in the public's spending for goods and services. Fiscal policy involves changes in government expenditures relative to its revenues. Monetary and fiscal policies are manipulated to help the government achieve its employment, income, and price level objectives.

Changes in monetary and fiscal policies affect a country's payments balance by altering international transactions in goods and securities. These policies lead to changes in national income; imports increase when national income increases, and exports may increase less rapidly. Moreover, the change in income may cause domestic prices to increase; if prices of domestic goods rise relative to prices of foreign goods, the country's international competitive position becomes less favorable. Then imports grow more rapidly, and exports more slowly. Monetary and fiscal policies also cause changes in interest rates; as domestic interest rates rise relative to interest rates abroad, imports of foreign securities fall while exports of domestic securities may increase.

Some countries change their exchange rate pegs relatively infrequently because their monetary and fiscal policies are geared to maintaining a particular peg. Haiti holds the longevity record, for the gourde has been pegged at 5 gourdes to the U.S. dollar since 1907. The Haitian record is no accident; Haiti's monetary and fiscal policies have been geared to maintaining a fixed parity. Similarly, the Mexican peso has been pegged to the U.S. dollar since 1953, for the central objective of Mexican monetary policy has been to keep the peso at 12.5 to the dollar. Haiti and Mexico have dependent monetary policies; increases in their money supplies depend on their balance-of-payments surpluses.

In contrast, Brazil, Israel, and Denmark change their parities relatively frequently because they direct their monetary and fiscal policies to domestic objectives, whether it be economic growth, full employment, or fighting wars in the Sinai or the Golan Heights. For these countries the retention of a particular exchange rate peg is neither an important objective of policy nor a significant constraint on the choice of domestic policies. Thus, Brazil adjusts its monetary and fiscal policies to raise its economic growth rate, Israel to finance its defense expenditures, and Denmark to pay for its welfare programs. Instead of adjusting its domestic economy to the prevailing exchange rate peg, each of these countries adjusts its exchange rate peg so that international payments and receipts will be roughly equal. The monetary policies of these countries are independent of their balance-of-payments positions.

The objectives of national economic policies change over time. U.S. history provides a good example. During the Civil War, monetary policies in both North and South were highly expansive, and both Federal and Confederate governments printed large supplies of bank notes to finance their war expenditures. Commodity prices rose rapidly. After the war, the U.S. government sought to offset the wartime inflation by pursuing deflationary policies. The objective was to peg the dollar again at its prewar parity with gold—which finally happened in 1878.

During World War I, as in the Civil War, the money supply

grew rapidly; again commodity prices increased sharply. Price stability did not become an important objective of U.S. policy until the 1920s. Substantial up-and-down price variations, tolerable in the largely agricultural society of the nineteenth century, were unacceptable in an industrial society; the impact of falling prices on business failures and urban unemployment was too acute. During World War II, full employment became an important objective of national policy. In the 1950s, largely in response to the threat of Soviet economic and technological achievements, economic growth became an important objective. The realization of the Great Society—raising the economic welfare of the millions of Americans who lived below the poverty line—became a prime objective in the mid-1960s. Shortly thereafter, the preservation of freedom and the stability of the dominoes in Southeast Asia meant that security expenditures went to the head of the list. As these U.S. objectives have changed, so have the targets for monetary and fiscal policies.

Several themes emerge. Wars lead to inflation, and inflation leads to sharp payments imbalances. No imbalance can persist forever; ultimately an adjustment is needed. As populations have become industrial and urban, governments have become increasingly concerned with economic welfare. Full employment, never a problem in an agricultural economy, has become a matter of crucial importance for the urban wage worker. The fiscal role of governments has increased; taxes in some countries may now amount to 50 percent or more of national income. As expectations of higher living standards have become more widespread, raising the annual economic growth rate has grown increasingly important as a national objective.

National economic policies have stressed domestic objectives in recent years, while maintenance of a particular exchange rate peg has been slighted. The international system has had to accommodate these increasingly inward-looking national policies. At first, the combination of domestically oriented financial polices and a pegged-rate system led to increasingly large international payments deficits—and surpluses. The size of these imbalances was limited by the ability of individual countries to finance larger deficits; eventually, changes in parities were forced. Now, to the extent that each country allows its currency to float in the exchange market, the diversity is reflected in movements in the exchange rates; the currencies of countries with relatively rapid inflation tend to depreciate. The movements in exchange rates are thus continuous rather than abrupt.

Fitting the Pieces: The Supply of International Money

A central bank can buy its own currency in the exchange market only by selling some other asset, and it can sell its own currency only if it buys other assets. By definition, any asset which central banks buy and sell when they support their currencies in the exchange market is an intervention asset. And the assets which central banks acquire by selling an intervention asset comprise the set of international monies. An international money is a necessary component of a pegged exchange rate system; a floating-rate system, in contrast, has no need for an international money.

One key question is what determines which assets qualify as international money: Why is gold an international money, while silver is not? Why are U.S. dollar assets considered international money, while Canadian dollar assets are not? A related question involves how much of each asset is held as international money.

Central banks need an international money whenever they peg exchange rates. Given this need, each central bank must then decide which asset has the most attractive combination of attributes in the form of interest income, future purchasing power, transaction costs, and storage costs.

Through 1965, holdings of gold were much the largest component of international money (see Figure 2–1). Then foreign holdings of dollars surged; gold shifted to second place in the 1970 ranking and has been an increasingly distant second ever since. The third and the smallest component remains monies produced by international institutions. Figure 2–1 shows that the value of gold as international money has increased only

FIGURE 2–1

The Supply of International Money
(billions of U.S. dollars, end of period)

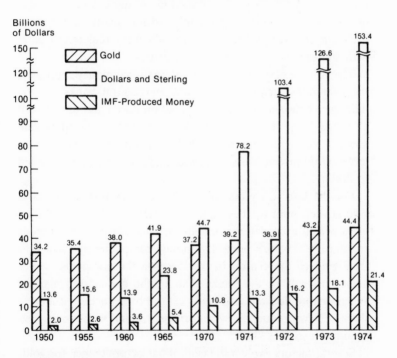

SOURCE: International Monetary Fund, *International Financial Statistics* (Washington, D.C.), 1975.

Note: Gold excludes holdings of international institutions. The increase in the gold holdings from 1970 to 1974 reflects the increase in the dollar price of gold. The dollar holdings are reported by foreign central banks and exceed those reported by the U.S. Treasury.

slightly over the twenty-four-year period, while the value of foreign exchange holdings increased sharply, doubling between 1965 and 1970 and more than tripling between 1970 and 1974. IMF-produced money also doubled between 1965 and 1970 and again between 1970 and 1974.

The use of gold as an international money is explained by its monetary history. (Chapter 5 examines gold's future as an international money.) For centuries, gold was the world's principal money. Gold bullion and then gold coins were used to make payments, both within countries and across national boundaries. Because gold was used in so many countries, payments between countries frequently did not involve any foreign exchange transactions, for foreign gold coins circulated together with domestic coins within many countries.

The volume of gold held as an international money represents the cumulative acquisitions of national central banks, or the difference between the amount of gold produced and the amount absorbed by jewelry, the arts, dentistry, industry, and private hoards. New gold discoveries led to sharp increases in price levels. Gold mining costs increased, and gold production tended to decline.

For the last 300 years, central banks have bought and sold gold at their mint parities. If the amount of gold produced during a period exceeded the amount demanded by private parties at the central bank's price, the mining companies in effect sold their gold to the central banks, because the companies got a higher price from the banks than in the commodity market. When private demand was weak, central banks acquired a large share of new production; when private demand was strong, they acquired a smaller share.

Several factors explain the central banks' preference for gold. A central bank holds gold because it feels it will be able to sell gold to some other central bank when the need arises. Even if this expectation should prove wrong, the gold could still be sold in the commodity market, perhaps at a price not far below its monetary price.

Over the last several hundred years, as national currencies have become more important, gold's role as a money in domestic economies has declined. Initially, national monies in the form of bank notes and deposits could be easily used to buy gold from central banks. But as the amount of national monies increased relative to the amount of gold, sovereigns found it difficult to maintain the national money and gold in circulation at the same time, for gold was often hoarded. This problem was eventually resolved by eliminating the use of gold in domestic transactions. In the last fifty years, monetary gold transactions have been increasingly restricted to dealings among national central banks. For example, the Bank of England would sell gold to the U.S. Treasury to get dollars to use in supporting sterling in the exchange market; conversely, the Bank of England would acquire dollars in the exchange market, knowing that it could use these dollars to buy gold at the U.S. Treasury.

The increasingly severe gold shortage of the 1950s and 1960s led to renewed efforts to reduce the demand for gold. U.S. citizens, who had been prohibited from owning gold domestically in 1933, were prohibited from owning gold abroad in 1961. Foreign central banks were encouraged to acquire dollar assets rather than gold to meet their demand for international money. A major international negotiation to produce a "paper gold"— an asset which was supposed to have all of the attributes of gold except its weight, durability, and glitter—was set in motion. The objective of all such measures was to forestall the sure cure for any shortage—an increase in the price.

These measures proved ineffective. As long as private parties could buy gold in private markets at $35, central banks were obliged to let private demand determine how much of new production would flow into various private uses and how much would flow to central banks. Indeed, maintenance of one price for both private parties and central banks meant that central banks would be required to sell gold from their own holdings to private parties if their demands exceeded new production.

The inevitable occurred: by 1965 private demand exceeded new production, and sales from central banks mounted to $2 billion by early 1967. The major central banks, following the U.S. lead, arranged a two-tier market: central banks would continue to buy from and sell gold to each other at $35, while private parties would buy and sell gold in a free market where the price might rise above the parity or fall below it. Gold producers would be tempted to sell new output to private parties if the price exceeded what the central banks would pay.

Soon after this two-tier system was adopted, the price of gold in private markets began to rise modestly above the official price. Paradoxically, the gold shortage intensified; central banks were reluctant to sell gold to another central bank at $35 if its value in the private market was $40. If gold was to remain in the system, an increase in the monetary price was necessary.

The gold shortage of the 1960s was similar to that of the 1920s; then, too, central bankers were concerned that there wasn't enough gold. Not enough gold was being produced, and too much of the production was going into commodity and other private uses because private parties paid a higher price for gold than central banks would. There was a similar search for substitutes for gold. Some countries began to acquire assets denominated in dollars. The Bank of Canada and the Bank of Mexico, for example, held most of their international money in the form of dollar assets—U.S. Treasury bills and time deposits in U.S. banks. Similarly, the Bank of Malaya held international money in the form of sterling assets in London.

Dollar assets had several attractive attributes for foreign central banks: they provided interest income, and they could readily be exchanged into gold at the U.S. Treasury. For a long time, U.S. dollar assets appeared more likely to remain acceptable and retain value than assets denominated in other currencies. Dollars could be used to buy U.S. goods and securities. The United States had a large, productive economy and seemed militarily secure and politically stable. And the dollar had—and still has—a better long-term record for retaining its purchasing power than any other currency. Whether dollar assets will continue to have these qualities is examined in Chapter 6.

As foreign holdings of dollar assets increased, countries became reluctant to acquire more dollar assets. In part, this was because the U.S. Treasury's ability to convert all of these assets into gold had come into question. Nevertheless, the dollar holdings of foreign central banks surged in 1970 and 1971, for business firms, banks, and private investors began to anticipate that the price of the West German mark, the Swiss franc, and the Japanese yen would rise in terms of the dollar, either because the dollar would be devalued in terms of gold or because these currencies would be revalued in terms of gold. So foreign central banks ended up with the dollars these other investors were selling; they were caught between their reluctance to acquire more dollar assets and their reluctance to revalue. The indecision proved costly, since the central banks first acquired the dollar assets and then revalued anyway.

International money also includes assets produced by international institutions. Such institutions are essentially groups of countries acting jointly. Negotiations among the members determine how much of each type of money will be produced each year and how the newly produced money will be distributed among the member countries.

The use of gold as money because of its underlying value as a commodity points to a unique problem of the international economy. In the domestic economy, paper money (in the form of bank notes and checks) has value because the government declares that it has value—sellers and tax collectors are obliged to accept it. No government has similar power in the international economy; no sovereign can compel another sovereign to accept an asset as money, and neither can any international agency. Some countries may be reluctant to acquire assets as international money unless they are confident that the assets will retain value and remain acceptable.

The persistent gold shortage, together with the reluctance of central banks to acquire more dollar assets, led some observers to suggest that the demand for international money should be satisfied by increased reliance on the monies produced by international institutions. Perhaps. But the question remains whether countries would have confidence in this money, an issue to be discussed in Chapter 8.

Who Fits the Pieces Together?

The gold and exchange crises of the last decade can be partly explained by the absence of institutions to ensure that the growth in the supply of international monies matches the growth in demand. The larger problem is that there is no mechanism to ensure that the three major components of the system—the exchange rate system, national monetary and fiscal policies, and the supply of international monies—are consistent with each other. Political forces within the major countries explain the change in orientation of national financial policies. The adjustment of the foreign exchange market and the supply of international monies to the increased diversity in national financial policies has lagged because of difficulties in securing agreement among the sovereigns.

"The Greatest Monetary Agreement in History"

The Smithsonian Institution in Washington, D.C., is the repository for the nation's artifacts. Lindbergh's *Spirit of St. Louis* hangs from the rafters. The Hope Diamond is there. So are George Washington's uniform and the largest blue whale ever caught. And in December 1971 the finance ministers of the largest non-Communist industrialized countries met at the Smithsonian and agreed to realign their exchange rates. President Nixon called the Smithsonian Agreement "the greatest monetary agreement in history."

The remarkable accomplishment of the agreement was that more exchange rates were simultaneously realigned in a multinational framework than ever before. In effect, the agreement meant that the existing machinery for resolving disputes about exchange rates could be sent to some monetary counterpart of the Smithsonian Institution to take its place alongside earlier monetary arrangements and agreements as yet another relic.

Rules and Myths of the Gold Standard

A hundred years ago, according to popular economic history, the world was on the gold standard. Participation in the gold standard was open to any country which pegged its currency to gold at a mint parity. There was no formal international agreement. The exchange rate between any two national currencies was set by the ratio of their mint parities, adjusted for any difference in the gold content of their money. For example, the mint parity for the U.S. dollar was $20.67, while the mint parity for the pound sterling was 3 pounds, 17 shillings, 10½ pence. The dollar-sterling exchange would be $20.67 divided by 3/17/ 10½, or $4.86 per pound sterling.

Moreover, each central bank would, on demand of private parties, readily buy and sell gold at its parity. Whenever exporters within a country acquired gold from their foreign customers, they could sell the gold to their central bank in exchange for domestic currency. The central bank would then print more money to pay for the gold; the domestic money supply and the central bank's gold holdings would increase. Conversely, the domestic money supply would decline whenever importers, in order to make payments abroad, sold domestic money to the central bank to buy gold.

The great attraction of the gold standard was its automaticity. Market forces automatically and simultaneously answered two important questions: How rapidly should the domestic money supply grow in each country, and how rapidly should the international money supply grow? The money supply increased when a country achieved a payments surplus, and it declined when there was a payments deficit. Exchange rate arrangements and monetary policies were compatible; there was never any risk that monetary policy would be so inflationary that the central bank might sell all its gold and not be able to retain its parity.

The flow of gold from new production meant that the gold holdings of all central banks could increase together; every country could have a payments surplus simultaneously. In some cases, the rapid growth in monetary gold holdings led to sharp increases in the supply of domestic monies and to worldwide increases in commodity prices. Increases or decreases in price levels were accepted as a natural part of economic life, much like the weather.

30

Market forces also determine how rapidly the supply of international money should grow. The amount of gold produced during any period depended on the relationship between the price that central banks would pay for gold and the costs of mining gold. These costs in turn depended on the general price level. When commodity prices increased, so would these costs. Gold production would then decline, since producers were caught between rising costs and a fixed selling price. The result was that gold holdings would increase less rapidly—and so would national money supplies. On the other hand, when the commodity price level declined, so would gold mining costs. Gold producers would then increase their output. Money supplies would grow more rapidly, thus checking the decline in commodity prices. In other words, the price level and the supply of gold were components of a consistent system. The pieces fit. In theory at least, the gold standard was a self-contained system.

In practice, the gold standard was less systematic than the model suggests. Often, changes in the gold supply reflected the chanciness of new gold discoveries and innovations in gold ore refining processes rather than changes in mining costs. Some central banks directed their monetary policies toward domestic objectives, especially during wars. Many countries were more frequently off the gold standard than on. Nevertheless, the automatic, anonymous, and consistent attributes of the system attracted numerous supporters who advocated adherence to the system as a basis for central bank policy.

Several developments associated with World War I reduced the relevance of the gold standard model. The war demonstrated that nationalism was a powerful force—in Britain and France as well as in Germany and Austria. The monetary counterpart of nationalism was that central banks directed their policies toward domestic objectives. The cohesiveness of the international system was fragmented.

Wartime inflation, moreover, pushed commodity prices in most countries to levels that during the 1920s were at least twice as high as in 1913. Higher prices meant both an increased demand for gold and, because of higher gold production costs, a reduced supply. A gold shortage ensued. Few countries were willing to accept the substantial reductions in commodity prices that would have been needed to raise gold output. If the demand for international money was to be satisfied, either the price of gold in terms of national currencies would have to be increased or new international monies would have to be developed.

Finally, the war brought about a sharp rise in U.S. economic power. The stimulus of the war had tied the regional economies of the nation together, a linkage that would otherwise have developed more slowly. The United States, moreover, escaped the war losses and the postwar turmoil of the European belligerents. After World War I, the U.S. economy was about as large as the combined economies of the ten next largest countries—a much more dominant position than Great Britain had ever enjoyed before the war.

The monetary problems of the half century after World War I revolve around these three themes: nationalism, the shortage of international money, and the dominant economic power of the United States. The disintegration of the international system in the 1930s resulted from the failure to adjust institutional arrangements to these realities.

The breakdown of the gold standard became starkly evident in the economic behavior of nations during the 1920s and 1930s. At the beginning of World War I, most European countries left the gold standard, since their rates of inflation exceeded that of the United States; indeed, the dollar was the only major currency that remained convertible into gold. During the early 1920s the European currencies floated in the exchange market, and they depreciated sharply in terms of gold and the dollar. Floating exchange rates were viewed as an interim measure; most governments in Europe wanted to return to the gold standard at their 1913 parities. But this objective could be achieved only if they permitted their domestic price levels to decline substantially—or if there was a substantial rise in the U.S. price level. Few countries were willing to adopt the deflationary policies needed to make a return to the 1913 parities feasible, and the United States was unwilling to inflate.

By the mid-1920s, most currencies were again pegged to gold. Sterling, the Swiss franc, and a few other currencies were again at their 1913 parities. Many more currencies had been devalued extensively in terms of both gold and the dollar. For example, the French franc, which had been worth 19.3 cents in 1913, sold for 3.9 cents in 1926.

This system of pegged rates held together for several years. But there were too many inconsistencies for the pieces to fit together for long. The gold shortage remained. Sterling was overvalued; the French franc was undervalued.

In the late 1920s, the central banks of the agricultural countries were again forced to stop gold sales because the prices and export earnings of agricultural products fell sharply. Then, in September 1931, the Bank of England suspended gold transactions, and sterling again became a floating currency. In 1933, immediately after President Franklin D. Roosevelt took office, the U.S. government ceased pegging the dollar to gold at the $20.67 parity. The dollar floated until early 1934, when a new $35 parity was established. Several years later, other currencies —the French and Swiss francs and the Dutch guilder—were also devalued in terms of gold. Within a six-year period, nearly every currency had been devalued in terms of gold, many by as much as 50 to 70 percent.

This sequence of currency devaluations—first by the agricultural economies and later by Great Britain, the United States, France, the Netherlands, and Switzerland—became known as the "beggar thy neighbor" policy. Each country devalued its currency in response to the worldwide shortages of international money and of jobs. Each country wanted to import international money—but no country wanted to sell gold. And each country wanted to import jobs by reducing the price of its goods in foreign markets and raising the price of foreign goods in its domestic market. But no country wanted to export jobs.

The Bretton Woods System

The interwar period demonstrated the need for an institutional framework that would enable countries to follow policies directed toward domestic objectives without exporting their problems. During World War II the United States and Great Britain took the initiative in developing an international treaty to constrain the financial behavior of industrial countries. This treaty—the Articles of Agreement of the International Monetary Fund (informally called the Bretton Woods Agreement after the New Hampshire resort where the final negotiations occurred)—had two major components. One was a set of rules or constraints directed at the exchange rate behavior of IMF members, especially their freedom to change their exchange rate parities. The second was a pool of member countries' currencies. The IMF would be a "lender of last resort," lending currencies to its members from this pool to help them finance payments deficits. These two components were part of a package; it was believed that members would be more likely to accept the constraints on changing their exchange rates if they were assured that they could borrow foreign currencies from the fund.

The thrust of the IMF Agreement was that unnecessary changes in exchange rates should be avoided, while desired and justifiable changes should take place in an orderly manner. The agreement proved to have two shortcomings. First, there was no mechanism to induce countries to change their parities when they became inappropriate. Second, the components of the system were not compatible: the agreement focused on the behavior of individual member countries, but not on consistency among national monetary policies, the exchange rate system, and the supply of international money.

The increasing emphasis of national monetary policies on the attainment of domestic objectives and the desire of most countries to retain pegged exchange rates subjected the Bretton Woods System to increasing stress. With most countries pursuing independent national monetary policies, changes in parities became inevitable. But national authorities were reluctant to recognize the implications of their monetary policies for their exchange rates; they retained the exchange market arrangements of the gold standard. The IMF rules sought to minimize unnecessary changes in the exchange parities. In fact, however, changes in parities proved too infrequent and too long-delayed; the adjustable pegs of the IMF system were sticky or frozen.

During the 1950s and 1960s, the supply of international money increased less rapidly than the demand. The analogy with the 1920s is strong. In both periods, the problem was aggravated by the sharp rise in national price levels during and after a world war; the higher prices meant an increase in the demand for international money. At the same time, higher production costs deterred increases in gold output. The increase in the central bank demand for gold was greater than the increase in monetary gold stocks resulting from new production. As a result, individual central banks could only satisfy their demand for gold by buying gold from other countries. Figure 3–1 shows gold output and the more rapid increase in the amount of gold demanded by private parties.

One alternative to increased central bank holdings of gold was increased foreign holdings of short-term assets denominated in dollars, sterling, and other major currencies. Foreign countries could add to their holdings of liquid dollar assets if, as a group, they achieved payments surpluses. This meant that the United States would incur payments deficits. Between 1950 and 1970, U.S. gold holdings declined from $23 billion to $11 billion, while

FIGURE 3–1

Gold Production and Private Demand
(millions of U.S. dollars at $35 per ounce)

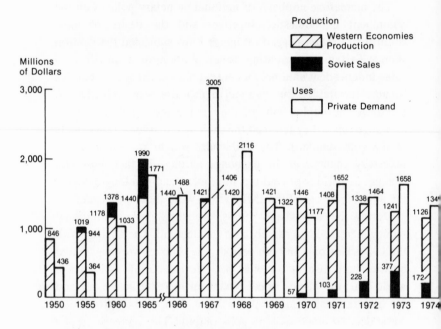

SOURCE: Bank for International Settlements, 1975.

foreign holdings of dollars increased from $8 billion to $47 billion.

The United States could supply dollars to meet the international money demands of other countries without limit; there was a virtually inexhaustible supply of U.S. Treasury bills and deposits in U.S. banks. But U.S. ability to supply gold to foreign central banks was limited; each million dollars of gold sold to foreign central banks was a million dollars less in the holdings of the U.S. Treasury. The U.S. dilemma was that it was unable to distinguish, in the design of its balance-of-payments policies, between those foreign countries that would satisfy their demand for international money by adding to their holdings of dollar assets and those countries that wanted to add to their gold holdings.

For most of the postwar period (probably until 1967 or even 1968), foreign holdings of dollars increased and the U.S. Treasury's gold holdings declined not because U.S. goods were overpriced or foreign goods were underpriced, but because foreign central banks wanted to add to their holdings of international money. During this period, the United States was the principal source of international monies because other sources were inadequate. But the United States could not sell dollars or gold to foreign central banks without incurring a payments deficit, at least as a payments deficit has been traditionally defined.

Numerous causes were given for the deficit: U.S. imports of Scotch whiskey, French brandy, and German beer, increases in U.S. military expenditures in Western Europe and Southeast Asia, and decreases in U.S. exports of automobiles and steel. But these factors derive from the foreign demand for dollars and gold. For if other countries want to add to their holdings of gold and dollars, they must underprice their goods relative to U.S. goods to secure a payments surplus.

The implication of the worldwide gold shortage was that the price at which central banks were buying and selling gold was too low relative to the production costs of gold. One solution was an increase in the price of gold in terms of all currencies. Gold production would be stimulated; the volume would increase, and the value of gold output would increase even more rapidly. And the private demand for gold would decline if gold were more expensive, so more of the newly produced gold would be sold to central banks.

If, on the other hand, the monetary price of gold were to remain unchanged, then the gold shortage would disappear only if demand fell. One way to reduce demand would be to stem the flow of dollars to foreign central banks, thus reducing the banks' ability to buy gold from the U.S. Treasury. A second way would be to induce foreign central banks not to buy gold.

During the 1960s the U.S. authorities adopted a series of measures to reduce the flow of dollars to foreign central banks. Foreign recipients of economic aid were obliged to spend the money on U.S. goods, even though foreign goods were cheaper. U.S. government agencies were directed to buy their goods from domestic sources unless foreign prices were lower than U.S. prices, first by 6 percent, then by 12 percent, 50 percent, and finally 100 percent. The U.S. Army began to ship Milwaukee beer to Munich. Purchases of foreign securities by U.S. residents were subjected to a tax, initially 1 percent, then 2 percent. Foreign investments by U.S. firms and U.S. financial institutions were subjected to voluntary controls in 1965; the controls became mandatory in 1968. Measures were also taken to increase U.S. receipts from foreigners—for example, U.S. domestic airlines offered special low fares for foreign tourists visiting the United States. Germany and several other countries were induced to buy more military equipment in the United States.

These measures effectively devalued the dollar by the "back door," for taxes and other barriers to U.S. purchases of foreign goods and securities raised their prices to U.S. residents. Individually, some of these measures were probably effective. But the U.S. payments deficits remained about as large as they had been in the late 1950s and early 1960s; these measures appeared to affect the composition of U.S. payments and receipts, but not the payments balance.

One explanation for the apparent failure of these measures was that U.S. tourist expenditures abroad were increasing; another, that U.S. firms were investing more abroad. The list of special factors is long. An alternative explanation is that other countries wanted to increase their holdings of international money at a combined annual rate of $2 billion to $3 billion a year and therefore took measures to counterbalance those taken by the United States.

FIGURE 3–2
U.S. International Monetary Position
(billions of U.S. dollars)

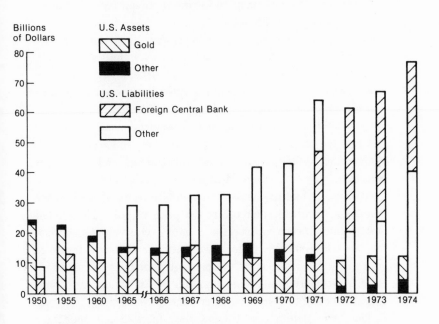

SOURCE: International Monetary Fund, *International Financial Statistics* (Washington, D.C.), 1975.
Note: The difference between U.S. liabilities to foreign central banks and dollar holdings in this figure reflect that the data here are from U.S. authorities, while the data for Figure 2–1 are from foreign monetary authorities.

The U.S. payments deficit was an inherent problem of the system: the demand for international money could not be satisfied without forcing the United States to incur a deficit. Numerous measures were taken to reduce the official foreign demand for gold. U.S. Treasury secretaries cajoled their foreign counterparts not to buy gold. The level of U.S. troops in Germany was tied to Germany's commitment not to buy more gold. The U.S. Treasury issued special securities denominated in marks, Swiss francs, and other foreign currencies for foreign central banks in the hope that they would find these securities an effective substitute for gold. By 1965 the U.S. government began to recognize that its payments deficit could be better explained by the foreign demand for international money than by the overvaluation of the dollar.

Devising new institutional arrangements that would satisfy the foreign demand for international money without forcing the United States to incur chronic payments deficits was a complex undertaking. The countries with surpluses were not convinced that the U.S. deficit was a problem of the system; rather, they believed that mismanagement of U.S. monetary and fiscal policies had led to the large deficits. Moreover, some countries—France, the Netherlands, Belgium, Switzerland, and to a lesser extent, Italy and Germany—had a strong preference for holding most of their international money in the form of gold. They favored a worldwide increase in the price of gold. The United States opposed such an increase, almost exclusively for political reasons. Domestically, a devaluation of the dollar in terms of gold might be regarded as evidence of poor financial management. And internationally, revaluation profits would go to gold speculators and to South Africa and the Soviet Union.

The U.S. government wanted the International Monetary Fund to produce a new international money. This money, colloquially termed "paper gold," would have the monetary but not the physical attributes of gold—it would not glitter. Paper gold could be produced at a rate which would satisfy demand; political negotiations would determine what this rate should be. European governments—especially the French—were reluctant to accept the U.S. initiative until the U.S. payments deficit was eliminated. But the U.S. deficit could not be eliminated until the foreign demand for international money declined, or until an alternative to the dollar as an international money was devised.

The U.S. view eventually prevailed, and an international treaty was signed providing for the production of a new international money, known as Special Drawing Rights (SDRs) within the IMF framework. Some $10 billion of SDRs were produced over the three-year period 1970–1972.

Perhaps the SDR arrangement would have been successful in resolving the system's needs. But the monetary events associated with the Vietnam war intervened, so that the SDR arrangement became irrelevant even before it became operational.

The Monetary Impact of Vietnam

The irony of the late 1960s was that just as the Europeans came to accept the view that their demand for payments surpluses might be connected with the U.S. deficit, the cause of the U.S. deficit changed. In 1969 the U.S. payments deficit of $6 billion was substantially larger than could be explained by the demands of other countries for international money. The overseas spending of U.S. military forces increased sharply. More importantly, U.S. prices rose rapidly, reducing the competitiveness of U.S. exports. As U.S. incomes rose rapidly, so did the demand for imports.

The United States wanted other countries to take the initiative in restoring the payments imbalance. Whenever the international money holdings of one or two countries increase at a faster rate than they wish—a not unlikely event in a world of more than 100 countries—these countries have an exchange rate problem which they can resolve either by revaluing their currencies or by taking other measures to increase their international payments. From time to time in the 1960s, Germany and perhaps Switzerland were in this position; so, in 1969 and 1970, were Canada and Japan. When a few countries have excessively large payments surpluses, it does not follow that the United States should limit its payments to all countries, as it did from 1960 on. But when many countries have excessively large surpluses, there is a much stronger case for the U.S. government to take the initiative to reduce the payments imbalance.

The European governments were in a delicate position. They wanted to force the United States to reduce its payments deficit. They might threaten to buy gold from the U.S. Treasury with some of their dollar assets, dollars that had initially been acquired in the belief that the U.S. Treasury would convert them into gold on demand. But this premise obviously was no longer tenable. A few countries might buy small amounts of gold—$10 million or $25 million at a time—from the U.S. Treasury. But for Germany, Italy, and Japan and other countries with large dollar holdings, the dollar was effectively inconvertible into gold. The European threat to convert dollars into gold was no longer credible, for the U.S. Treasury might formally stop selling gold.

If the Europeans could no longer buy gold with their dollars, the wisdom of their acquiring substantial amounts of both gold and dollars would be questioned. Their holdings of dollars would be criticized because the dollars would no longer be convertible into gold. And their holdings of gold would be criticized because a decision by the U.S. Treasury not to buy or sell gold would cloud the future of gold as an international money.

From 1969 through the summer of 1971, the underlying issue was whether the United States or the European countries and Japan would take the initiative in altering the exchange parities. Germany revalued the mark in October 1969. Canada returned to a floating rate in June 1970. Through late 1970 and the beginning of 1971, speculative pressure against the dollar began to mount, as it became increasingly likely that the European currencies and the Japanese yen would rise in price in terms of the dollar. What remained unclear was when the change would take place.

In May 1971 speculative pressure increased still further; Germany and the Netherlands followed the Canadian example and shifted to a floating rate, while Switzerland and Austria each revalued its currency by about 5 percent. But speculators were not assuaged, and the pressure against the dollar increased further. Within three months, speculators converted billions and billions of dollars into yen, marks, Swiss francs, sterling, and other strong currencies.

The crisis came to a head in early August. The leading U.S. congressional authority on international finance, Representative Henry Reuss, suggested that the dollar price of gold be raised slightly. Speculative pressure against the dollar greatly intensified. Finally, on August 15, President Nixon announced that as part of his New Economic Policy the Treasury would suspend gold sales and purchases, inducing other countries to revalue their currencies. The government also imposed a surcharge of 10 percent on dutiable imports. U.S. government officials made it clear that the surcharge would remain in effect until the exchange rate structure was realigned, discriminatory trade barriers against U.S. imports were reduced, and Europe and Japan agreed to begin negotiations toward a new international system. The Europeans and Japanese stopped pegging their currencies in terms of the dollar, and their currencies began to rise in price in terms of the dollar. The U.S. authorities were content with a floating-rate system; the pressure for returning to the pegged-rate system—and eliminating the U.S. tariff surcharge—came from abroad.

Monetary Artifacts and the Smithsonian

The suspension of U.S. gold sales was inevitable; the 10 percent surcharge was not. The surcharge was levied in a period when most countries were in a recession—and, as in the 1930s, these countries found it attractive to import jobs by increasing their exports of goods. But they could only do this by maintaining an undervalued currency. In the first test in twenty years of its ability to prevent "beggar thy neighbor" policies, the Bretton Woods System had failed.

Two complex questions complicated the realignment of exchange rates. One was whether European and Japanese currencies should be revalued around the dollar while the dollar remained pegged to gold at $35, or whether the dollar price of gold should be increased so that the dollar would depreciate in terms of some of the European currencies. The second was the amount of the revaluations of the various currencies in terms of the dollar. The first question involved political issues, while the second question involved economic issues.

The political aspect was especially clear in the context of U.S.-French relations. President Nixon would lose points with his domestic constituency if the dollar were devalued in terms of gold, while President Pompidou would gain support with his Gaullist followers if it appeared that the dollar had been dethroned as the center of the international system. An increase of 10 or 15 percent in the dollar price of gold and other currencies would have no significant impact on the gold output. But such an increase would win points for Pompidou.

The economic issues involved the effect of changes in the exchange rate structure on the competitive position of firms in different countries. Germany, for example, would not set a new parity for the mark until Japan had set a new parity for the yen. The Germans wanted to be sure that the yen would be revalued by a larger amount than the mark, so that German producers would be in a more favorable position relative to their Japanese competitors in world export markets. And the French would not set a new value for the franc until the rate for the mark had been set.

In mid-December 1971, agreement was reached on a currency realignment: the United States would increase the dollar price of gold by 8 percent, to $38; the other countries would realign their exchange rate pegs about the dollar. The yen was revalued by 17 percent from its May 1971 parity, the mark by 14 percent. But U.S. authorities would still not sell gold.

Thus, the Smithsonian Agreement—"the most important agreement in history"—may have resolved the imbalances resulting from Vietnam war inflation, but it did not solve the gold problem or resolve the inconsistencies between national monetary policies and the exchange rate system. While it was agreed that a new monetary system was needed, there was no agreement on what such a system should look like.

Any new system, regardless of its name, must accommodate itself to several realities. Most countries continued to prefer the pegged to floating exchange rates, and more and more countries were giving greater priority to independent monetary policies. Increasingly, countries were adjusting to external disturbances by adjusting international payments through controls. There was a widespread belief that the international role of the dollar would have to be diminished—a euphemism for attempting to reduce the economic power and influence of the United States. And somehow the new system would have to be built through multilateral agreement.

In June 1972 a speculative attack against sterling forced British authorities to stop supporting the pound, which promptly floated to its pre-Smithsonian parity. Speculation against the dollar increased in early 1973; in a day or two, the Bundesbank was obliged to buy $6 billion. It was too much: the monetary authorities permitted their currencies to float, while U.S. authorities agreed to increase the dollar price of gold to $42. The "greatest monetary agreement in history" lasted little more than one year.

A new Smithsonian-style accord was virtually out of the question; while the national monetary authorities might again commit themselves to a new set of pegged rates, few investors would believe in their commitments to these rates. So national treasuries were obliged to adopt floating rates because there was no feasible alternative. And so, beginning in late February

1973, the major currencies began to float against the dollar, with quite mixed results.

The movement of the U.S. dollar in terms of European currencies was much sharper than in terms of the Japanese yen or the Canadian dollar. The Bank of Japan extensively intervened to support the rate, the Bank of Canada rarely if ever. The large swings in the rate movements of European currencies took place despite extensive intervention by the various central banks.

The Committee of Twenty Exercise

The signers of the Smithsonian Agreement concurred on the need for monetary reform. Monetary reform required a plan—a proposal for how institutional arrangements should be revamped. To develop such a plan, a small secretariat was established within the IMF; the staff members would serve the national representatives. They met frequently in 1972 and were about to propose a more relaxed form of pegged rates when currencies began to float in February 1973.

4

"The Gnomes of Zurich"—A London
Euphemism for Speculation
Against Sterling

Between 1967 and 1973, speculators in foreign exchange—
private firms, banks, and individuals—netted nearly $8 billion.
In 1967 they sold sterling; in 1969 they sold French francs and
bought German marks. From 1970 on they sold massive amounts
of U.S. dollars to buy most European currencies and the
Japanese yen. Few banks or firms admit that they speculate; it
sounds antisocial. Rather, they maintain that they are solely
engaged in hedging their risks. Everyone points instead to the
"Gnomes of Zurich."

The brotherhood of Gnomes is worldwide. There are chapters
in London, Paris, Tokyo, New York—indeed, in every financial
center where banks and firms deal in foreign exchange. Membership in the brotherhood is open to anyone willing to take the
risks; all that is necessary is a willingness to play by the rules of
the market economy. The Gnomes are on *Fortune*'s lists of the
500 largest U.S. corporations and the 300 largest foreign
corporations.

Successful currency speculation is highly profitable. Speculators who bought dollars with sterling near the $2.80 parity
just before the November 1967 devaluation and then repur-
chased sterling near the new $2.40 parity made a 16 percent
profit. In the months prior to the revaluation of the mark in

September-October 1969, speculators sold dollars to get marks at a parity of about 4 marks to the dollar. After the revaluation they bought dollars at about 3.67 marks, giving them a profit of 8 percent. Note that many speculators secured these profits in a month or two, so on an annual basis their profit may have been as high at 50 or 100 percent. If, for example, a speculator sold sterling for dollars in the middle of September 1967, about two months before the devaluation, his profit of 16 percent on the investment of two months equals an annual profit rate of 96 percent. In a world in which annual rates or returns of 8 or 10 percent are the norm, such extremely high annual rates of profit attract risk takers.

Someone must pay for the revaluation profits earned by the Gnomes. In part, one Gnome loses what another wins; speculators deal with each other. Still, the $12 billion earned between 1967 and 1973 is the net overall estimate of the Gnomes' profits. These profits were earned at the expense of central banks. In the months prior to the devaluation, for example, the Bank of England sold $2 billion from its own holdings of dollars and $3 billion of borrowed dollars. Various firms and investors earned $800 million on their transactions—the product of the 16 percent devaluation and the $5 billion change in their position. After devaluation the Bank of England bought $3 billion from British exporters to get the dollars to repay its foreign creditors; in effect, it paid £1 for $2.60, whereas before devaluation it had sold $2.80 for £1.

The revaluation losses of the Bank of England—and of the Bank of Japan, the Bank of France, the Bundesbank, and numerous other central banks—fall on their stockholders. And since these institutions are owned by their governments, the taxpayers pay the bill. Despite massive losses, the taxpayers rarely complained. Perhaps this explains why, despite the increased search for speculative profits by firms during the latter 1960s and early 1970s, the authorities were slow to revise obsolete exchange market arrangements.

Foreign exchange speculation is not a certain gamble. Nor is it costless—anticipated changes in exchange rates may not occur, or they may be long delayed. But at least under the exchange market arrangements that prevailed until the end of 1971, the risks and costs were low.

The Gnomes of Zurich were a handy scapegoat for the problems besetting sterling in the mid-1960s, problems that had their source in London, not Zurich. Sterling's weakness was a result of British monetary policy; $2.80 had ceased to be a viable parity by 1964, if not by 1962. Speculators sought revaluation profits at low risk because the British authorities retained archaic exchange market arrangements with an increasingly overvalued currency.

With the move to floating exchange rates in early 1973, central banks greatly reduced their subsidy to business firms willing to speculate in the exchange market. Many firms and banks had developed great confidence in their ability to predict changes in exchange rates during the pegged period. When currencies began to float, they continued to speculate. The losses incurred by a few were so substantial that they went bankrupt. For others, the experience was only a public embarrassment.

Gnomes and Non-Gnomes

Gnomes (and non-Gnomes) who deal in foreign exchange buy and sell bank deposits denominated in different currencies. A turn of events—an election, the quarterly report on exports and imports, a dock strike, this month's report on changes in wholesale prices—can alter expectations about the future price of a currency. Gnomes sell and buy in order to profit from anticipated price changes.

A market in national monies is inevitable as long as there are separate national currencies. Domestic monies—primarily bank deposits—are traded against similar deposits denominated in other currencies. In New York, U.S. dollars are traded against Canadian dollars, sterling, French francs, Swiss francs, marks, and more than 100 other currencies. In the United States, there are foreign exchange dealers in New York, Chicago, and San Francisco; in Switzerland, in Zurich, Geneva, and Basel. But in reality, New York, London, Brussels, Zurich, and the other financial centers are the geographic extensions of one international market.

Because the cost of transporting money across national borders is very low, the sterling-dollar exchange rate in New York is virtually identical with the rates quoted in Zurich, London, and every other center at the same moment; foreign exchange traders find it financially rewarding to keep the rates in different centers in line whenever deviations appear. Assume an extreme example: the dollar price of £1 sterling is $2 in New York and $3 in London; that is, sterling is cheap in New York and dear in London. Foreign exchange traders buy sterling with dollars in New York: they receive a sterling deposit in a bank in London which they pay for with a dollar deposit in New York; each pound costs them $2. At the same time, they buy dollars with sterling in London and receive $3 for each pound; they receive a dollar deposit in New York and pay with a sterling deposit in London. Thus, their profit per "round trip" for each $2 investment is $1. Their activity is riskless, for the two transactions occur simultaneously. Riskless transactions designed to take advantage of price discrepancies in different geographic centers are known as arbitrage.

Investors cause the dollar prices of sterling in New York and London to converge until the remaining spread between them is insufficient for any additional arbitrage to be profitable. In practice, this means that the spread can be as low as several thousandths of 1 percent.

Arbitragers also ensure that the exchange rate between the guilder and the mark is consistent with the price of the dollar in terms of the mark and in terms of the guilder. Once the price of the dollar in terms of each of these currencies is known, then the guilder price of the mark (the cross-rate) can be determined arithmetically. Arbitragers see to it that the arithmetic is correct. Assume, for example, that the dollar costs 4 marks, the mark costs 2 guilders, and the dollar costs 6 guilders. These rates are inconsistent; the cross-rate for the mark in terms of the guilder, given their rates against the dollar, is 1.5 guilders to the mark. So the arbitragers sell guilders to buy dollars, then sell the dollars to buy marks, and finally sell marks to buy guilders; 6 guilders buy $1, which buys 4 marks, which in turn buy 8 guilders. Arbitrage continues until the riskless profit opportunities are eliminated. The mark price and dollar price of the guilder decline, while the dollar price of the mark rises.

Some foreign exchange dealings are spot transactions: buyers and sellers agree to transfer bank deposits immediately after they enter into the contract, which in practice means two days later. Other dealings are forward transactions, which differ from spot transactions in only one important respect—the exchange of deposits occurs at a more distant future date, often thirty days or ninety days after the date of the contract.

Gnomes often prefer forward transactions because they can buy a foreign currency without having to make an immediate large cash payment. But Gnomes can only buy forward contracts if some non-Gnomes sell forward contracts. If, for example, speculators believe that sterling will depreciate, they may want to sell sterling forward, which means they will want to buy dollars forward. Most participants in the exchange market would be reluctant to buy forward sterling if they thought sterling might depreciate. Some arbitragers, however, may buy forward sterling, but only after selling sterling in the spot market. By combining a sale of sterling spot with the purchase of spot sterling, they protect themselves against a loss from a depreciation of sterling. Thus, the arbitragers might sell sterling at $2.20 and at the same time buy forward sterling at $2.15.

Regardless of changes in the dollar price of sterling, they would profit, since the forward contract protects them against any loss from a change in the exchange rate. While speculators seek to profit from anticipated change in the exchange rate, arbitragers (who are reluctant to bear the risk associated with changes in the exchange rates) profit from the differences in the price of foreign exchange in the spot market and the forward market.

As long as the exchange rates are pegged, the risks that exchange speculators run center around government policy toward the exchange rate. The foreign exchange market is distinguished from the commodity, stock, and bond markets by the pervasiveness of the government's role, especially through central bank intervention to maintain the foreign exchange price of the national currency within a narrow "band" around par value. Under the old IMF rules, support limits of the band could be no greater than 1 percent on either side of par; these limits were increased to 2.25 percent under the Smithsonian Agreement.

Speculation about changes in the exchange rate centers largely on changes in the central bank's parity. Exchange speculators buy and sell foreign exchange with the large commercial banks. But these banks are not eager to hold large amounts of currencies which might be devalued. They are more likely to be sellers of the weak currency; indeed, many qualify for senior membership in the Brotherhood of Gnomes. Since for every seller there must be a buyer, the central bank must buy its own currency to prevent its price from moving beyond its support limits.

While countries may be reluctant to change the parity *formally*, they cannot avoid or even postpone changes in the *effective* exchange rate. So ad hoc measures are adopted to prevent exceptionally large and persistent losses in central bank holdings of international money. Purchases of foreign exchange may be restricted, taxed, delayed, and licensed. Supplemental tariffs may be levied on commodity imports. A ceiling or tax may be placed on overseas spending by tourists. Government agencies may be directed to supply their needs from domestic sources even though foreign sources are cheaper. Such taxes and restrictions increase the effective price of foreign exchange. In effect, the currency is devalued through the back door.

Once the ability to buy foreign exchange freely at the established price is restricted or taxed, a black market in foreign exchange almost inevitably develops. Rather than pay the taxes or wait in line at the central bank to buy the foreign exchange at the legal parity, some importers decide that it is cheaper to buy it in the black market. Some exporters will seek to increase their income by selling their foreign exchange earnings in the black market. Some governments seek to profit by offering to sell foreign exchange to importers at the artificially low price, and then taxing their purchases. And various government officials in the agencies which ration foreign exchange and import licenses may place individual importers in a favored position in the queue in return for side bets, private payments, or commissions.

Surprisingly, most governments tolerate black markets in foreign exchange. Legal penalties are rarely imposed in spite of the pervasiveness of apparently illegal transactions. In many cases the black market in effect permits the government to delay the political costs of formally devaluing the rate, while minimizing the economic costs of maintaining an overvalued currency.

The Source of Exchange Crises

Speculation about devaluations—or, in the case of the mark, the Canadian dollar, and the yen, revaluations—involves a game of wits between the authorities and private parties. The authorities must always deny that they will ever change a parity. To do otherwise, or even to offer a halfhearted denial, almost inevitably leads to a surge of speculative demand. The participants in the exchange market must constantly decide how much importance to attach to the official denials.

Crises in the exchange market reflect two underlying factors. The first—and necessary—factor is the desire of many countries to pursue independent monetary policies. Price levels rise rapidly in some countries and slowly in others. The resulting changes in price level relationships, in turn, have an impact on trade. The imports of countries whose prices are rising increase more rapidly, while their exports increase at a slower rate or may even fall. Their international money holdings decline, and ultimately a devaluation is necessary. Meanwhile, in the countries with more stable prices, exports grow more rapidly than imports and holdings of international money increase. A revaluation of currencies may be necessary in countries with payments surpluses.

The second factor in the exchange crises of the past is that the IMF rules for regulating exchange rates were archaic, if not when they were adopted in the 1940s, then by the early 1960s. These exchange rate provisions—a combination of narrow support limits around the parity and measures that sought to prevent countries from changing their parities—were designed for a monetary world based on the gold standard, where the chief danger was to avoid excessive changes in exchange parities.

The anomaly of the Bretton Woods System, which ultimately led to its breakdown, was that the exchange market arrangements of the gold standard were retained even though many central banks had switched from dependent monetary policies under the gold standard to independent monetary policies. Predictably, an exchange rate system designed in accordance with the gold standard worked less well in a period of greater national monetary independence.

54

The Politics of Parity

The decision to change an exchange parity is ultimately political. Necessary changes in parities have often been delayed because of the political costs. One hangover from the gold standard era was the notion that there is something sacrosanct about a parity and that devaluation is an admission that domestic financial policies have failed. The monetary authorities always hoped that events would somehow save them from the need to devalue —that next month's trade data would show a healthy rise in exports, or that other countries would revalue their currencies so that their own devaluation would be unnecessary.

No one needs any private knowledge to recognize when a currency is overvalued or undervalued. Because changes in parities are usually delayed, investors do not need remarkably accurate foresight to anticipate them. With a narrow band between the support limits, the cost of guessing wrong was minimal, since investors' transactions could be easily reversed. And because the authorities were often reluctant to change the parities by small amounts, speculators could be confident that the eventual changes would be substantial.

Take sterling. By 1964 sterling was clearly overvalued. British prices had been rising more rapidly than those of Britain's competitors, the British share of the world export market was declining, and the payments deficit was large. Many observers felt that the Labour government should have devalued immediately on winning the election and coming to power in October 1964, for at that time the need for the devaluation could have been blamed on the outgoing Conservatives. But the Labour party did not take advantage of its opportunity. Labour governments had been in power before when sterling was devalued—in 1931 and again in 1949—and party leaders were fearful of being tagged as the "devaluation party." For at

55

least three years, Britain's economic policies, as well as its international and national security policies, were affected by the need to defend an overvalued parity.

By November 1967 nearly everyone except Harold Wilson admitted that sterling would have to be devalued. While the precise amount of the devaluation needed could not be determined, it was almost certain to be greater than 10 percent, since a smaller change would not have seemed worthwhile. And it was almost certain to be smaller than 20 percent, since a larger change would almost surely have resulted in retaliatory devaluations by other European countries whose trade positions were excessively threatened.

As it turned out, sterling was devalued in November 1967 because the British authorities could no longer maintain the parity; their holdings of international money were exhausted. Moreover, they had already borrowed the maximum possible amount from the IMF and were negotiating for large loans from other countries. But the conditions on British domestic policy attached to these credits, especially by France, were deemed too onerous.

The devaluation of the French franc in August 1969 was similarly influenced by political factors. To restore the domestic peace and harmony that had been threatened by the student riots of May 1968, the French government approved nationwide wage increases of 15 percent. Price increases were inevitable; firms could not othewise afford to pay the higher wages. The prospect of a one-shot increase in the price level of 10 to 15 percent meant that the franc would have to be devalued. The anticipated price increases and the political uncertainty associated with the riots triggered a sharp speculative attack against the franc.

Yet the necessary change in the parity was delayed for political reasons. President de Gaulle would not devalue the franc; after all, he had given France ten years of price stability (1959–1968) following 50 years of inflation. To maintain that stability,

---

The Brussels Caper

In the mid-1960s, a foreign exchange trader in the Brussels branch of a major New York bank fell in love with sterling. The Gnomes were bearish on sterling; they anticipated a devaluation. Forward sterling was at a substantial discount—when spot sterling was at $2.79, forward sterling was cheaper. Moreover, the discounts on 12-month forward contracts were substantially larger than on one-month forward contracts. So the trader bought the long sterling contracts, which were cheap, and sold one-month forward sterling contracts, which were more expensive. Thus, his position in sterling was more or less even, at least for one month; from the beginning of the second month until the end of the twelfth, he was long sterling. And he had a potential profit, which was the difference between the cheap sterling he had bought and the dear sterling he had sold.

A month later, he again bought one-month sterling forward to offset his position in the long forward contract, which had eleven months to run until maturity. At the same time, he bought more long sterling contracts and sold an equal amount of short sterling contracts; his position was even and he still had a nice potential profit.

A month later he repeated the process; he repeated it for several more months. The potential profit kept increasing.

When the bank learned of its extremely large position in long sterling contracts, the position was closed, at a loss of $8 million.

---

the payments abroad had been restricted; in effect, the franc was being devalued by the back door. Only the date of "front door" devaluation and the amount of the change remained uncertain. Less than four months after de Gaulle resigned, the franc was devalued.

The way election results can influence an exchange parity was dramatically shown by the revaluation of the West German mark in October 1969. The Christian Democrats wanted to maintain the existing parity until the German parliamentary elections in September. The business community, an important supporter of the Christian Democratic Party, favored retaining the 4 mark parity with the dollar, since a revaluation of the mark would mean that the prices of German goods in the United States and other foreign markets would rise relative to the prices of U.S. goods, and that German export sales and the profits of German firms would decline. Revaluation of the mark would also lead Germans to buy more foreign goods, since they would be cheaper in relation to German goods. Thus, the mark prices of German goods competing with imports would have to fall, and the profits of domestic firms producing these goods would decline.

The major constituency of the Social Democrats was—and is—the workers, who are interested in higher incomes and lower prices, not in business profits. Thus, a revaluation would benefit the Social Democrats, and a revaluation was widely expected— if the Social Democrats won. Had the Christian Democrats won, the outcome would have been more uncertain, for their constituency and the economic realities were pulling in opposite directions.

As soon as preliminary election results indicated that the Social Democrats would win, the speculative demand for the mark soared. On September 29 the Bundesbank ceased pegging the mark at the parity of 4 marks to the dollar, and the mark floated upward until October 24, when it was pegged at 3.67 marks by the newly installed Social Democratic government.

On two occasions in twenty years the Canadian government shifted from a pegged exchange rate to a floating rate. In both instances, the cause was the same: Canada wanted to minimize the increase in the Canadian price level resulting from wartime inflation in the United States. Both in 1950 and in the late 1960s, as a result of the U.S. booms, Canadian exports surged and large payments surpluses brought about large increases in Canada's money supply. In each case, the Canadian government sought greater monetary independence by shifting to a floating exchange rate system.

Now, the dominant factor in Canada's exchange rate policy is the economic fit of the Canadian economy with the U.S. economy. The close economic and geographic relationship with the United States means that Canada has an automatic tendency to import U.S. problems. Moreover, because Canadian exports to the United States are largely raw materials, U.S. economic developments have an exaggerated impact on Canada. When the U.S. economy has a little boom, U.S. imports of raw materials soar, and the Canadian economy has a big boom. Thus, in June 1950, the Canadian dollar (which had been pegged at the rate of $1.10 Canadian to $1.00 U.S.) was floated, and it shortly appreciated by 10 percent. Similarly, when in June 1970 the Canadian authorities again freed their dollar from a parity of $1.08 Canadian to $1.00 U.S., it appreciated by 8 percent.

Canada wants more independence from the United States. Since Canada cannot readily move to Europe or to the Far East, it has sought mechanisms that would disengage its economy from the U.S. economy. Both in 1950 and in 1970, the Canadians hoped that a floating rate would provide increased insulation from U.S. inflation. Conversely, when in 1962 both the U.S. and Canadian economies were in recessions, the Canadian government returned to a pegged exchange to stimulate its economy; the Canadian dollar was pegged at a rate below the market level in order to increase Canadian exports.

Until 1971 most exchange crises involved only one country; there was no systematic relation between the problems of sterling, the Canadian dollar, and the French franc. But the exchange rate changes of May 1971 and of February 1973—both those that did occur and those that should have occurred but did not—involved more than ten countries. The U.S. payments deficit associated with the Vietnam war indicated that foreign central banks were acquiring more dollars than they wished. As a result, their domestic money supplies were growing rapidly; they imported the U.S. inflation. One of the few options open to foreign central banks was to use the dollars to buy gold from the U.S. Treasury and hope that the gold losses would force U.S. authorities to take measures to reduce the payments deficit. Another option was for the other industrial countries to revalue their currencies and incur the costs in terms of their own constituencies.

Murphy's Law—anything that can go wrong will go wrong—went to work. The other industrial countries imported the U.S. inflation and *then* they revalued. Their price levels increased about as rapidly as the U.S. price level, because the revaluation was too long delayed.

By mid-1971 the U.S. gold position was precarious, for the large payments deficit had led foreign central banks to come to the U.S. Treasury for gold. Once it became obvious that the $35 parity would not be viable until November 1972, it was in President Nixon's domestic political interest to advance the suspension of U.S. gold sales as far as possible before the 1972 election.

But the decision to suspend gold transactions did not automatically lead to changes in the exchange rates. Most foreign countries were reluctant to appreciate their currencies because of the adverse impact such revaluations would have on jobs and profits in their export industries. Because of this concern, the U.S. government adopted a surcharge of 10 percent on all imports subject to tariffs as a way to raise the dollar price of these goods. The bargain was that the surcharge would be removed when they had revalued their currencies.

The Search for Flexibility—Floating Rates and Sliding Parities

Since 1960, more than thirty countries have devalued their currencies. A few—including West Germany, Austria, the Netherlands, Switzerland, Japan, Canada, France, Italy, and Great

Britain—have revalued. Small wonder that speculators appear increasingly sensitive to the possibility of changes in exchange parities. Whenever it has appeared likely that a parity might be changed, the volume of funds shifted in anticipation of such a change has increased greatly year after year. The odds in the game have increasingly favored the speculators.

Inevitably, the central bankers have been forced to deny they would change their parities; not to deny is to admit. But the sequence of a succession of denials followed by a succession of parity changes quickly reduced the value of their denials. Central bankers' public statements about the exchange rate have lost credibility.

The inconsistency between national monetary policies and the exchange rate system—and the resulting speculation—might be reduced by a return to a gold standard monetary policy, that is, by returning to dependent national monetary policies. For many countries, however, monetary independence is the essence of sovereignty. In the Age of Aquarius, each country wants to do its own thing.

Given each nation's desire for monetary independence, greater flexibility is obtained through floating exchange rates, or with more frequent changes in the parity so as to reduce the scope for speculative profits. Under a floating exchange rate system, the exchange rate varies like any other price in response to market forces. Central banks are not required to support their currencies in the exchange market, although they do intervene to smooth movements in the exchange rate so as to accommodate the needs of traders and investors. Changes in the exchange rate are less sudden and discrete than under the pegged system. New information about future events—and hence about the exchange rates in the future—is immediately reflected in the exchange rate. Thus, as the domestic price level increases or the foreign demand for domestic products declines, the price of foreign exchange increases. Firms can still speculate on changes in the exchange rate, but they no longer have the relatively riskless one-way option available under the pegged exchange rate system. For one thing, the amount of the change is smaller, since the rate is adjusted continuously. And the costs of being wrong can be much greater, since the currency may appreciate by a larger amount if speculators are wrong. The need to apply controls and restrictions to limit purchases of foreign exchange should disappear, as should the currency black markets.

Academic economists—perhaps a majority of them—favor floating exchange rates. Some—those who advocate monetary rules that the money supply grow at a rate of 5, 6, or 10 percent a year—favor independent monetary policies; they abhor the idea that the growth of the money supply within a country should be affected by whether the country has a payments surplus or deficit. And the economists who do not accept a fixed monetary rule want to eliminate the external constraint on the choice of domestic policies and the need to balance international payments and receipts at one particular exchange rate. Most economists believe that the variations in exchange controls needed to maintain individual parities indicate either that the system was badly managed or that it was obsolete—and that even the best central bankers could not make it work effectively.

Yet floating exchange rates have been extensively criticized by men of affairs. Their reasons differ. Some believe that daily, weekly, and monthly movements in the exchange rate retard the growth of international trade and investment because the increased uncertainty about future exchange rates deters some individuals and firms from undertaking international transactions.

The rationale for pegged exchange rates is that central bankers are more astute in setting the price of foreign exchange—in speculating in the exchange market—than are private parties. Central banks are government-owned public utilities, and they are supposed to provide public services—if necessary, at a loss. Their transactions and presence in the exchange market are thought to reduce uncertainty, so that traders will have greater confidence in the future exchange rate. Exporters and importers benefit from the reduction of uncertainty. And since their costs decline, the benefits are passed on both to those who produce export goods (and would thus have a larger foreign market) and to those who consume imports.

The rationale for floating exchange rates, on the other hand, is that changes in the exchange rate should be depoliticized. Even if the foreign exchange traders in the central banks are more skillful than their private-sector counterparts, they cannot alter the exchange peg on their own; these changes reflect a political decision. The needed changes in parities are long delayed. Thus, in most periods, any reduction in exchange market uncertainty from central bank intervention is more than offset by the sharp rise in uncertainty whenever expectations develop that the exchange parity must be altered—and that politicians are mustering the political will to make the change.

In general, proponents of floating exchange rates emphasize the ease with which the market rate changes over time. Critics of floating exchange rates emphasize the unnecessary and avoidable fluctuations in the market rate, and the associated costs.

In choosing between pegged and floating exchange rates, one of the major questions concerns the impact of uncertainty on trade and investment. Ideally, the effects and relative costs of uncertainty under the two systems might be measured and compared. Yet until 1973 the opportunities for comparison were infrequent and the task complex. Floating exchange rate systems did not work well in the 1920s, but the relevance of this experience is questionable, as is the failure of the pegged-rate system during the 1930s. The twelve-year Canadian experience with floating exchange rates between 1950 and 1962 was generally acknowledged a success, except by the governor of the Bank of Canada, who in 1962 shifted back to a pegged system. Lebanon has used a floating exchange rate since 1950, and the system has worked well despite wars, revolutions, and other sources of political uncertainty in the Middle East. But Lebanon has not followed an independent monetary policy.

Another issue in choosing between these two exchange rate systems concerns the likelihood that a floating exchange rate will be manipulated by governments. The fear is that some countries might manipulate their exchange rates to enhance their national advantage. Without established parities, governments cannot be prevented from manipulating the foreign exchange price of their currency. International rules could be developed that would define acceptable and unacceptable forms of central bank intervention under a system of floating exchange rates. Perhaps—but the likelihood that such rules will be adopted seems low. And the likelihood that they will be followed even if adopted is lower still.

The postwar experience has been biased. Since most countries have been on pegged rates, the problems of this system have been evident. The exchange crises have been dramatic; drama aside, their economic cost may not have been so great. In any case, the cost derives from delays in changing the exchange rate, and from changing the effective rate by administrative controls—in effect, with the way the system has been managed rather than with the system itself.

Strong resistance to floating rates stimulated the search for greater flexibility within the pegged-rate system. The widening of the support limits around parities to 2.25 percent either side of parity was a response to this search. The advantage of a wider spread is that it tends to lessen shifts of funds between assets denominated in various currencies, since the possible exchange losses are greater; investors have less of a one-way option. Whether 2.25 percent is sufficient is not yet clear—a somewhat wider spread, perhaps 4 or 5 percent, might be preferable. But even if there were international agreement on a wider spread, some central banks might intervene to hold rate movements within a narrower range.

Even with wider margins, exchange crises might still arise because independent monetary policies tend to make established parities obsolete. Unless authorities manage to change their parity before they are forced to do so by speculative pressure, crises are inevitable.

Another approach toward greater flexibility involves various mechanisms which make it easier to change parities. Such devices, called sliding parities, crawling pegs, or gliding rates, are all minor variations on a single theme: when a country begins to move into a position of persistent payments surplus or deficit, the parity should be changed quickly. Small, frequent changes in parity then replace large, infrequent ones. These changes can be triggered automatically by changes in a country's holdings of international money, since a formula approach might circumvent the reluctance of the authorities to change the peg.

Brazil and Colombia have been using a floating peg; every six or eight weeks each devalues its currency by 2 or 3 percent. The amount of the change is so small and its exact timing so uncertain, that investors have not found it worthwhile to seek to profit from the predictably small change in the peg. But most governments are skeptical of using a formula to determine the amount and timing of an exchange rate change; the domestic political consequences might be too severe. And many governments have shown an unusual reluctance to use any variant of the sliding parity approach.

That the Bretton Woods System would break down was inevitable; the system had become obsolete in a world of independent monetary policies. It became too easy for investors to profit from changes in parities. Central bankers continued to play by the Bretton Woods rules even while they sought to negotiate changes. Changes in institutional arrangements occur slowly, especially when the number of participants is large and their interests diverse. The negotiations proved unsuccessful; currencies were allowed to float because agreement could not be reached on any alternative.

Floating Rates—The Arguments and the Experience

The months since February 1973 provide the most extensive experience since the 1920s for testing the arguments for floating rates. Even so, most currencies remain pegged; the floating currencies are almost exclusively those of the industrialized countries. And there have been wide differences in the freedom of currencies to float, with some central banks intervening extensively in the exchange market in support of their currencies.

At one extreme stands the Bank of Canada which takes a hands-off approach to the exchange rate; at the other stands the Bank of Japan, which smooths the daily movements in the rate and seeks to moderate the tendency toward sharp cyclical swings. Sterling has been another managed floating currency. The U.K. authorities have decided on the range within which they want sterling to trade and have sold enough foreign currencies to achieve their objective. In both the Japanese and British cases, floating has largely meant the absence of a commitment to a particular parity.

The continental European countries have participated in a joint float as an initial step toward the eventual unification of European currencies. In effect, countries participating in the joint float peg their currencies to each other, and these currencies appreciate and depreciate together in terms of the dollar. The percentage changes from peak to trough and from trough to peak are sharp in terms of the dollar, as much as 15 or 20 percent in a relatively short interval. Moreover, these currencies also float relative to each other within range of little more than 2 percent (see Figure 4–1).

France dropped out of the joint float in January 1974 because the reserve losses associated with pegging within the snake were too large; France rejoined in August 1975. In the summer of 1973, Germany revalued the mark in terms of other

FIGURE 4–1

The EEC "Snake" and the French Franc vis-à-vis the Dollar*
(weekly averages of daily figures)

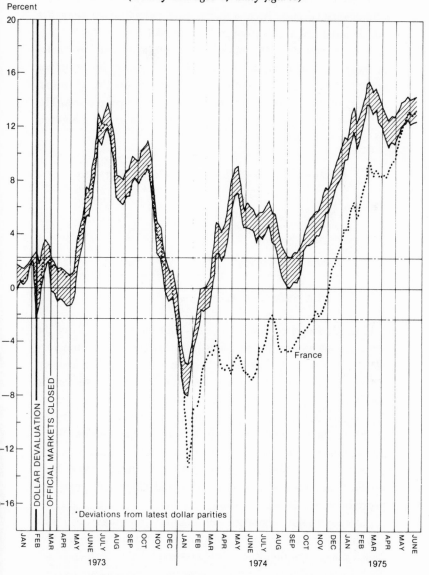

SOURCE: Organisation for Economic Co-operation and Development, *OECD Economic Outlook* (Paris), July 1975.

currencies. Great Britain has delayed joining the joint float, while Norway and Sweden participate even though they are not members of the European Economic Community.

The movements of the mark, the guilder, and other currencies in the joint float in terms of the dollar are shown in the upper portion of Figure 4–2, while the movements of the French franc, sterling, the yen, and the lira are shown in the lower portion. The percentage deviations from the Smithsonian rates are measured on the vertical axis.

Forecasting Exchange Rates: The Known Scorecard

Herstatt	$171 million
Union de Banques Suisses	56
Westdeutsche Landesbank	114
Franklin National	46
Lloyds Bank	77
Banque de Bruxelles	100

SOURCE: *The Banker* (London), May 1975.
Note: These figures represent losses.

One advantage of floating rates is that the movements of the rates are no longer the occasion for great crises; the monetary authorities are no longer subject to the political embarrassment associated with changes in parities. But the quieter life for the authorities is not a free lunch; business firms and investors have had to give much concern to the impact of exchange rate movements on their competitive position and on their profits. While international trade and investment have not declined, it seems plausible to assume that their rates of growth have been smaller than they would have been had currencies remained pegged.

Another major argument for floating rates has been that countries would be able to pursue independent monetary policies. Perhaps they tried. Yet one remarkable feature of the period since 1973 has been the similarity of movements of price levels and incomes among the major countries.

FIGURE 4–2

Exchange Rates Against the Dollar:
Percentage Deviations from Dollar Smithsonian
Parities of December 1971
(weekly averages of daily figures)

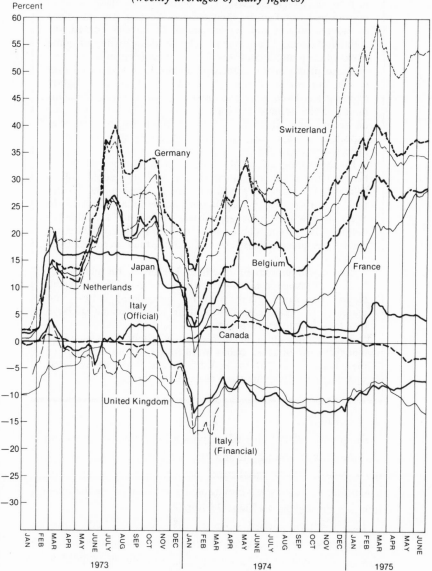

SOURCE: Organisation for Economic Co-operation and Development, *OECD Economic Outlook* (Paris), July 1975.

The move to floating exchange rates meant a boom for foreign exchange traders. The demand for their services skyrocketed—and so did their salaries. Success was measured by advancement, and advancement by profits earned for their employees. The foreign exchange departments of some banks made a major contribution to the bank's profits.

These profits arose from two sources. One was that banks bought currencies at one price and sold them at a slightly higher price. Even when the bid-ask spread is small, the sums mount if the volume of business is large. The second source of profit came from holding long positions in currencies expected to appreciate and a short position in currencies expected to depreciate.

In the spring of 1974, traders in a number of banks believed the dollar would appreciate, so they bought dollars forward. The dollar depreciated; they incurred losses. Rather than take these losses, they bought more dollars forward; in effect, it was the exchange market equivalent of double-or-nothing. The dollar depreciated further, so they doubled up again. The greater their losses, the more they increased their positions.

Two questions remain unsettled. The first is the number of foreign exchange traders—and the number of banks—who played the same game, incurred unrealized losses, and managed to break even before their losses became so large that they had to be revealed.

The second question involves the extent to which the managements of these banks were aware of the activities of their traders—and, if so, how they could have believed that such large profits came from the bid-ask spread.

Frequently, the choice of exchange rate systems seems much like the choice among automobiles or brands of soap—any of the available brands might do. But the analogy is misleading, since floating rates were inevitable in the context of the general inflation during the 1973–1974 boom.

The historical record suggests that countries will move to floating rates whenever rates of price change—or intended price change—deviate sharply. Sterling floated in terms of gold from

1803 to 1815 during the Napoleonic Wars. The U.S. dollar floated from 1862 to 1879 because Civil War finance was highly inflationary and the dollar remained overvalued for a substantial period after the war ended. That most European currencies were floating in the early 1920s was not an accident; floating rates were necessary as long as countries sought to deflate their price levels relative to the U.S. price level as a prelude to pegging their currencies to gold at the 1913 parities.

As long as the world economy continues to be subject to the disruptions of inflationary booms or sharp recessions, floating rates are likely to be retained. The major uncertainties then revolve around the extent of central bank intervention in the exchange market and the possibility that some countries might adopt exchange controls.

Which Way After Floating?

If historical experience suggests that floating rates are inevitable in an era of double-digit inflation and major recession, it also suggests that countries will move back toward some form of pegged rates once the monetary environment is more stable. Individual countries will decide on their own when the time is appropriate to peg their currencies. Such a move might follow an international conference or agreement which concludes that a move toward pegged rates is desirable; alternatively, individual countries might unilaterally peg their currencies after they have achieved monetary stability.

Ultimately, a new agreement might be reached on pegged rates. Such an agreement would differ from the Bretton Woods System in several important ways. The support limits are likely to be wider, probably even wider than the 2.25 percent limits of the Smithsonian Agreement. The rules concerning parity changes will place greater emphasis on the need to change rates which are inappropriate. And the rules are likely to be more permissive, so that some countries might permit their currencies to float while others might peg their currencies.

Just as it is predictable that there will be a move back toward pegged rates and a new exchange rate arrangement, so it is inevitable that this agreement too will eventually become outdated and will be shelved with the gold standard and the Bretton Woods System in the monetary counterpart of the Smithsonian. Monetary agreements are matters of convenience which last for a decade or two; as the economic conditions which made the agreement feasible change, the agreement becomes obsolete.

 **5**

Gold—How Much Is a Barbarous Relic Worth?

President John F. Kennedy once observed that the U.S. balance-of-payments problem was one of the two most complex issues he had to deal with; the other was avoiding nuclear war. What worried him about the payments problem was that he might have to change the dollar price of gold. Yet when President Richard Nixon suspended gold sales by the U.S. Treasury in August 1971 and then agreed to increase the dollar price of gold to $38, the domestic political fallout was extremely mild. Actually, the Nixon decision was ironic. In his 1960 bid for the presidency, Nixon had suggested that the dollar would be devalued if Kennedy were elected President. Nixon was right— Kennedy was elected president and the dollar was devalued! Kennedy was wrong to be distressed by the thought of changing the gold price. A variety of U.S. decisions have proved more costly, including Nixon's temporary tariff surcharge of 10 percent, U.S. quotas on textile imports, and the invasion of Cambodia.

Gold's role in monetary affairs has periodically been subject to such ironic twists. John Maynard Keynes called gold a "barbarous relic." De Gaulle said only gold could be the cornerstone of a new international monetary system. Both were probably right.

The U.S. government's suspension of gold transactions in 1971 raised the question of whether gold could continue as an international money. Demonetizing gold would greatly reduce the supply of international money. The credibility of future U.S. commitments about the international monetary system would decline. And indefinite suspension of the U.S. Treasury's gold transactions, even at a $42 parity, would amount to effective demonetization.

In the mid-1960s, one solution for the gold problem was to double the monetary price; the U.S. gold parity would have been $70. The rationale was that since the world commodity price level had more or less doubled since the monetary gold price was last increased, it was appropriate that the monetary gold price should also be doubled. Then, as world inflation proceeded, the gold bugs began to talk about a $100 parity.

In 1973 and 1974, when the price of gold in the private market began to rise, first to $100 and then to $150, the newspaper explanation was that investors around the world were losing confidence in paper monies. Perhaps. But an alternative explanation is that they were betting that the monetary price of gold would increase. No one would pay $100 for gold unless he expected the price to rise; no one would pay $150 unless the future anticipated price was even higher.

At the end of 1974 the gold price approached $200. In the first months of 1975 gold traded in the range of $160–175. These market prices are viable only if central banks decide that gold should remain an international money. When and if gold is demonetized, the market price will tumble. For better or worse, investors have indicated what they anticipate the outcome will be.

Before Gold Was a Barbarous Relic

The use of gold as money predates written history. How did gold develop its monetary role? Two questions are relevant here. One is why a money was necessary. The second is why gold satisfied this need better than the alternatives.

5 / Gold—How Much Is a Barbarous Relic Worth?

Without money, goods must be exchanged through barter, a time-consuming process. First, an individual who wishes to sell his output has to find a buyer with a desirable product to exchange. Next, buyer and seller must agree on a price, since there is no standard way to determine prices. Finally, the values in the transaction have to match—if buyer and seller agree that the fair price for one horse is three cows, the seller of the horse might acquire one or two more cows than he wishes.

Someone must have realized that an intermediate good might lead to more efficient transactions. Producers could sell their output in exchange for the intermediate good, so that they need not spend the time finding a buyer for their product. Prices of goods might be expressed in terms of the intermediate good. If the intermediate good was divisible into small units, the amount of the payment could be matched to the price. The intermediate good thus performed the several functions of a money—it served as a medium of exchange, a unit of account, and a store of value.

Gold has several attributes that enhanced its attractiveness as the intermediate good. Gold is durable; it does not "wear out." Gold is homogeneous; one unit is virtually identical with another. Its value-to-weight ratio is high, so transport and storage costs are relatively low. Gold can be manufactured into large coins and small coins. Because of the high costs of gold mining, moreover, the supply of gold does not change rapidly— which means that the price of a market basket of commodities is likely to be more stable in terms of a unit of gold than in terms of other commodities whose supplies change more rapidly. So gold became a commodity money.

Other commodities with an attractive set of attributes also have been used as money. Silver, for example, has a somewhat lower value-to-weight ratio than gold, so it proved more useful for coins and transactions of lower value. The costs of transporting silver were many times the costs of transporting gold of equal value.

A major problem with using several different types of commodity money was that efficiency in transactions required that the price relationship between the different monies remain constant; otherwise, producers would have to quote a price for each good in terms of each of the monies. A constant price relationship could not simply happen; government policies were necessary to peg the price of one commodity money in terms of any other.

Over the last several hundred years, the authorities in most countries have supplemented gold's domestic role with paper monies—note issues and bank deposits. Such paper monies were easier to use in making payments than gold, for their storage and transportation costs were lower. Initially, individuals were dubious about the value of paper monies. One concern was that excessive production of paper monies might raise the commodity price level and lead to a reduction in their value. So to gain acceptance for the paper monies, governments had to agree to convert them into gold at a fixed price; this requirement was supposed to insure against excessive production of the paper money. The free convertibility of paper monies into gold constrained the monetary authorities in their attempts to have independent monetary policies—that is, to produce money at the rate which satisfied their domestic objectives.

When the constraints on independent policies became too severe, the monetary authorities eliminated gold from the domestic monetary system; central banks stopped converting their domestic monies into gold. In September 1931 the Bank of England stopped pegging sterling to gold; the British authorities wanted the freedom to pursue a more expansive monetary policy. In 1933 the U.S. government required all U.S. residents to sell their gold to the government; the government wanted to eliminate the pressure on U.S. commercial banks to convert their liabilities into gold.

Today gold retains a monetary role in only a very few countries, principally some Arab sheikhdoms. In most countries outside the United States, private parties have been free to hold gold as a commodity, although they cannot buy it from their central banks. From January 1975 on, U.S. residents could once again buy and deal in gold domestically.

Nations continue to demand gold as international money because they believe it to be a better store of value than other international monies. Each central bank buys gold in the belief that at some future date it will be able to sell the gold to the monetary authorities of other countries. Obviously the argument is circular—central banks buy gold because they believe other central banks will in turn buy gold. This circularity is what confidence in any money, including the various paper monies (such as U.S. Treasury notes), is all about.

Gold's monetary functions have gradually declined. Private parties rarely use gold as a medium of payment and almost never as a unit of account; they hold gold as a store of value— or as an investment. This change in gold's role is not a result of planning or government decree; it is more efficient to use various national monies as a medium of payment and to state prices in terms of national currency units than in terms of ounces of gold or various gold coins.

Similarly, gold's role as an international money has gradually declined, so that now it is used primarily as a store of value. Gold is no longer used as a unit of account for central banks; the parities for most national currencies are stated in terms of some other national currencies. Nor has gold had any significant impact on commodity price levels for over sixty years. Central banks use gold infrequently as a means of payment; instead, payments imbalances are financed by transfers of dollar deposits.

That some central banks prefer gold to dollars or other international monies as a store of value may seem irrational, for gold earns no interest, while these other monies do. One explanation often given is tradition; central banks got used to holding gold during the gold standard era, and their preference remains unchanged, even though the system has changed. But this explanation isn't very convincing. What needs to be explained is why central banks hold gold and thus forgo the opportunity to hold their international money in assets yielding 6 or 8 percent. One advantage of gold over other assets is greater acceptability; gold may be acceptable as money by other central banks when dollars or other international monies are not. Another advantage is gold's underlying value as a commodity; gold has retained its value despite wars, revolutions, and spendthrift sovereigns.

In the short run, other monies may prove more attractive. But gold has remained, while numerous national monies have come and gone. The continuing demand for gold reflects confidence in its future value and the belief that no one sovereign can diminish this value significantly.

The Persistent Gold Shortage

The suspension of gold transactions by the U.S. Treasury in 1971 reflected a shortage of monetary gold which has now persisted for most of the last 60 years. The supply of gold available to central banks has been smaller than desired because, while production has grown slowly, the private demand for gold as a commodity—for use in jewelry and industry and for hoarding—has grown rapidly. Monetary demand and private demand compete with each other; when more gold is demanded for one use, the amount available for the other use falls. Thus, if private demand for gold increases, less gold is available to central banks. Similarly, if the central bank demand for gold increases—that is, if the banks agree to pay a higher price for gold—they will bid gold away from private users.

The persistent shortage of monetary gold reflects the fact that the commodity price level has increased more rapidly than the price of gold in terms of the dollar, sterling, and other national currencies. Between the outbreak of World War I in 1914 and 1950 the U.S. wholesale price index increased by 125 percent and the monetary price of gold by 70 percent. From 1950 to 1970 the wholesale price level increased by 35 percent; the monetary price of gold remained unchanged. Through most of the postwar period until 1973, gold producers have been squeezed between a much sharper increase in production costs than in their selling price.

The gold shortage first became apparent immediately after World War I, and it persisted until the currency devaluations of the 1930s. The increase in the dollar price of gold in 1934 was not designed to resolve the world shortage but to stimulate the U.S. economy. President Roosevelt was convinced that if the dollar price of gold were raised from $20.67 an ounce to $42 an ounce, the U.S. economy would be pulled out of the Great Depression. The rationale was that gold production would increase sharply, and so would the money supply. The ultimate choice of a new gold parity for the dollar of $35 an ounce was an accident.

As it turned out, the increase in the gold price led to a glut, for the amount of gold produced exceeded the amount demanded. Excess gold flowed to central banks, especially in the United States; U.S. gold holdings increased from $7 billion in 1934 (valued at the $35 price) to $20 billion in 1939.

The inflation of World War II rapidly eliminated the gold glut, and so the possibility of a gold shortage reappeared. Wholesale commodity prices doubled during the 1940s. Gold mining firms were again squeezed between higher production costs and a fixed selling price. The private demand for gold again increased, since gold was cheaper in terms of other commodities.

Postwar concern with the gold shortage first became acute in the late 1950s. Between 1949, when the U.S. Treasury's gold holdings peaked at $24 billion, and 1960, U.S. gold holdings

---

$35 an Ounce and 3.1416 Are Not the Same Kind of Numbers

The choice of $35 as the parity for the dollar in January 1934 was a historical accident; the price might have been $30 or $40. President Roosevelt had been convinced that the way to move the U.S. economy out of the Depression was to greatly increase the gold price. Gold production would be stimulated. More gold would be sold to the U.S. monetary authorities. The U.S. money supply would increase, and so would commodity prices. As a result, business firms would no longer incur losses because of declines in the value of their inventories, and banks would no longer be threatened with insolvency because of the declining value of their assets.

To increase the dollar price of gold, a subsidiary of the government-owned Reconstruction Finance Corporation bought gold in New York. The price of gold in the United States then tended to exceed the price, at the prevailing exchange rates, in London. Arbitragers had an incentive to buy gold in London for sale in the United States. But they had to buy sterling first. And their purchases caused the price of sterling to rise in terms of the dollar and numerous other currencies, weakening the competitive position of British firms in the world market. The British objected. The U.S. authorities stabilized the dollar price of gold when the free market price was near $35. Had the British objection been delayed until the free market price was $40, the U.S. gold parity would have been $40.

---

declined by $8 billion. This redistribution of gold among the world's central banks was deemed necessary to provide the financial basis for the postwar growth in world trade. But by 1960 there was growing recognition that the total supply of gold available for central banks as a group was too small to meet their demand.

The impending gold shortage was an issue during the 1960 presidential election campaign. Nixon had tagged Kennedy as an inflationary spender—higher prices were around the corner. The first threat of a dollar devaluation appeared when a small number of investors increased their gold purchases in the London market. For several weeks their purchases exceeded the flow from new production. Under such circumstances, the Bank of England would normally have sold gold from its holdings to keep the price from rising above $35; it would then have used its dollar receipts to buy gold from the U.S. Treasury. This time, however, someone in the U.S. Treasury had led some British officials to doubt that the Bank of England could buy gold from the U.S. Treasury to replenish its gold holdings after sales to private parties in the London market. So the Bank of England stopped selling gold. A combination of a nervous demand and the absence of a steadying supply led to a rise in the gold price to about $40, an increase which seemed extremely sharp when it occurred but which pales into insignificance when compared with the increase in the monetary price in 1973. Eventually, the Bank supplied gold to the market and the London price fell back to $35. Still, the first signal of an impending gold shortage had appeared.

Two kinds of measures might have resolved the shortage: either the private demand for gold might have been reduced by lowering the commodity price level, or the supply might have been increased by raising the monetary price of gold. The scope for reducing the private demand was small. U.S. gold regulations were changed to prohibit American citizens from buying or holding gold outside the United States, but congressional efforts to induce foreign governments to apply similar measures to their residents were rebuffed. And attempting to increase the supply by reducing the world price level—the classic approach of the gold standard—was ruled out by the high cost of a deflation in terms of unemployment, business failures, and lost elections.

By 1965 the private demand for gold had increased above the level of production; central banks sold $50 million of gold from their reserves to hold the price at $35. Uncertainties about the future sterling parity led to a surge in the private demand for gold. In 1967 central banks sold $1.6 billion of gold to private parties to prevent the price from rising above $35. And in the first ten weeks of 1968, sales to private parties reached $700 million.

Investors were alarmed lest the experience of the 1930s be repeated; they feared that the devaluation of sterling would force a devaluation of the dollar in terms of gold. They believed that, at a minimum, the dollar price of gold would be doubled. Hence the potential for revaluation gains was attractive. Altogether, private parties bought more than $3 billion of gold from central banks in the 1965–1968 period. Much of their demand was supplied, indirectly, from the U.S. Treasury.

Then, in March 1968, the monetary authorities in Europe and the United States agreed to separate the private gold market from the monetary gold market in which central banks buy and sell gold to each other. Under this two-tiered arrangement, monetary and nonmonetary gold became "separate" commodities; the tie between the private market and the official market was severed. Newly produced gold was to be supplied to the private market, from which private demands had to be satisfied. Initially, central banks continued to deal in gold with each other at the price of $35 an ounce. In the private market the gold price might rise above $35 or, conceivably, fall below $35.

The adoption of the two-tiered system raised the problem of marketing South Africa's $1 billion annual gold output. South Africa naturally wanted to get the largest possible revenues from its output; it wanted to sell between one-half and two-thirds of its gold output to private parties, at prices of perhaps $38 or $40, and the rest to official institutions at the $35 price. The European central banks liked the South African proposal, since they could continue to add to their gold holdings. At the same time, their own gold holdings would appear more valuable if the price in the private market climbed above $35.

The U.S. authorities, in contrast, wanted South Africa to sell all its gold in the private market, in the belief that the price would then fall to $30 or $32. According to the U.S. scenario, central bank confidence in the future of gold as international money would thus be shaken. At the same time, the preference for other types of international money (including dollars) would increase, and countries would become more receptive to the need for a new international money.

Eventually, a compromise was reached. Under certain conditions, South Africa was permitted to sell limited amounts of gold at $35 to central banks. But this compromise became irrelevant almost as soon as it was concluded, for the increase in private demand in response to worldwide inflation meant that nearly all of the output could be sold to private parties at about $40.

After the August 1971 suspension of gold transactions, the price of gold in the private market began to rise; by mid-1972 the price had approached $70; by late 1974, as it became possible for U.S. citizens to buy gold, the price reached $200. Many investors were betting that the monetary gold price would be increased to an even higher price.

The Choices Now Available

The objective of the U.S. game plan for gold had been to avoid, largely for political reasons, a change in the dollar price of gold. Every U.S. president since Eisenhower—Kennedy, Johnson, and then Nixon—had said that the dollar price of gold would be fixed forever. The retention of the $35 gold parity was a U.S. commitment like the Monroe Doctrine, access to Berlin, and free school lunches. Altering one U.S. commitment would undermine the credibility of other U.S. commitments.

The adoption of the $38 parity and then the $42 parity by the Nixon Administration helped resolve the impasse about exchange rate structure, but it made no dent in the gold problem.

Yet one advantage resulted from this minor change: it demonstrated that while a few economists and government officials were vitally interested in the gold price, the public at large was bored. The price of gold was not a domino; changing its price had no significant adverse reaction, at home or abroad.

The U.S. response to the gold shortage was that gold should be gradually phased out of the international monetary system; if gold were demonetized, it would not appear as if the United States had altered its parity. After the parity was changed, first in the Smithsonian Agreement and again in February 1973, the commitment to phasing out gold was retained, even though the costs of altering the $35 parity had already been incurred.

One of the primary alternatives to the $42 parity is a substantial worldwide increase in the price of gold, if not to the $125–175 price prevailing in the free market, at least to a much higher price than $42. The gold shortage would then be resolved by increasing the supply and reducing the private demand. The other basic option involves demonetizing gold in terms of the dollar and other currencies which remain pegged to the dollar; in that case, the monetary gold shortage would be resolved by eliminating gold's monetary role for a large number of countries.

Nearly every country has a vested interest in the monetary price of gold. An increase in the gold price—or gold demonetization—makes some groups better off and others worse off. And those who are worse off—or who feel worse off—would probably blame the United States, since the change in the price would be seen as a U.S. policy, even though much of the initiative arose in Europe. Since the United States produces and consumes minimal amounts of gold, the direct U.S. economic interests are trivial. The central U.S. interest is in the functioning of the international monetary system and its consequences for U.S. foreign relations.

Changes in the gold price have an impact on gold producers,

the owners of gold mines and their labor force, and on the producers of competitive monies and commodities. When gold is valued at $150, speculators' holdings may be valued at $30 billion. Should the monetary price of gold rise, both the producers and speculators would gain, while the consumers and the producers of competitive monies would lose. If, on the other hand, gold is demonetized, the pattern of winners and losers is reversed.

The price of gold in the private markets is shown in Figure 5–1. From the 1930s on, the price of gold remained unchanged, and even after the move to the two-tier gold market in 1968 the gold price remained relatively stable. Then, in 1973 and 1974, the price soared. The increase in the demand for gold is sometimes said to reflect a distrust of national monies. The argument is unconvincing, since in that case other commodities would also increase in price. The more convincing explanation is that investors expected that the authorities would again peg the price of gold.

Several questions remain. One is what will happen to the price of gold if it is demonetized. A second involves the future monetary price, should gold be retained as an international money. A third involves the process by which gold would be demonetized or retained as an international money.

Demonetization is likely to represent the gradual realization by central banks that their holdings of gold would be of greater value and utility if they sold gold in the commodity markets than if they continued to hold on to gold, which cannot be sold to other central banks.

Central bank gold sales in the commodity markets would sharply depress the price. The underlying explanation is that the stock of gold held by central banks, 37,000 metric tons, is exceedingly large relative to the annual production of gold, which is less than 1,000 metric tons. Sales which seem small relative to central bank holdings would be quite large relative

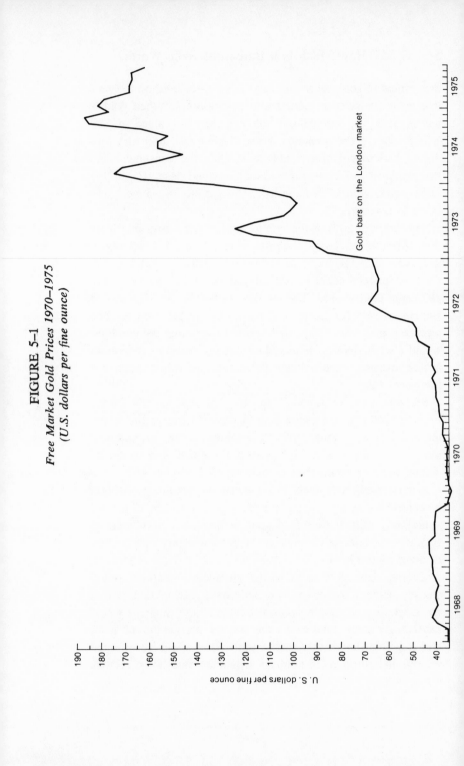

FIGURE 5-1
Free Market Gold Prices 1970–1975
(U.S. dollars per fine ounce)

Gold bars on the London market

U.S. dollars per fine ounce

to the supply from new production. Once the price began to fall, numerous private holders would sell, and the price would fall sharply; how rapidly and how far would depend on how large central bank sales were. Almost immediately, the six or eight central banks that are the major holders of gold would seek to establish an agreement regulating their sales in the commodity market.

What would be the international consequences of demonetizing gold? Gold-producing countries and those European countries which hold large amounts of gold as international money would clearly lose, since the value of their holdings would decline. The gainers would include the consumers of gold, since the commodity price would fall. Moreover, to the extent that manpower and materials would no longer be needed to produce a commodity money and could therefore be used to build dams, bridges, and schools, all countries would gain. But this gain would have to be balanced against the cost of having a smaller supply of international money than was formerly deemed optimal.

Gold demonetization would force countries to rethink how they might peg their currencies. Some might continue to peg their currencies to the U.S. dollar; in that case, they too would in effect be demonetizing gold. Together with the United States, they would constitute a dollar bloc. Pegged exchange rates would prevail within the bloc.

A few countries might continue to peg their currencies to gold; they would constitute a gold bloc. Exchange rates would also be pegged within this bloc; their currencies would float together in terms of the dollar. The gold bloc countries would probably charge that the United States, after having played the gold standard game to its own advantage, had violated the spirit of the game. Some would pick up the Gaullist argument that the United States had financed its purchases of European industry by selling gold to buy European currencies. Then, when U.S. gold holdings were much smaller, the U.S. government had abandoned gold, leaving the United States with a sizable investment in Europe while Europe was left with non-monetary gold.

Which countries would belong to what currency bloc? Most or all of the western hemispheric countries and Japan would undoubtedly join the dollar bloc. The gold bloc countries would include most western European countries.

It seems unlikely that the two blocs, one based around the dollar and the other based on gold, would live in peace and harmony forever after. The gold bloc countries would be under strong pressure to peg their currencies in the exchange market. Yet the only viable alternative to gold as a peg would be the dollar, and the Europeans would fear that the United States might unilaterally alter the rules of the "dollar standard" world and reduce the "moneyness" of European-owned dollars. So while the Europeans might find it necessary to peg to the dollar, they would be reluctant to add to their dollar holdings.

The combination of sharply reduced supplies of international monies (as a result of the demonetization of gold), European reluctance to acquire dollars, and European unhappiness with floating exchange rates would lead to more direct controls in the international payments system. This would please the bureaucrats in Europe, although the Americans, who place a somewhat higher value on payments freedom, would be unhappy. Thus, the international system would be further fragmented.

Assume, on the other hand, that gold is retained as an international money; then the price at which gold is traded must be set. In January 1975 the Bank of France valued its monetary holdings at $170 an ounce; it has voted to retain gold as an international money. In the latter part of 1974, Italy arranged a balance-of-payments loan from Germany; Italian gold, supposedly used as collateral, was valued at $120 an ounce. Rumor has it that other European central banks have informally revalued their gold holdings.

A move to a higher monetary price seems unlikely to occur as a result of a formal international agreement. Rather, the U.S. Treasury would gradually come to recognize that an important U.S. foreign policy interest would be served by retaining gold in the system.

The Treasury would then have to calculate the appropriate price for gold, but it would recognize the chanciness of trying to determine the right price. It would seek to avoid too low a price, which would occur if the private price continued above the monetary price. Too high a price would be inflationary. If the new price was $140, existing monetary gold holdings would be worth $160 billion and the monetary value of current output would be $6 billion. A higher market price for gold would in the long run stimulate production, so new output might reach $7–8 billion annually. If private expenditures on gold remained unchanged—the percentage decline in the number of ounces purchased approximating the increase in the market price— monetary gold stocks might increase by $5–6 billion annually.

These are rough estimates, not definite projections. Clearly there is a dollar price of gold which would enable both official and private demands to be satisfied adequately, at least for a few years. If the target for the annual increase in monetary gold holdings is $4 billion rather than $5 billion, then the appropriate monetary gold price might be $120. But since demand and supply will change over time, that price would inevitably become obsolete, sooner or later.

The monetary price of gold might be set initially at a level at which the amount supplied exceeded the amount demanded. In that case—if the gold supply were initially excessive—gold would flow into the U.S. Treasury, as happened in the late 1930s. Because of the higher value of the gold output, other countries could satisfy their gold needs without forcing the United States to sell gold. Indeed, every country might add to its gold holdings at the same time out of the $4 billion of new production.

Some economists have argued that an increase in the gold

price would be inflationary: private parties would spend more as a result of their revaluation gains. This concern might be valid if gold were still used as a domestic money; it has much less force now, with gold's monetary role limited to transactions among central banks and with private gold holdings such a small fraction of private wealth. Some central banks might follow a somewhat more expansive monetary policy as a result of their revaluation gains. Any increase in commodity price levels from an increase in the monetary price of gold would be small relative to the increases resulting from other sources.

When Keynes called gold a barbarous relic, he meant that mining gold to produce international money is unnecessarily expensive. Producing $6 billion of gold uses labor and machinery which might produce other goods with a value of $6 billion. If the IMF or some other international institution produces $6 billion of paper gold, the costs are minimal—the time of some government negotiators and a few clerks to record which central banks owe what to whom. And the labor and machinery otherwise used to mine gold for monetary purposes could then be diverted to dams, schools, and hospitals.

The cost of producing $6 billion of gold falls on those countries which prefer to hold gold in their reserves when they might otherwise hold IMF-produced money, since these countries must earn the gold by exporting goods and services to the gold-mining countries. The European countries with a strong demand for gold would acquire most of the newly produced gold. They would also bear most of this cost.

What about the *political* consequences of changing the gold price? At one time, it was feared that raising the gold price would give substantial windfall gains to the Soviet Union and South Africa; that's bad, the argument went, because the former is part of the Sino-Soviet Communist conspiracy and the latter practices apartheid. Reducing the gold price inflicts losses on the Soviet Union and South Africa, and that's good. Of course, as long as South Africa manages its gold sales so as to keep the price in the private market high, the Russians have already secured the windfall.

If gold is demonetized, South Africa's ability to maintain the price would indeed decline. But the impact of changes in the gold price on South African apartheid is a complex issue, not to be resolved by armchair sloganeering. If gold is valued at $160 an ounce, South Africa's gold production accounts for 15 percent of its GNP and 35 percent of its exports. At this gold price, the blacks gain in economic welfare; if the gold price were much lower, unemployment among blacks would increase. True, government revenues would also rise from taxes on the profits of gold-mining companies. Even so, it is not obvious that the impact of fixing a higher monetary gold price would change the level and distribution of income in South Africa so as to give the supporters of apartheid greater power. But even if the evidence showed that a gold price increase strengthened apartheid, this cost would have to be weighed against the advantages of resolving the inadequacy of the supply of international money—and the advantages and costs within each country of a higher gold price.

Most European central bankers have a strong preference for increasing the gold price over gold demonetization—indeed many prefer a higher gold price to other approaches to re-vamping the system. For some, the two approaches are complementary, not competitive.

As far as the credibility of U.S. commitments is concerned, an increase in the dollar price of gold is preferable to gold demonetization. If gold is demonetized, then the credibility of the commitments required to satisfy the world's demand for international money by producing paper gold would be low. (This issue is more fully discussed in Chapter 9.) Raising the gold price would also be more nearly consistent with the structure of the IMF and its Articles of Agreement than would gold demonetization. Gold demonetization would impose substantial losses on those now holding gold, whereas retaining gold by increasing the monetary price imposes losses on no one, although those central banks that hold dollars and other reserve assets might be upset because they did not share in the gains.

The move toward increasing the gold price would occur only after exchange rates were again pegged. At that time, the United States would again need to concern itself with its payments position. Both demonetization and a gold price increase would help reduce any U.S. payments deficit. Demonetization would work because the U.S. authorities would no longer have to worry about the deficit, since foreign official institutions could no longer require the U.S. Treasury to sell gold. And the gold price increase would work because the annual increase in the gold supply would be large enough to enable other countries to satisfy their demand for international money without forcing the United States to incur a deficit.

It is true that reliance on gold is an inefficient way to meet the demand for international money; there are less costly alternatives. The problem, however, is not with gold, but rather with the attitudes and preferences of central banks around the world—and their experience with the credibility of commitments made by foreign governments. The European preference for gold *is* archaic. But it *is* their preference—and they pay the costs of retaining gold in the system.

Ultimately, the choice, as de Gaulle knew, is a U.S. choice. The United States must decide whether the payments system will function more smoothly and U.S. interests will be better served if the European preferences are satisfied or frustrated. For a decade or more, U.S. authorities focused on trying to wean the European central banks away from their preference for gold. The effort was not notably successful. At some stage, U.S. officials may seek to build a system around these preferences.

5 / Gold—How Much Is a Barbarous Relic Worth?

In monetary affairs, the authorities cannot afford to be ambiguous; to do so would point toward profit opportunities open to private investors. So they can never hint that they will change a parity, shift from pegged to floating rates, or favor a change in the monetary gold price. When the timing seems appropriate, however, they can suddenly reverse their policies.

The Dollar and Coca-Cola
Are Both Brand Names

The money-producing industry is like the soda pop industry; a large number of firms make a similar product. Soda pop is basically carbonated, colored water. One brand of pop is a good substitute for another. Each pop-producing firm strives to make its brands attractive: the product is available in large, small, and medium-sized packages, and the packages are attractively designed. Coca-Cola has been so successful in its marketing strategy that a gallon of Coke—caramel colored fizzy water—sells for $1, or more than four times the pretax price of a gallon of gasoline. The market leaders strive to distinguish themselves from their competitors; thus, they have brand names that are protected by copyrights. High profits automatically attract competitive imitators who frequently choose a similar name (Royal Crown Cola, Pepsi-Cola) and in other ways try to infringe on the market position of the brand leader.

So it is with money. Each national central bank produces its own brand of money. Each of these national monies serves an identical set of functions—as a medium of payment, a store of value, and a unit of account. Each national money is a differentiated product. U.S. dollars and Canadian dollars are not perfect substitutes for each other, and neither are French francs and Swiss francs, or English pounds and Irish pounds. One national money may be a good substitute for another as a means of payment, and even a better substitute as a store of value or a unit of account.

The analogy between the soda pop industry and the money industry may seem invalid within the United States, for while the supermarkets carry numerous brands of pop, the banks carry only one brand of money. Nearly all transactions are settled by payments in dollars. But some U.S. firms and some U.S. residents hold large amounts of money in London, the Bahamas, Zurich, and elsewhere for business convenience, or to avoid U.S. monetary and fiscal regulations (see Chapter 7 on the Eurodollar market and Chapter 11 on tax avoidance). More importantly, foreign residents have had a much greater incentive to hold dollar assets because of the brand leadership position of the U.S. dollar.

The U.S. dollar has been the leading brand name in the money industry. In the immediate postwar years, U.S. currency notes circulated extensively in Europe. In Europe, Latin America, and Asia, many firms and individuals hold a substantial portion of their money and other financial assets in dollars. And some foreign firms with substantial international business interests keep their books in dollars. Another favored brand of money, one which appeals to a specialized and small segment of the market (like the Ferrari in automobiles, or Chivas Regal in Scotch whiskey), is the Swiss franc.

Some central banks have changed the brand name of their product to the dollar to increase its attractiveness; this name change is sometimes accompanied by changes in packaging. When Australia, Jamaica, and Malaysia shifted to the decimal system from pounds and shillings, they named their currencies dollars, a tribute to the preeminent standing of the U.S. dollar. But there is only one U.S. dollar; the other central banks are poaching on the established market position of the U.S. producer.

Central banks, like the soda-producing firms, sell their product. The public "pays" for the money produced by the central

95

bank by supplying goods and services. When Brazil's central bank produces more cruzeiros, the public acquires these cruzeiros by selling goods, services, and securities to the central bank and to its owner, the Brazilian government. The larger the public's demand for money in the form of cruzeiros, the larger the volume of goods and services that the Brazilian government can buy without having to raise taxes. Each government, like each firm in the soda pop industry, has a vested interest in increasing the demand for the product of its central bank.

The production of commemorative postage stamps, Green Stamps, Plaid Stamps, and other trading stamps provides a good analogy to the production of money. Like money, these stamps can be produced at very low cost; the only expense is developing designs and paper that are costly to imitate. The producers of these bits of colored engraved paper want the public to hold more and more of their stamps; they much prefer to have them pasted into collectors' books than onto letters. Liechtenstein would go broke if its postage stamps were used to mail letters. Similarly, the producers of Green Stamps and Plaid Stamps want the public to collect their stamps rather than redeem them; therefore they offer high-priced "gifts" in exchange for thirty or forty books of stamps to lengthen the period between the time the stamps are sold and the time they are redeemed. In the meantime, the stamp companies have free use of the public's money. Similarly, the producers of traveler's checks profit handsomely, for they use receipts from the sale of such checks to buy interest-paying assets while paying no interest on the checks.

Each central bank has a marketing strategy to strengthen the demand for its particular brand of money. Just as each of the soda pop firms wants the public to buy more of its pop and less of its competitors', each central bank wants the public to buy, use, and hold more of its money. The greater the demand, the more readily the product—the national money—can be sold.

Packaging is one element in the marketing strategy—two or three colors may be used in the printing. The bank notes carry the portraits of favorite kings, presidents, and other national heroes. Frequently, the central bank even provides a money-back guarantee; that is, it may offer to repurchase its own money in exchange for a leading foreign money at a set price, the exchange rate.

The packaging arrangements in the soda pop industry are a component of pricing policy; the more attractive the package, the higher the price. In some cases, the firm sells a package or a way of life or a self-image rather than a product.* In much the same way, the packaging arrangements in the money-producing industry are designed to enhance the attractiveness of a particular brand name, and thus to reduce the interest rate on assets which carry that brand label. Finance ministers and Treasury secretaries want interest rates to be low to minimize their borrowing costs, and therefore the taxes that must be raised to pay the interest costs. In Britain, holders of certain Treasury securities can participate in a special lottery; the Treasury can sell these securities at a lower interest rate. The lottery prizes supposedly cost less than the savings in interest costs. Similarly, holders of some U.S. Treasury securities receive special tax advantages which are intended to reduce the interest rates necessary to attract lenders. From the Treasury's point of view, the cost of the tax advantages should be smaller than the reduction in interest payments. Some countries link the interest rates on domestic securities to the price of gold or to the price of the U.S. dollar, so as to increase the attractiveness of their issues to borrowers. All such devices are marketing gimmicks designed to create investor interest in particular brands—the central bank counterpart of Green Stamps and baseball cards.

In the money industry, just as in the soda pop industry, over-production occurs. In the soda pop industry, any firm which

---

* This technique conforms to Michael Aliber's First Theorem, "When you buy baseball cards, you get the gum free."

increases its output very rapidly may have to cut its prices to avoid seeing its cans and bottles pile up on supermarket shelves. In the case of money, overproduction leads to price increases; central banks can produce more money, but they cannot force people to hold it. When too much money is produced, people may shift from domestic money to goods—or to other brands of money.

Authorities frequently take more direct measures than packaging to enhance investor demand for the national brand of securities. Most governments stipulate that only the national money is legal tender within their boundaries; the national tax collector will not accept payment in foreign monies. Ministers of finance and secretaries of the Treasury continually "talk up" the national brand by waving the flag. When the voluntary approach proves inadequate, compulsory measures are often used, and purchases of monies and securities denominated in foreign currencies may be taxed, licensed, or otherwise regulated.

The Market Position of Currency Brands

The contrast between the number of brand names in money— more than 100—and in automobiles and jet aircraft is strong. While every country except the very small ones—Luxembourg, Panama, Liechtenstein—has its own currency brand, most countries import their jet aircraft and their automobiles from foreign producers. Thus, the German and Canadian airline companies buy U.S.-produced jet aircraft because they are cheaper than domestically produced jets would be. Their national airlines—which must vie with Pan Am, TWA, Japan Air Lines, and other foreign airlines—are reluctant to incur the additional cost of buying domestically produced aircraft, for they would then be at a competitive disadvantage in the world market.

Why then does nearly every country insist on producing its own money? One reason may be that none sees any cost to having a national money. But for most countries, the decision to have a national money raises the interest rate of its domestic loans. If Denmark, for example, were to give up its own money and adopt the Swedish brand or if Canada adopted the U.S. brand, the interest rates to borrowers in Denmark and Canada would probably decline. Having a national currency clearly puts firms in these countries at a cost disadvantage in the international marketplace.

Indeed, many Canadian firms, as well as the Canadian provincial governments, come to New York or Chicago and issue U.S. dollar securities to reduce their interest cost below the rates they would pay if they borrowed in Canada. To the extent that the higher interest rates charged to Canadians are a result of having a national money, there is a real cost to Canada, for some investment projects which might profitably be undertaken if interest rates were lower are never launched.

Yet governments continue to incur the costs of a national money; few, if any, have decided to abandon their national brands. For there are offsetting advantages. One is prestige. Only with a national money can a country have its own monetary policy. And kings and presidents want their constituents to be proud of their heritage: the prouder they are, the less reluctant they will be to pay taxes.

The government profits from having a national money, for the cost of producing the money—printing the bank notes or issuing the deposits—is less than its purchasing power in terms of goods and services. These profits from the production of money are an indirect form of taxation. Indeed, issuing money is often a less costly way of taxing the public, especially if the administrative fiscal apparatus is inadequate or corrupt. It is also a way of circumventing parliamentary opposition to higher tax rates.

In market economies, interest rates on financial assets vary continuously in response to changes in the supply and demand of securities. Prices adjust to find sellers or buyers. If the prices are sufficiently low, buyers can be found even for such risky securities as the bond issues of Penn Central and the Czar Bonds of 1912. Within a country, investors continually shuffle the ownership of monies, short-term debts, long-term debts, growth stocks, and public utility stocks as their assessment of the future changes. Similarly, they continually compare the attractiveness of monies with different brand names.

All financial assets—bank notes, demand deposits, government bonds, corporation bonds—must have a brand name. The buyers of these assets must choose among one of the twelve kinds of dollars, eight kinds of francs, the cruzeiro, the baht, the kip, and numerous other national currency brands. They must calculate whether the currency brands which are not attractive will remain so. Possible changes in the market position of the various brand names—and in their exchange rates—are closely examined.

In part, interest rates on assets denominated in Danish kroner exceed those on assets denominated in Swedish kronor because investors anticipate that the Danish currency will depreciate; they want the additional interest income to offset any loss from holding a depreciating currency. If there were complete confidence in predictability of future changes in exchange rates, then arbitragers would shift funds between Danish and Swedish securities until the difference between the two interest rates reflected the anticipated change in the exchange rate. If they expected Danish kroner to depreciate 1 percent a year more rapidly than Swedish kronor, they would shift funds until interest rates on Danish assets were 1 percent a year higher than on Swedish assets. Examination of the data suggests that investors do a rather effective job of pricing assets.

Currency brands can be ranked like songs on a hit parade, with the standings based on interest rates on assets which are similar except for currency of denomination. Investor preferences for currency and checking account money—assets which usually carry no explicit market yield—can be inferred from their preferences for short-term, interest-bearing assets denominated in the same currencies. For example, if the interest rates on short-term U.S. dollar assets are below those on short-term U.K. sterling assets, then the dollar stands above sterling on the hit parade. Investors, in other words, will only hold assets denominated in sterling if interest rates are sufficiently high to compensate them against the risk that sterling may fall in value relative to the dollar. Higher interest rates are necessary in order to find buyers for money and other financial assets denominated in sterling—that is, to adjust for overproduction of sterling. Higher interest rates are the money-market counterpart to price cutting in the soda pop market.

True, some borrowers seemingly ignore the brand name problem when issuing liabilities, as do some lenders when acquiring assets. Most investors simply deal in securities denominated in the national brand, the currency of the country in which they live. Similarly, most individuals vote for the same party in election after election. Candidates for office pitch their campaigns to the 10 or 20 percent of the electorate whose fickle preferences may swing the results. Brand loyalty is—or once was—strong in cigarettes and beer. Producers within these industries—money, politics, and tobacco—market their products toward the swing voters and the swing buyers. Convenience, ignorance, uncertainty about exchange rates, and exchange controls help explain the preference for the domestic brand of money.

Still, some borrowers calculate the advantages of issuing securities denominated in foreign currencies, just as some lenders calculate the advantages of acquiring such securities. The smaller the country, the more likely that its residents will compare foreign alternatives to domestic monies and securities. Dutch and Swiss investors, for example, are very much aware of assets denominated in foreign currencies; many U.S. dollar securities are listed on the stock exchanges in Amsterdam and Zurich.

For most of the last fifty years, dollar-denominated assets have been at the top of the brand name hit parade. In contrast, currencies which have been more or less subject to continuous devaluations have ranked low; the yields of assets denominated in such currencies have been correspondingly high. Thus, interest rates on assets denominated in sterling, the Canadian dollar, the yen, and even the mark have been higher than interest rates on assets denominated in dollars because investors believe that assets denominated in these currencies are riskier.

One exception is Switzerland: interest rates on assets denominated in Swiss francs have been lower than those on dollar assets. Switzerland is attractive to investors for a variety of political reasons, including low tax rates on interest income and lenient official attitudes toward the origins of large funds.

It was not always thus. Before World War I, London was the world's principal financial center and sterling was at the top of the currency hit parade. At that time, borrowers from around the world found it cheaper to issue sterling-denominated securities than to borrow in their domestic markets. American firms went to London to borrow; London was the center of the international capital market.

The dollar displaced sterling for several reasons. In the first place, the dollar was the only currency which remained pegged to gold during World War I. Moreover, U.S. prices had risen less than those in various European countries during the war. Wartime overproduction of sterling led to a loss of investor confidence and a downward shift of sterling. U.S. financial markets offered investors a wide range of securities, and the United States took on a dominant role in the international economy. Central banks in Europe and elsewhere began to acquire dollar assets as a form of international money.

The question today is whether the successive devaluations of the dollar in terms of gold and the concurrent appreciation of the mark, the yen, and the Swiss franc may lead to a displacement of the dollar from the top spot, much as sterling was displaced earlier. Whatever the short-run outlook for the dollar, that the dollar will still be at the top several hundred years from now seems unlikely.

A Dollar Standard World?

The dollar has been a workhorse currency in the postwar period. It has been the currency used by central banks in their exchange market intervention. Holdings of dollar assets have been the largest component of central bank reserves since 1970. International firms and investors have used the dollar as a vehicle currency; many international trade transactions are denominated in dollars. These multiple roles reflect the dominant size of the United States among the market economies.

Since the United States plays such a major role in the world, it follows that what happens in the United States will have a substantial impact on what happens in the world. The U.S. money supply is a large part of the world money supply. Changes in the U.S. price level necessarily have a major direct impact on the world price level; the indirect impacts are so extensive that a change in the U.S. price level may have a greater effect on the world price level than is suggested by the U.S. share of world GNP.

Because of the central importance of the United States, the dollar is frequently the numeraire currency, or the unit of account. Thus international airline fares are stated in terms of dollars; the price of tickets in the sterling area is the product of dollar price and the sterling-dollar exchange rate. The prices of many international commodities—the price of gold in Zurich, of petroleum in the Persian Gulf—are stated in terms of dollars.

From this it is easy to conclude that the world is on a

103

dollar standard, especially if the term is not clearly defined. One meaning of the term is that the rest of the world is obliged to hold the U.S.-produced dollars that U.S. residents won't hold. In fact, by almost every measure, the U.S. payments deficit since 1950 has been large. In some years the deficit was only $2 or $3 billion; in 1971 it reached $30 billion.

The cumulative U.S. payments deficit between 1950 and 1970 was between $50 and $70 billion, depending on how it is calculated. The deficit or surplus is measured by sales and purchases of gold and liquid dollar assets to foreign central banks, commercial banks, and private parties. But economists disagree on whether all sales of dollar assets to foreigners should be included in the calculation of the payments balance.

Formerly, U.S. authorities included all purchases and sales of gold and other international monies held by U.S. authorities together with purchases and sales of liquid dollar assets by foreign central banks, foreign commercial banks, and foreign private parties in the computation of the payments balance; this is known as the *net liquidity balance*. This meant that if a large U.S. bank exchanged deposits of $100 million with its London branch, the payments deficit would increase by $100 million. Why? Because the increase in the dollar holdings of the London bank was included in the calculation of the U.S. payments balance, while the increase in the London deposit of the U.S. bank was excluded. In a period in which foreign commercial banks and foreign private parties were adding to their dollar holdings, this measure tended to overstate the deficit.

A second approach, known as the *official reserves transactions balance*, was then adopted; the modification in this approach was that only the purchases and sales of liquid dollar assets by foreign official institutions were included in the calculation of the payments balance. This definition differs from the net liquidity balance in that changes in the liquid dollar assets of foreign commercial banks and foreign private parties are excluded from the calculation.

The problem with both definitions is that they fail to recognize the unique role of the United States as a producer of international money. The United States exports money to satisfy the needs of foreign customers, just as Germany exports Volkswagens, Ecuador exports bananas, and South Africa exports gold. As long as investors retain confidence in the dollar brand name, the use of the term "deficit" to describe intended and voluntary increases in dollar holdings by foreigners is misleading. Realistically, these increases in dollar holdings could be excluded from the calculation of the U.S. deficit.

Of course, separating intended from unintended increases would be difficult. But any errors that might arise in making this distinction operational are likely to be smaller than those resulting from a more misleading concept.

Thus, until 1968 or so, the U.S. balance-of-payments deficit was primarily an accounting phenomenon which reflected the desire of other countries to have payments surpluses; the problem was a "system" problem, not a country problem. No one was really upset about U.S. monetary policies or U.S. price level performance, and dollars were not being overproduced. In the absence of data on payments balances, no one would have been upset about the performance of the U.S. economy on the world scene.

One of the apparent paradoxes of the late 1960s was that just as the U.S. payments deficit began to increase, some analysts asserted that the world was on the dollar standard. The meaning of the term was vague; the implication was that changes in the dollar money supply, like changes in the monetary gold supply sixty and seventy years earlier, determined the world price level. True, the U.S. government's policies for financing the Vietnam war led to sharp increases in U.S. prices and in the U.S. payments deficit, and the parallel increases in the payments surpluses of other countries meant that their own domestic money supplies increased sharply, so that prices abroad rose almost as rapidly as did U.S. prices. The United States was exporting inflation. But the logical implication of the phrase "the world is on the dollar standard" was that foreign central banks had shifted to dependent monetary policies and were unwilling to revalue their currencies.

The dollar standard view of the world was shattered by the moves of Canada, Germany, and the Netherlands toward floating exchange rates, and by subsequent revaluations of various European currencies and the yen relative to the dollar —or, as the French would say, by the devaluation of the dollar.

Do the changes in the exchange rates' structure mean that it is "Afternoon on the Potomac" for the dollar? The answer involves disentangling two overlapping but distinct relationships. The first concerns the market position of all national currencies —the dollar, sterling, the Swiss franc, the mark—relative to gold. The second concerns the market position of the dollar relative to these other currencies.

Both relationships can be analyzed in terms of interest rate structures. Interest rates on assets denominated in dollars, sterling, Swiss francs, and other currencies increased substantially in the 1960s and were substantially higher in the 1960s than in the 1950s. The market position of all national currencies as a group declined relative to that of gold, as was evident from the increasing shortage of monetary gold and the rise in the price of gold in the private component of the two-tier system to $50, $100, and then $200. From 1960 on, all currencies were overvalued relative to gold.

Throughout the 1960s, U.S. gold sales and the increase in foreign-owned dollars led many observers to conclude that the dollar was overvalued in relation to other currencies. If a currency which served as international money was overvalued, then the currencies of some other large countries—perhaps Germany, Japan, France, or even Britain—must have been undervalued; that is, either the international money holdings of these countries were too large, or they were increasing at too rapid a rate. One test of whether the dollar was overvalued is to ask: What would have happened if the dollar had been devalued in terms of gold by 10 or 15 percent? How many countries would have maintained their exchange rates against the dollar (thus also devaluing their currencies in terms of gold), and how many would have allowed their currencies to appreciate in terms of the dollar?

The answer would depend on when the question was asked. During the early 1960s nearly every country, with the possible exception of Germany, the Netherlands, and Switzerland, would have maintained its exchange rate peg against the dollar. In contrast, if the currency of a small country, say Denmark, had been devalued, few if any other countries would have devalued their currencies. Most would have permitted their currencies to appreciate relative to the Danish krone.

Until 1969 the international payments imbalances could more easily be explained in terms of the demand of foreign central banks for international money and the undervaluation of several currencies—primarily the mark—than in terms of an over-valued dollar. The statement that the dollar was overvalued was wrong in the early and mid-1960s. The statement was correct in 1970 and 1971.

The surge in the dollar holdings of foreign central banks in the early 1970s led to great concern about the stability of the system, for some of these holdings were undesired. Several relevant questions arose. One involved determining how much of the total reserve holdings of foreign central banks was excessive. A second was how much of the dollar holdings was excessive (there was great concern with the dollar overhang).

Because increases in central bank holdings of international money lead to corresponding increases in their domestic money supplies, excess reserve holdings tend to disappear. A country can reduce its reserves only if it runs a payments deficit; its imports of goods or securities increase. Few countries were willing to make the exchange rate changes necessary to increase their imports of goods, in part because of the impact this would have on domestic producers of similar goods. Few figured out how to increase their imports of foreign securities.

While there was concern that the dollar component of reserves might be too large, there were no ready alternative assets, given that the United States would not sell gold to buy back the dollars. One view was that the short-term dollar holdings should be consolidated into long-term dollar securities; any foreign central bank that wanted these securities could easily buy them. One analyst suggested that the foreign central banks simply write off part of their dollar assets as a reverse form of Marshall Plan aid.

The dollar overhang, like most hangovers, proved transient; the system adjusted to its reserves. Part of the adjustment resulted from the increase in world commodity prices. Total reserves doubled between 1970 and 1973; the world wholesale price index increased by more than 50 percent. The increase in prices resulted in part from the increase in reserves. And the reverse was true—the increase in reserves contributed to the increase in prices. When the oil-producing countries quadrupled the price of crude in the fall of 1973, the oil-importing countries faced massive payments deficits. All of a sudden, their large reserve holdings seemed providential. Even though planning or market forces could explain the wisdom of acquiring the reserves, it began to seem as if everything was working out for the best.

The Dollar on the Hit Parade

The demise of sterling as the world's preeminent currency suggests one possible future scenario for the dollar. When Britain entered World War I, the Bank of England immediately withdrew its money-back guarantee; sterling was no longer convertible into gold. Exchange controls limited imports of goods and of foreign securities. British prices rose rapidly as a result of an inflationary monetary policy. At the end of the war, official sentiment was strongly in favor of a return to the gold standard at the prewar parity. But sterling was then overvalued by at least 10 or 15 percent. Throughout the early 1920s, British economic policy was geared to reattain the 1913 gold parity. This target was reached in 1925; then the problem was to maintain the parity, since sterling was still overvalued. Investors were increasingly apprehensive that a change in British policy would lead to a depreciation of sterling relative to the dollar and gold. But these factors were all monetary, the result of overproduction of sterling during the war. They should be distinguished from the real factors: the sharp decline in British foreign investments and the sluggish British industrial performance.

The error of the British authorities seems clear: they confused a pegged exchange rate for sterling with a particular rate at which sterling should be pegged. In retrospect, it seems clear that Britain should have pegged its currency to gold soon after the war, perhaps at a parity which left the dollar-sterling exchange rate at $4.00 or $4.20. Moreover, the British should have taken the initiative in increasing the monetary price of gold in terms of the dollar, sterling, and other currencies. Interest rates on sterling assets would then have been much lower, since there would have been no need to pay a high interest rate to investors concerned about the risk that sterling might be devalued. Business in Britain would have boomed, and foreign capital would have flowed to London.

Whether sterling could have retained its brand leader position with even the most sensible of policies is doubtful; the war hastened a move of the dollar to the top of the hit parade which seemed inevitable in any case. The U.S. economy was growing very rapidly, and U.S. financial markets were developing depth, breadth, and resiliency. Investments in Europe seemed riskier than investments in the United States, partly for political reasons.

109

Just as sterling was displaced by the dollar, so the dollar can only be displaced from its dominant position by another currency brand. In the past, every country whose currency has been at the top has had attractive financial markets, an economy open to international trade and investment, relative price stability, and great international economic power. Today no country appears to satisfy all these criteria. Switzerland is too small and lacks adequate financial markets. Japan is too peripheral and its economy too closed to foreigners. Germany's long-run record for monetary stability is poor—as is its record for political stability; its remarkable performance in the 1960s and 1970s follows two massive inflations. No country other than the United States appears to combine economic size and a record for financial stability.

True, the new European currency planned by the members of the European Economic Community might eventually go to the top of the hit parade. But the new Europe would still be smaller in economic size than the United States. And its financial markets, even if integrated, would be considerably smaller than the U.S. market. Anyhow, the European countries must first succeed with the plan to merge their currencies—that is, they must give up monetary sovereignty. Then the new currency will have to establish a record for monetary stability. Finally, if this record proves impressive, investors will have to decide whether this advantage is sufficient to outweigh the advantages of the larger U.S. financial markets. And in 1976 the prospects for currency unification in Europe were less encouraging than they appeared in 1970; nationalist sentiment has been increasing.

The future position of the dollar will be affected by policies directed toward the $160 billion held by foreign central banks and by the future role of gold in the monetary system. In 1970 and 1971 foreign central banks acquired more dollar assets than they wished, because of the delays in changing the exchange rates. Yet they have held on to these assets; they have been built into the international monetary structure.

One of the major European demands after the Smithsonian Agreement was that their dollar holdings be convertible into some other international money, so as to restrain excessively expansive U.S. monetary and fiscal policies. Such convertibility would force U.S. authorities to take the initiative in reducing the U.S. deficit, relieving the Europeans of the need to reduce their own surpluses. More importantly, if dollars were to become convertible on a substantive rather than a symbolic basis, then a worldwide increase in the price of gold would be almost essential. Such an increase appeared desirable to the French and other Europeans as a way of diminishing the attractiveness of the dollar as an international money.

The future attractiveness of the dollar will be directly affected by decisions about the future role of gold. A worldwide increase in the gold price would remove the uncertainty about the future of gold as a money. The U.S. international monetary position would be stronger, since U.S. gold holdings would increase greatly in relation to foreign holdings of dollars. The U.S. Treasury would be in a very good position to sell gold in exchange for any excess dollar holdings of foreigners. And for some time thereafter, the United States would no longer need to produce international money in large amounts to satisfy the demands of other countries.

The impact of formal demonetization of gold on the market position of the dollar is less clear. The reduction in the supply of international money and the removal of the uncertainty about possible changes in the dollar-gold relationship would make dollar assets more attractive. At the same time, a unilateral move by the United States to demonetize gold might make some foreign investors wary of accumulating any more dollar assets.

One lesson that can be learned from the British experience is that decisive action, whether in the form of a worldwide increase in the gold price or a formal demonetization, is preferable to continued piddling with minor changes in the dollar price of gold. The British paid an extremely high price for attempting to avoid or delay changes in the sterling parity that were inevitable. Throughout the 1960s, U.S. authorities followed a similar strategy of trying to avoid what proved inevitable—initially a change in the monetary price of gold, then a change in the exchange rate structure.

The real factor—the size and wealth of the U.S. economy—suggests that the dollar will continue at the top of the hit parade. The monetary factors are uncertain, however. Economic mismanagement could tarnish the dollar's attractiveness to world investors.

From time to time, the committees which choose the Nobel laureates may decide that no one should be awarded the Nobel Peace Prize in a particular year. Some currency, however, must always be in a commanding position. While U.S. inflation and devaluation have reduced the attractiveness of the dollar, inflation rates in other countries have exceeded those of the United States. And the depreciation of the dollar may be a one-shot event, rather than a continuing state of affairs.

Radio Luxembourg and the Eurodollar Market
Are Both Offshore Stations

Radio Luxembourg is a commercial broadcasting station based in Luxembourg whose programs are beamed primarily to two markets, Britain and France. A few years ago, neither country permitted commercial broadcasting; each relied solely on government-owned stations. Programs within each country reflected what the producers—the bureaucrats of the British Broadcasting Corporation or Radiodiffusion Française—felt the public should have.

Perhaps these government officials had correctly gauged the public's wants. If so, they would not have needed their monopoly power.

Radio Luxembourg, which produces consumer-oriented programs as a way of selling commercials, was created to fill this gap in the market—and to generate profits. Although the radio signals were produced in Luxembourg and "consumed" in Britain and France, neither country raised its "tariffs" or other barriers to the imports of foreign commercial broadcasts. (Only the Russians jam airwaves.) Transport costs for this product are low. And so Radio Luxembourg prospered. Predictably, numerous competitive stations were established. Radio Caroline, for example, had its transmission facilities parked on a tugboat which sat just outside the 3-mile limit of British jurisdiction.

Radio Luxembourg is a classic example of an externalized activity—that is, a good or service produced in one jurisdiction but consumed and used in another. Another example is the sale of alcohol, tobacco, and other tax-free products at airport shops; these sales are taxed differently from domestic sales, since the product is consumed abroad. The traveler does not pay either transport costs or customs duty on his imports. Similarly, in Washington, D.C., external transactions on sales of alcohol and tobacco take place. Residents of Maryland and Virginia can buy these products in Washington, where the taxes are lower; and imports of these untaxed products into the adjacent states, while illegal, are not significantly regulated.

Externalized activities occur because governments—national, state, or local—often regulate the same transaction or activity in different ways. Thus, production will often occur in jurisdictions with low taxes or minimal regulation to meet the consumption needs of people in jurisdictions with higher taxes and more severe regulation. Differential regulation, while necessary, is not enough to bring about an externalized activity; the cost of transporting the goods or services from the production area to the consumption area must be low.

The External Currency Market

Today the largest, most rapidly growing external transactions involve the production of dollar bank deposits in London, Zurich, and other centers outside the United States; of Swiss franc deposits in London, Amsterdam, and other centers outside Switzerland; and of mark deposits in centers outside West Germany. The generic term for all these transactions is the "external currency market"; the popular terms are the "Eurodollar" or "Eurocurrency" market. The unique feature of this market is that banks produce deposits denominated in currencies other than those of the country in which they are located.

The banks which produce external currency deposits are known as Eurobanks. Thus banks in London become Eurobanks whenever they issue deposits denominated in dollars or Swiss francs or German marks—or, indeed, in any currency other than sterling. Similarly, banks in Zurich are Eurobanks whenever they issue deposits denominated in currencies other than the Swiss franc. Eurobanks need not be located in Europe. Singapore, for example, is a thriving center for the Asian dollar market, which is really the Asian branch of the Eurodollar market; Panama City performs the same function in the Latin American dollar market.

Eurobanking is only one activity of a commercial bank. Banks in London which produce dollar deposits also produce sterling deposits and mark deposits. Altogether, there may be 300–400 Eurobanks; for most of these, Euro-transactions are a sideline to their primary activities as domestic banks.

Today some of the leading Eurobanks are branches of the Bank of America, the First National City Bank of New York, Morgan Guaranty and other U.S.-based banks in the major European financial centers. Participation in the Eurodollar market is the primary activity of most of the forty or so London branches of U.S. banks.

That banks in London conduct some of their business in dollars, marks, Swiss francs, and guilders may seem strange. It seems more natural for banks in each country to produce deposits and make loans in the domestic currency, for banks in Switzerland to deal in Swiss francs and banks in the Netherlands to deal in guilders. But dealing only in the domestic currency is a traditional bank practice rather than a legal necessity.

Banks outside the United States issue dollar deposits in response to investor demand. The dollar is a unit of account

—one of the yardsticks in the world of money, a measure comparable to the gallon or meter. The "real" meter—the piece of metal about 39-plus inches long, which is one ten-millionth of the distance between the equator and the North Pole—remains in the International Bureau of Weights and Measures near Paris. The French could not prevent Americans or Swiss from using the meter as a measurement even if they wished. Similarly, the U.S. government cannot prevent banking offices outside the United States—including the offshore branches of U.S. banks—from issuing deposits denominated in dollars, since these banks are outside U.S. legal jurisdiction. These are London dollar deposits or Zurich dollar deposits, and perhaps one day even Peking dollar deposits; they are not U.S. dollar deposits. The adjective is important, for dollar deposits in London are subject to British regulation, while dollar deposits in Zurich are subject to Swiss regulation.

Note that banking readily satisfies the requirements for an externalized activity. The transportation costs for money are extremely low. A million dollars, a billion dollars, or even a trillion dollars can be moved across the Atlantic at the cost of a couple of telegrams or phone calls. And bank regulations differ widely among countries; regulation of banks in the United States, for example, is much more restrictive than in Britain. In most countries, moreover, deposits denominated in foreign currencies are less extensively regulated than deposits in domestic currency. In London, for example, dollar deposits are not subject to the reserve requirements or interest rate ceilings applied to sterling deposits. In the United States, Federal Reserve regulations stipulate that commercial banks cannot pay interest on demand deposits (the ceiling is zero). In London, Zurich, and other major centers for external currency transactions, the interest rate ceilings applicable to deposits in the domestic currency do not apply to deposits denominated in foreign currencies. Finally, most of the developed countries have been reluctant to apply barriers to the importation of funds from external currency banks located abroad.

Thus, certain borrowing and lending activities are externalized in the Eurodollar market—that is, shifted from the U.S. political jurisdiction to the less severely regulated foreign or offshore markets. Depositors shift funds from dollar deposits in New York to dollar deposits in London and Zurich primarily for higher interest income. A U.S. firm borrows dollars in London and Zurich because the interest rates paid there are lower than in the United States. U.S. banks set up branches in London and Zurich to "intermediate"—to bring borrowers and lenders together—because this activity is profitable.

Where Eurodollars Come From

By the end of 1974, bank deposits denominated in external currencies totaled $220 billion, compared to only $1 billion in 1961. Most external currency deposits are denominated in dollars; the other principal currencies in the external market are Swiss francs, German marks, and Dutch guilders. Modest amounts of deposits are also denominated in sterling, the French franc, the Italian lira, and the Japanese yen.

London is the principal financial center for Eurodollar business, followed by Zurich. The volume of foreign-currency deposits in U.S. banks is extremely small, not because they are prohibited but because U.S. regulations make such transactions unprofitable.

There is no mystery to the production of Eurodollar deposits. In principle, the process is the same as when a bank on the west side of Fifth Avenue in New York transfers funds to a savings and loan association on the east side. The only difference is that the Eurobank in London is across the Atlantic Ocean rather than across the street.

FIGURE 7–1

External Currency Deposits by Currency, for
Eight Reporting European Countries
(in billions of U.S. dollars)

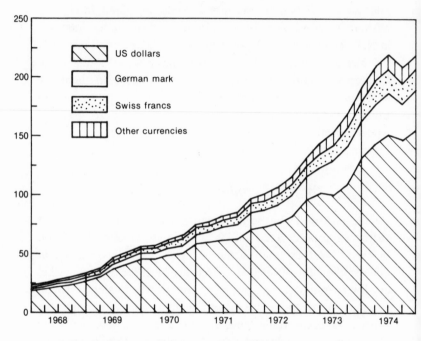

SOURCE: Bank for International Settlements, 1975.

Two aspects of this growth in external currency deposits are
especially noteworthy. The proportion of dollar-denominated
deposits to total external deposits has remained about 80 percent of the total, which is about the share of dollar deposits in
the total. And external deposits have grown at an average
annual rate of 30 percent.

Eurodollar deposits are produced in response to two different initiatives. First, an investor may shift funds from a bank
in New York to a bank in London. He writes a check on his
New York account and deposits it in his account in the London

118

bank. The London bank may then deposit this check in its account in a U.S. bank. The investor now holds a dollar deposit in a bank in London rather than a bank in New York. The total deposits of the U.S. banks are unchanged; however, individual investors hold smaller deposits in the United States, while London banks hold larger deposits. And the increase in the deposits of the London bank in the New York bank is matched by the increase in its deposit liabilities in London. Note that there is an increase in dollar deposits for the world as a whole: the volume of dollar deposits in New York remains unchanged, while the volume in London increases. Note also that the dollar deposit of the investor is in London, while the dollar deposit of the London bank is in New York.

The second initiative leading to the production of Eurodollar deposits occurs when the London bank increases its loans. Assume, for example, that Worldwide International Conglomerate (WIC) borrows from the London bank. WIC signs a promissory note or transfers a mortgage on some tankers to the London bank; the London bank "pays" by increasing the size of WIC's deposit in the bank. Note that this process of deposit creation is identical with the process that occurs whenever anyone borrows from a U.S. bank; the only difference is that the bank is in London rather than New York.

The London bank must be concerned that it will lose reserves if WIC decides to make a payment to some other firm. Domestic banks have the same concern. Yet they do not worry excessively, for they can take advantage of the law of large numbers: while some depositors will be reducing their balances, others will be increasing theirs.

In the domestic economy, the capacity of banks to expand their deposits is limited by the monetary authorities, who both determine the reserve base (the supply of high-powered money) and the reserve requirements. In the external currency market, in contrast, there is no formal reserve base, and no reserve requirement. Eurobanks add to their loans whenever their deposits increase. The relationship is set by business prudence rather than regulation.

The Eurobank system in dollars is an offshore extension of the domestic banking system, just as the Eurobank system in marks is an offshore extension of the domestic mark banking system. While there are no explicit reserve requirements relating changes in Eurobank liabilities in particular currencies to the reserves of the banks in these currencies, business prudence suggests that banks limit their expansion.

An interesting question is why U.S. banks should be so eager to set up branches in London and Zurich, considering that they usually pay higher interest rates on deposits and receive a lower interest rate on loans than they do in the United States. One answer is that they wish to grow, and branch expansion abroad is easier than in the United States. Another is that if they do not expand abroad, they may lose dollar deposits to foreign banks and to domestic competitors who have expanded abroad. A third is that even though the interest rate costs are higher in London than New York, the other costs may be lower. Most domestic banks are required to hold reserves, usually in the form of a non-interest-bearing deposit in the central bank. This requirement is a "tax" on their earnings, since otherwise the bank would have invested nearly all these funds in income-earning assets. As a rule, Eurobanks are not subject to reserve requirements. Moreover, the costs of Eurobanks are low because the market is a wholesale market; the minimum deposit size is $50,000, and the average deposit is much larger. Thus, banks are willing to pay a higher interest rate on external deposits than on domestic deposits so long as this additional interest cost is outweighed by the savings.

Finally, the growth of the external currency market enables some non-U.S. banks to enter the market for U.S. dollar deposits at less cost than if they were to establish branches in the

United States. U.S. banks have responded to this competitive challenge by setting up branches abroad that are prepared to offer the same terms on such deposits.

What remains to be explained is why investors continue to hold domestic deposits when, with minimal inconvenience, they can earn higher interest rates on external deposits. The answer is that external London deposits are subject to risks not encountered on domestic deposits, and these risks deter depositors from seeking the higher interest rates. The British authorities might restrict banks in London from fulfilling their commitments on foreign currency deposits. For example, the Eurobanks might be told that depositors could withdraw deposits only if they satisfied conditions X, Y, and Z. Or they might subject the external deposits to exchange controls, requiring depositors to sell their deposits to the Bank of England in exchange for sterling.

London dollars, in other words, differ from New York dollars in terms of political risk: they are subject to the whim of a different set of government authorities. Those who continue to hold dollars in New York believe that London dollars are too risky, that the additional interest income is not justified in terms of the loss if shift of funds back to New York were somehow restricted. The continued growth in external deposits during the 1960s reflected increasing investor confidence that the additional risks attached to external deposits were small, and the risks of holding funds in Europe seemed small.

External currency transactions probably go back to the seventeenth century, when one sovereign would counterfeit the gold coins of another. One popular explanation for the recent growth of the external market is that during the early years of the cold war, the Russians wanted dollar deposits because the dollar was the most useful currency for financing their international transactions. But they were reluctant to hold these deposits in New York because of the threat that the U.S.

authorities might "freeze" the deposits. In effect, the Russians believed that the political risk of dollar deposits was lower in London than in New York.

While the Russians may be the cause of rapid market growth during the 1950s, the remarkable growth in the 1960s reflects three additional factors: the steep climb in interest rates, which made it profitable to escape national regulation; the spread of multinational firms; and the great competitive expansion of banks.

Depositors contemplating a shift of funds to the external market must decide whether to acquire external deposits in London, Zurich, Paris, or some other center. Depositors choose among centers on the basis of their estimates of political risk. Moscow and Peking seem risky—the heavy hand of bureaucratic regulation is all too evident. Even though there is undoubtedly an interest rate which would induce lenders to acquire Moscow dollar deposits, banks issuing these deposits might not have the investment opportunities to justify paying such high interest rates.

The U.S. payments deficit contributed to the growth of the Eurodollar market, since some foreign central banks acquiring dollars decided to hold dollar deposits in London and Zurich rather than New York. Paradoxically, measures taken by the U.S. government to reduce the payments deficit led to a more rapid growth in the overseas money market. In 1965 the U.S. authorities adopted a voluntary restraint program to stem the outflow of U.S. capital; firms were asked to shift less money abroad, and financial institutions were asked to reduce their foreign loans. So both U.S. and foreign firms tried to borrow more dollars overseas. The increase in the demand for external dollar loans induced shifts of funds from New York to London in response to the higher interest rates offered by banks not directly affected by the U.S. controls. In 1968, the restrictions of U.S. capital outflows were tightened, and the incentive to borrow dollars abroad increased proportionately.

122

The tight U.S. monetary policy of 1969 and 1970 also contributed to the growth of external deposits. U.S. banks wanted to make more loans to foreigners but were unable to raise the funds to finance these loans. So they bid aggressively for dollar deposits in London. And as London deposit rates rose relative to New York rates, some nonresident holders of New York dollars sold them to buy London dollars.

The Links Between External Deposits in Different Currencies

External deposits denominated in dollars, Swiss francs, and other currencies are closely linked by the Eurobanks engaged in interest arbitrage. Eurobanks bid for deposits in six or seven currencies, not because they wish to make loans in each of these currencies but because funds received from selling deposits in one currency can be used to buy loans in any other currency. For example, a Eurobank might issue a deposit in Swiss francs. Finding relatively few attractive loan opportunities in marks, the bank would sell the Swiss francs for marks in the spot exchange market and make a loan in marks. To protect itself against the exchange risk, the bank would buy Swiss francs forward at the same time that it sold Swiss francs in the spot market. Because banks are willing to arbitrage in this way, the interest rates they offer on deposits in various currencies differ by the interest equivalent of the spread between the forward exchange rate and the spot exchange rate.

The external currency market provides a new set of links among the national money markets in the five or six largest Atlantic countries. Funds flow continuously between the domestic and external markets. By increasing the links between national money markets, the growth of the external currency market has tended to reduce further the scope for national monetary independence.

123

In 1969 and 1970, when credit conditions were extremely tight in the United States, interest rates on Eurodollar deposits rose to 10 percent at a time when interest rates on comparable domestic dollar deposits were 7 percent. These high interest rates led to an increase in the external deposit rates of the various other European currencies. Holders of domestic deposits in Swiss francs, marks, guilders, and other currencies were attracted by the high interest rates on external deposits; and the volume of external deposits denominated in Swiss francs, marks, and guilders rose rapidly. The Eurobanks used some of the funds received from the sale of deposits denominated in marks, Swiss francs, and guilders as the basis for loans in dollars; they sold some of their holdings of European currencies to buy dollars in the exchange market.

In 1971, the process was reversed; dollar-denominated deposits provided the basis for acquiring assets in other European currencies. They also provided the impetus for the currency revaluations since interest rates in various European currencies were then high while dollar interest rates were low. So Eurobanks—and currency speculators—found it attractive to borrow dollars and use the funds to make loans or acquire assets denominated in marks and Swiss francs.

Internationalizing Regulation

Central bankers lie awake at night worrying about the wheelers and dealers trafficking in their currency in jurisdictions outside their direct control. Dollar deposits in London seem outside U.S. control because they are in London, and outside British control because they are in dollars. The authorities are worried that much of the growth in Eurodollars has resulted from an expansion of credit, arranged in an inverted pyramid. Thus, each transfer of $1 million from New York to bank *A* in London may lead to a much larger increase in Eurodollar deposits, for bank *B* in London might borrow dollars from bank *A* to lend to bank *C,* and so on. The borrower from one Eurobank may deposit the proceeds in another Eurobank—or buy goods, services, or securities from a seller who deposits his proceeds in a Eurobank. As a result, the total of London dollars might increase by much more than the initial transfer from New York to London—perhaps as much as three or four times the initial amount—as banks lend to each other and to customers who borrow from one bank and shift the funds to other banks. The worry of central bankers is that a shock to the base of the pyramid could have a disastrous impact, bringing the whole credit pyramid down with a crash.

Assume that bank *A* decides to ask bank *B* to repay the loan. Where will *B* get the money? Perhaps from bank *C*. Ultimately, some bank in the system will ask a nonbank borrower to repay. If he can't, then the ability of the banks to repay declines. And the weaker the banks appear, the quicker their depositors will be to shift funds to those banks in the system which seem safer.

Several years ago, the pyramid began to shake when a German steel company that had borrowed extensively from Eurobanks went bankrupt. It was feared that if the firm was unable to repay these banks, the banks in turn would be unable to repay their depositors; then a run on the Eurobanking system would begin, and Eurobanks would have to call their loans. The cliché image is that of a tumbling house of cards. In fact, the Eurobanks *are* high-risk operations—and in the central banker's eyes, they are high-risk operations simply because they are unregulated.

How sensitive the system is to a major collapse is debatable. Two factors suggest that a collapse is unlikely. The first is that many Eurobanks are branches of U.S., Swiss, German, and other major banks; these banks will not permit their branches to fail. Second, the central banks would be likely to step in if

125

they thought a general collapse of credit possible. Nevertheless, central banks might delay their assistance, since they must feel less than completely responsible for the survival of banks whose raison d'être has been the avoidance of regulation. Moreover, the various central banks might not be able to agree on who has responsibility for the failure of banks in Luxembourg, the Bahamas, and other monetary havens.

The authorities are also concerned that access to the Euro-dollar market enables borrowers, lenders, and intermediaries to circumvent domestic monetary control, thus reducing the effectiveness of regulation and creating inequities between banks that participate in the market and banks that do not. Someday a clever entrepreneur might establish a Eurobank on a tugboat 5 or 10 miles from New York in the Atlantic Ocean; this would be the monetary equivalent of Radio Caroline. U.S. residents would shift funds to the Tugboat Bank because it would offer higher interest rates; borrowers would seek loans from the Tugboat Bank rather than from banks in New York. The Tugboat Bank would be in a favored competitive position relative to regulated U.S. banks, since it would be beyond the scope of U.S. regulation.

So, increasingly and inevitably, the long arm of regulation is reaching out to Eurobanks and to external currency transactions. The Bank of England and the Bundesbank control the foreign currency activities of banks within their legal jurisdiction, although the British do so in a very relaxed way. U.S. authorities apply a reserve regulation to funds received by U.S. banks from their foreign branches. These controls have usually been applied only to commercial banks, for only these entities are within the functional jurisdiction of the central banks. Since regulations reduce the profitability of Eurobanking in London and Zurich, the inevitable next step is for the commercial banks to shift to less extensively regulated jurisdictions.

Just as Radio Luxembourg can satisfy its customers because of official reluctance to disrupt its signals, so Eurobanks can flourish in Luxembourg and Nassau as long as depositors and borrowers are free to do business there. The Eurobanks will survive and flourish as long as one country with substantial political stability exerts only minimal controls on transactions in foreign currencies and as long as borrowers and lenders have relatively unrestricted access to the Eurobanks. So the next inevitable step would be for the authorities to regulate access —to tighten their controls on international capital movements.

One day, perhaps, countries will unify their regulations both for radio broadcasting and for commerical banking. Radio Luxembourg will fade away, and the Eurobanks will disappear. That day, however, does not seem imminent. For the central bank authorities have had the choice of harmonizing their regulations to reduce the incentives for Eurocurrency transactions or of regulating these transactions; they have chosen the latter path. Monetary independence and the central banks' own viability as institutions are the issues at stake.

Central Bankers Read Election Returns,

Not Balance Sheets

For most of the last few years, finance ministers of the world have been pursuing the grail of monetary reform. They've met each other at the annual meetings of IMF, at the monthly meetings of BIS, at the ad hoc meetings of the OECD, at the Group of Ten and the Committee of Twenty, at UNCTAD and the United Nations, at the Four and then the Five. In Brussels, the finance ministers of the countries of the European Economic Community have met, and there have been scores of meetings on a bilateral basis. Moreover, the deputy finance ministers have met. Somehow the prize is elusive.

Yet without reform, the system survives. Whatever is, is a system. The push for reform is a push for a System with a capital S—a set of rules which would govern the exchange rate policies of the system's members and the supply of international money.

Reform of the international monetary system could be accomplished with changes in a few key arrangements. The exchange rate system should allow for more flexible responses to payments deficits and surpluses, with only a minimal increase in the uncertainty felt by international traders and investors. And a mechanism must be found to produce the appropriate amount of international money without forcing the United States to incur payments deficits.

Stated in this way, the reform problem does not sound difficult. Surely it should be possible to obtain the agreement of central bankers and finance ministers to such modest proposals. But this ignores the politics of the problem. The most dramatic solution to the shortage of international money and the various other problems raised by the existence of more than 100 national monies would be to adopt a common worldwide money. Since there would be no exchange rates, crises associated with pending changes in exchange rates would disappear. There would be no further need to coordinate the monetary policies of various central banks, for there would be only one central bank and one monetary policy. Nor would there be any need to be concerned with the relationship between the rate of growth of national monies and international money, since the distinction between the two would disappear. Indeed, the advantages of a worldwide money appear so overwhelming that one wonders why national monies are retained.

Once there was a common worldwide money—gold. The move away from the gold standard suggests why the idea of a worldwide money is now somewhat utopian. The twentieth century is one of nationalism. National governments have given increased priority to domestic objectives. The growth in the power of the state and the increase in attention to purely national objectives are not accidents. First monetary policy was manipulated to help finance World War I expenditures. Then, during the Great Depression, national governments geared monetary policy to expand their domestic employment. In the final analysis, the gold standard faded because governments wanted the advantages of national money.

The library shelves are lined with books containing plans for reforming the monetary system and reducing its susceptibility to various crises. These plans are full of articles, paragraphs, sections, and subsections which spell out in detail when a country can change its exchange rate and when it can't, when it can borrow from other countries or international institutions

129

and when it is obliged to lend to them. In reality, all of these articles, paragraphs, sections, and subsections are proxies for issues that are rarely discussed formally. For what each national government wants to know is how the proposed arrangements will affect its ability to achieve its own national objectives— full employment, a stable price level, rapid growth, higher business profits, and more exports. Each wants to know how any plan will affect its ability to keep its constituents sufficiently happy to win the next election or forestall the next coup. When adjustments must be made, national governments want to be sure that the burdens and costs fall elsewhere. If some event occurs that adversely affects their constituents, they want to be able to show that the event, like the weather, was imported and beyond governmental control.

Many countries are concerned that an international monetary agreement might limit their freedom to set domestic policies, thus making it more difficult to satisfy their domestic constituencies. When the British joined the European Common Market, for example, they worried over what would happen to employment in Birmingham and Conventry once bureaucrats in Brussels set monetary policy. They feared that the Bank of England might lose its independence and eventually become a branch office of a European central bank, much as the Federal Reserve Bank of Atlanta is a branch of the Federal Reserve System in Washington.

Every government would readily sign an agreement for international monetary reform if it were allowed to write the treaty, select the management for the institution, and formulate its policies. Each would then design the arrangements so as to minimize any external constraint on its choice of domestic policies. In this case, membership would impose no cost on the government generating the proposal. The inevitable costs of adjustment would fall on other countries. Naturally, the proposals of various nations would be inconsistent. What is good for General Motors is not necessarily good for Ford. And what

130

is good for France is not necessarily good for Germany—as the Germans have learned, at some cost, in Brussels.

Two facts of political life explain why efforts to establish new rules have not proved very successful. One is that the residents of different countries frequently have conflicting interests. The second is that foreigners don't vote in domestic elections.

Nations compete for markets. Importers and exporters squabble over a fair price. Oil producers and oil consumers contest the fair price for oil—and so it is with rice, wheat, bauxite. Whenever payments imbalances occur, there is sporadic conflict over whether the deficit countries or surplus countries should take the initiative in making the necessary adjustments. Political leaders talk about the virtues of international cooperation, but domestic factors frequently merit priority, especially when the next election may be only months away. Monetary reform has a limited constituency.

Ideally, it would be nice if we were able to predict the positions of each of the major countries on the major issues of international monetary reform: the arrangements for producing international money and for adjusting to payments imbalances. Someplace, somewhere, there may be some systematic knowledge about this question. But in the absence of such knowledge, we must content ourselves with anecdotal evidence about differing national attitudes toward inflation, bureaucracy, economic openness, and the market.

Inflation Is No Accident

Britain and Germany have different positions toward reform of the system, largely because Britain has run payments deficits while Germany has had surpluses. Since the late 1940s the dollar price of sterling has fallen by a half, while the dollar price of the mark has almost doubled. The payments positions of the two countries reflect their price level performance: prices have risen rapidly in Britain and slowly in Germany. This difference is no accident. In fact, the financial policies pursued by each country during the 1960s and 1970s can be traced to its economic performance during the early 1920s. In the period following World War I, Great Britain's unemployment rate reached nearly 20 percent. Ever since, British economic policy has sought to maintain full employment, regardless of the impact on domestic prices. Germany, on the other hand, has been almost paranoiac about increases in its price level, as a result of German experience with the hyperinflations of 1922–1923 and 1944–1948, during which its currency and most of its financial assets became worthless. These national experiences fostered attitudes that directly affect their payments positions and indirectly affect their positions on reform.

Countries whose prices rise more rapidly than the average, such as Britain and Denmark, tend to have payments deficits; they also have more ambitious approaches toward international monetary rules than do countries with greater price stability, such as Germany and the Netherlands, which tend to have surpluses. The deficit countries want foreign loans and credits made available on an automatic basis, without strings and lectures about good financial behavior; they want to avoid the need to devalue, and they hope their currency will not depreciate. If changes in exchange rates are necessary, then they want the surplus countries to take the initiative. If the deficit countries themselves must take the initiative, then they want to be able to restrict their foreign payments without subjecting themselves to the criticism or surveillance of other countries or of international institutions.

Countries with payments surpluses, on the other hand, do not want to commit themselves to extending large credits to deficit countries; they fear that if they do, their payments surpluses will become even larger and they will in effect import inflation. Nor do they want to be put in the position of having to revalue to avoid having to inflate.

Substantial payments imbalances result from differences among countries in the rates at which their prices increase and, indirectly, at which their national money supplies grow. Differences among countries in rates of monetary growth are likely to reflect institutional differences in their tax systems or in their union-management relations.

The common explanation of rising prices—too much money chasing too few goods—describes a situation known as demand-pull inflation. Annual price increases of 50 or 100 percent, as in some Latin American countries, are neither mistakes nor accidents; they result from government expenditure and credit policies that are not consistent with price stability. Few governments are perpetually ignorant of the financial policies needed to produce price stability. When prices continue to rise, it is because anti-inflationary policies are deemed more expensive than those that permit a continuation of the inflation.

Demand-pull inflation occurs because the government wants the profits from the production of money, either to finance its own expenditures or to divert them to its supporters. Because the government is unwilling to raise its tax rates, expenditures within the public sector are financed with newly produced money. The Vietnam inflation in the United States and the U.S. inflation in Vietnam both reflect increased government spending based on monetary expansion. The Johnson administration evidently believed that it was less costly politically to finance the full costs of an unpopular war through debasement of the money than by raising tax rates.

Similarly, within Vietnam the Thieu government financed its local expenditures and those of U.S. forces by "printing press" money; the money supply grew at the rate of 40 or 50 percent a year. Both governments in effect increased their expenditures, just as if they had raised their income and sales tax rates. In both the United States and Vietnam, the holders of money were taxed—the widows and orphans and pensioners who held savings bonds and other fixed-price assets, like cash, savings accounts, and life insurance policies. Even those individuals who did not have to pay the higher income and sales taxes nevertheless had to "pay" the inflation tax.

An alternative explanation for rising prices, especially in countries with well-organized, independent, and militant labor unions, is cost-push inflation. The scenario begins with a strike or the threat of a strike. To obtain labor peace, firms grant large wage increases. Since their labor costs rise, they must raise their prices to avoid sharp declines in their profits or, more likely, to avoid substantial losses. The national authorities may decide that the solution to the cost-push problem is to wait until the higher prices reduce the demand for the firms' product and the consequent demand for labor.

At that point, the higher unemployment rate might be sufficient to dampen further upward pressure on wages, and the power of the unions might be broken. But the unemployed vote. Elections may occur long before the union structure is weakened. So the authorities may adopt an expansive monetary policy to reduce unemployment; the increase in the money supply leads to an increase in demand for goods and for labor, sustaining the higher prices. When the unemployment rate falls, unions will again be in a good position to strike for another wage increase.

In Britain, which has a large number of decentralized unions, local strikes have been frequent. British employers have been prepared to buy labor peace, knowing they can pass on the higher costs by raising prices. Germany, in contrast, can afford its inflation paranoia because its labor force has been relatively docile and has not pressed aggressively for large wage hikes. Moreover, Germany, unlike Britain, has been a willing importer of foreign labor. Germany could not have achieved its relative price stability with a British-type industrial structure. And British prices would have risen much less rapidly if its labor union leaders had Germanic attitudes toward authority. The economic structures in each country have thus reinforced the importance that each attaches to price stability and full employment. If the European Economic Community moves seriously toward a common currency, then either the British or the Germans—and perhaps both—will be in for a shock. There is no one rate of monetary expansion which will leave both happy, and a compromise rate might leave both unhappy.

National central banks respond to their own fiscal and labor market structures. That is why greater harmonization or unification of the economic structures in various countries may be necessary before a comprehensive international monetary agreement, limiting monetary independence in individual countries, can be negotiated. If a comprehensive reform agreement were negotiated while these economic differences remained substantial, the agreement would break down when the national views about the appropriate rate of monetary growth diverged sharply. Institutions must adjust to national diversity, for national diversity will not adjust to institutions.

Bureaucracy Is a Growth Industry

Change is as inevitable in economic life as it is in biological life. Individuals go through a sequence of stages of growth. At some stages they grow rapidly; then they mature, stabilize, degenerate, and eventually die. Throughout the life cycle, they are subject to shocks of disease and accident, which may alter the growth process.

Economies also go through stages, although the distinction among the stages may be less clear. Moreover, the length of particular stages in the various economies may differ. Finally, economies are subject to shocks—both natural, such as crop failures, and accidental, such as wars. Technological change is a shock to individuals and firms within an economy, since it may result in a decline in the demand for their products. Competition—foreign as well as domestic—may also be a shock.

Shocks require adjustments and adaptations. Few people welcome shocks, and an increasingly large part of governmental activity has involved reducing shocks or minimizing their costs. Frequently, what government does is to reallocate the costs of a shock among various elements in the economy.

Countries differ sharply in the way they respond to shocks. Countries also have their traditional economic styles, as is evident from the different roles played by government in determining price, wage, credit, and investment decisions. In Japan (and in France, to a lesser extent) the bureaucracy plays a major role in setting the target growth rates and the investment levels of particular industries and firms. In other countries these decisions reflect market forces. Americans, for example, favor decentralized decision making; it is felt that government should be responsible for monetary and fiscal policy, households should make the consumption decisions, and business firms the investment decisions. The mix of goods and services to be produced and who is to produce them are the outcomes of millions of private decisions. A few other countries, such as Germany and Switzerland, share the U.S. perspective, but elsewhere governmental authorities are more fully involved in production and investment decisions.

National attitudes toward government intervention are closely related to the prestige enjoyed by the bureaucracy. In Japan and France the brightest graduates of the most elite universities vie for careers in government service; in these countries bureaucratic intervention in investment and production decisions is readily accepted. A strong central government is deemed desirable, and the bureaucrats are regarded as highly competent.

As a general rule, the more powerful the bureaucracy, the smaller the scope for market-oriented decisions. Bureaucratic intervention is justified on various grounds, from reducing uncertainty associated with free markets to minimizing excessive competitive waste or reducing business conflict. The bureaucracy affects decisions in several ways—for example through control over the allocation of credit, through taxes, and through the issuance of building, investment, and import permits. Clearly, moves toward a more open economy will tend to weaken bureaucratic control and thus may threaten the future of the bureaucracy.

The views of most politicians about how the international economy should be managed are, not unexpectedly, an extension of their views about how their domestic economies should be managed. Countries which place a low value on the bureaucracy tend to favor an open international economy, with minimal barriers to the free flow of goods and capital internationally. They feel either that exchange rates should be allowed to float freely so as to balance international payments and receipts, or that the supply of international money should be so managed as to satisfy the needs of individual countries. In either case, individuals and firms should be free to choose between domestic and foreign goods on the basis of price, without arbitrary restrictions at the border.

Countries with strong centralized bureaucratic controls over their domestic economies, on the other hand, tend to favor the use of bureaucratic controls to manage international payments. International monetary reform usually has a lower priority for such countries, since their bureaucrats are in a position to correct payments imbalances by tightening or easing controls on purchases of foreign exchange and on imports.

Thus, it is no accident that U.S. government officials are likely to be more favorable to floating exchange rates than are French or Japanese government officials. Nor is it surprising that U.S. government officials are more intensely concerned with the adequacy of international money than officials in other

137

countries, for the officials in other countries are more willing to make arbitrary decisions regulating international payments at their borders.

Inevitably, government officials in other countries are concerned about the costs to the system of two types of errors: one is too small a supply of reserves, the other too large a supply. If the supply is too small, as it was in the early 1960s, other countries may still be able to earn payments surpluses by forcing the United States to incur a payments deficit. If the supply is too large, as in the late 1960s, these countries import inflation, perhaps from the United States. Foreign bureaucrats believe the cost to their countries of adjusting to too small a supply of reserves is much less than the cost of adjusting to too large a supply. The U.S. authorities, not surprisingly, come to the opposite conclusion.

The New Mercantilists

One of the conflicts in the international economy is the attitude toward openness: are foreign residents treated on a par with domestic residents, or are they discriminated against in access to markets, jobs, investments, and tax relief? In earlier periods, nationalism was the opposite of openness; at an earlier stage, mercantilism was the term for nationalistic behavior. The mercantilists were interested in hoarding gold as a basis for enhancing their country's power and reducing that of other countries. An open international economy threatens, almost by definition, the advocates of nationalism. Nationalism means that the economic interests of domestic producers are preferred over those of foreign competitors. It means that domestic residents have preferred access to markets, products, and jobs. Tariffs, quotas, and restrictions on the ownership of domestic assets by foreigners reflect nationalist pressures.

Countries subject to strong nationalist pressures are likely to place substantial barriers in the way of imports of foreign goods and services, as well as the sale of domestic securities by foreigners. Japan has a strong nationalist bias. The Japanese rush toward modernization in the last third of the nineteenth century reflected the fear that foreign imperialists would begin to dismember Japan into colonies or enclaves, as they had China. Thus, Japan became a strong industrial power in order to resist a perceived external threat. Japanese attitudes toward trade and investment decisions continue to reflect this strong desire to maintain the nation's cultural identity. That is why Japan resists foreign investments and is reluctant to liberalize its import policies; domestic residents should not be injured or inconvenienced for the sake of international harmony. Rather, U.S. textile workers should lose their jobs so that Japanese textile workers can produce for the U.S. market.

One pervasive worldwide tendency of the last fifty years has been an increase in the government's role in production. Often, when private entrepreneurs find a particular industry increasingly unprofitable, foreign competition further reduces the number of domestic producers. Yet the government, while reluctant to subsidize private entrepreneurs, usually wants to maintain domestic production. So the activity is shifted to the public sector. Many of the "private" firms in Italy are owned by one of three large holding companies, IRI, ENI, and ENEL, each of which is largely owned by the government. Sometimes national ownership may be justified on grounds of national security. General de Gaulle insisted that France needed a computer industry for national security, and so part of Machine Bull, the largest French computer firm, was absorbed by the government when it would otherwise have been liquidated. Similarly, the Conservative government in Great Britain nationalized Rolls Royce because the immediate unemployment in areas near the company's factories would have been excessively high.

As government assumes a bigger role in production, open-

139

ness to foreign competition declines. Even more than those in the private sector, firms and industries in the public sector demand protection from foreign competition; almost of necessity, the government-owned firms are unprofitable. British Leyland, the last major domestically owned auto firm, is becoming progressively nationalized; given the productivity of its laborers and their wages, if Leyland prices its cars to cover its costs, it won't be able to sell any cars. If it sells at a lower price, then it needs a subsidy. But government's ability to pay subsidies is limited because the ability to tax is limited. So tariffs and other import barriers are levied to protect domestic producers and to minimize the necessary subsidies for public sector industries. The result is that countries with a large number of government-owned firms in manufacturing are reluctant to reduce barriers to external competition or to further integrate the international economy; such moves jeopardize the survival of these domestic firms or raise the cost of the subsidy to the Treasury.

Although other countries may seem more nationalistic than the United States, the differences may be partly an illusion. The large U.S. economic size means that any direct foreign threat to the United States is small; foreign economies have a minimal impact on the level of U.S. business activity. While Canada and France may worry about U.S. domination of their economies and of their national institutions, size alone protects the United States from foreign domination. Foreign ownership of firms located in the United States or of shares in U.S. firms is small. But the relatively liberal U.S. position toward foreign ownership would almost certainly change if foreigners tried to acquire a sizeable proportion of major U.S. industries or of large U.S. firms like IBM or General Motors. Shifts in U.S. foreign economic policy in the last ten years to more and higher import barriers—such as quotas on imports of textiles, apparel, steel, beef, and petroleum—suggest that the United States is not immune from nationalist pressures. The threat that various Arab countries might use some of their new-found wealth to buy up various U.S. firms sends a number of congressmen up the wall.

Who Takes the Consensus?

International monetary reform would be a cinch if countries were homogeneous—if each were made in the same image. But most national borders are not arbitrary; rather, they tend to segregate economies with different industrial and institutional structures and electorates with different values. Conflicts in interests are inevitable and complicate monetary reform.

Moreover, the increasing priority given to national interests is a worldwide phenomenon; the pull of nationalism intensifies the growth of the bureaucracy and domestic demands for monetary flexibility. In time, perhaps, the strength of these national pulls may diminish. In the meantime, efforts at monetary reform which are inconsistent with these pressures are not likely to succeed.

They Invented Money So They Could
Have Inflation

One hundred years ago, a mile was a mile, a dollar was a dollar, a liter of water weighed a kilo. While the 1875 kilo is identical to the 1975 kilo, the 1875 dollar was much more valuable then than it is now. All the national monies in 1975 measure less than they did in 1965; they were less valuable in 1965 than in 1955. And nearly everyone believes they will be less valuable in 1985.

One hundred years from now, the mile and the kilo will be unchanged as units of distance and weight. It's equally certain that the dollar will have a smaller value, as will the mark, the Swiss franc, and all other "strong" currencies. While the measurement of the value of money may be less scientific than the measurement of the speed of light or the distance to the moon, the error in the measurement is not in question—the orbit of the moon around the sun also varies within a range. Rather, the question is why, of all the measures in the world, money is the only one which generally shrinks, usually at an uncertain rate.

From time to time, the monetary authorities in various countries acknowledge the debasing tendencies of their predecessors —they knock two or three zeros off the money units. In 1959 the heavy French franc replaced the light French franc; 1 new franc was set equal to 1,000 old francs. Similar adjustments have been made in Argentina, Brazil, Chile, and numerous other countries in which inflation is rapid.

Traditionally, shrinkage in the value of money is associated with wartime finance; the sovereign finds it expedient to print money to pay his army. The U.S. consumer price level nearly doubled during the 1915–1920 period, and the annual rate of increase averaged 15 percent, about as high as during the Civil War period. From 1940 to 1948 the annual rate of price increase averaged 7 percent. During the Korean War the rate of price increase averaged 5 percent for about two years. From the beginning of major U.S. involvement in Vietnam in 1965 to the climax, in 1970, the annual increase in the U.S. consumer price index averaged 4 percent. The progressive decline in the annual rate of price increase over these four wartime episodes suggests that the U.S. government has been more successful in putting wars on a pay-as-you-go-basis.

Increased confidence in the ability of governments to control inflation has been shattered by the world inflation of 1973–1974, virtually unprecedented in peacetime. A new term, double-digit inflation, hit the newspaper headlines. Prices were increasing nearly as rapidly in peacetime as they had in our most severe wars. By almost any peacetime standard, the four-year interval 1972–1975 was unprecedented: the U.S. consumer price level increased by 36 percent, or nearly 10 percent a year, more rapidly than during World War II.

The world inflation of the early 1970s should be distinguished from the Vietnam inflation of the late 1960s. Tight money policy in 1969 pushed the economy into recession. The U.S. commitment in Vietnam and U.S. inflation were winding down together. Whereas during the late 1960s U.S. price levels increased more rapidly than those in other industrialized countries, inflation in the 1970s was worldwide. Price levels abroad were increasing as rapidly as U.S. prices—or more so. In Japan, prices were increasing at a rate of nearly 30 percent; in Great Britain, at a rate of 25 percent. Germany was the principal exception; price increases were several percentage points lower than in the United States.

While inflation has been around as long as money, there remain sharp disagreements about its causes. Is the cause economic, sociological, or psychological? If economic in origin, does inflation reflect supply shortages of a natural or artificial kind, or expansion of demand? The worldwide inflation has been attributed to the growth of the Eurodollar market, to the floating exchange rate system, to the loss of confidence in money, to the fourfold increase in the price of oil. Indeed, some experts have gone so far as to say that of the 10 percent increase in U.S. prices, 2 percentage points represent the increase in oil prices, 4 percentage points the devaluation of the dollar, and so forth. Some Englishmen talk about a sociological theory of inflation; they mean that strong unions—the railway workers, miners, electrical workers, and other public sector employees in Britain—raised the selling prices for their product.

Many things happen at the same time in the worlds of business and money. Distinctions must be made between causes and consequences, between causes and associations, between causes and definitions. A frequent pairing of two events sometimes leads to a "scientific truth" or rule, as if causation could be inferred from association. An exception then leads to the statement, "This is the exception that proves the rule." But the statement should read: "This is the exception that proves the rule wrong." It is a fact that the money supply increases with great statistical regularity toward the end of the year, but it would be risky to suggest that increases in the money supply cause Christmas. Casual observation suggests that fire trucks frequently are found near fires, but it would be risky to suggest that fire trucks cause fires, or that the fires caused the fire trucks. These relationships involve association, not causation.

To say that inflation is caused by rising prices is like saying that death is caused by the failure of the heart to beat; all deaths are associated with the stoppage of heart movement, but heart failure has not yet put cancer, strokes, and accidents out of business. A definition is not a statement about causation. Brain stoppage measures death, just as rising prices measure inflation; the questions to be answered are why the brain stopped and why prices increased.

Whether an alleged example of economic cause and effect is another example of argument by association can sometimes be determined by asking whether the relationship holds over a variety of years. While the quadrupling of oil prices in the fall of 1973 may have led to a more rapid increase in world price levels thereafter, it does not explain the rapid increase in prices that had previously occurred—nor does it explain why the prices of sugar, copper, groundnuts, and other primary products also increased sharply. The move to floating rates may explain why prices increased more rapidly in some countries than in others—yet the move to floating rates would not have been necessary if prices had not already been increasing more rapidly in some countries than in others. Floating exchange rates may have been a result of differential rates of inflation rather than a cause, or at least so many Germans believe. While the growth of the Eurodollar market may have been inflationary, the market grew no more rapidly in 1973 and 1974 than it had in earlier years, when the rate of price increase across countries was much less rapid.

In the long run, inflation will not occur without an increase in the money supply. But an increase in the commodity price level may occur in response to shortages, even if the money supply is constant. A failure in the corn crop frequently leads to higher corn prices, for the increase in price is one way to ration the reduced supply among competing buyers. Nevertheless, these factors lead to one-shot (or perhaps two-shot) increases in the price level, rather than continuing increases.

The question is not what was happening in 1973 and 1974, but rather what happened in 1973 and 1974 that had not happened before. A second question is why rates of price in-

Bank failures were commonplace in the nineteenth century. Banks closed their doors when their deposit liabilities exceeded their loans, mortgages, and assets. Once the word got out that a bank might be in difficulty, the depositors rushed to get their money, much more rapidly than if they were to sell a currency about to be revalued. If the bank closed, the depositors might receive 30 or 40 cents on the dollar, depending on how badly the bank was managed.

In some cases, the run on the bank caused an otherwise good bank to fail. Banks were forced to sell assets to meet their depositors' demand for money. Such sales further weakened the banks' position, for inevitably the best assets were sold first. The failure of one bank had a domino effect on the stability of others; bankruptcy became contagious. Credit systems collapsed when the public lost confidence in the banks. Bank failures also meant that the money supply fell, so recessions resulted.

Several institutional innovations were adopted to minimize failure. The National Banking Act of 1863 provided for a comptroller of the currency to protect banks and depositors by ensuring that the assets held by banks were good. Yet there were substantial bank failures in 1883, 1896, and 1907. The Federal Reserve was set up in 1913 to act as a lender of last resort, supplying funds—newly printed money—to banks in distress so they could pay depositors who sought to reduce or close out their accounts. Nevertheless, nearly 6,000 banks suspended deposits in the 1920s, 1,352 in 1930, 2,294 in 1931, 1,456 in 1932, and 4,000 in 1933. To dampen the snowball effect of deposit withdrawal, the U.S. government set up the Federal Deposit Insurance Corporation. Initially, individual deposits were insured to $10,000, then $20,000; in 1975 the ceiling was raised to $40,000. Banks pay a premium to the FDIC, and it has built up reserves over the years. At the end of 1974, capital accumulated by the FDIC from these insurance premiums totaled $9 billion; the FDIC supposedly has an open credit line at the Treasury if its losses should be larger.

A few banks have failed recently despite these institutional safeguards. U.S. National Bank in San Diego failed for $90 million; the bank managers made high risk loans to captive firms. Franklin National Bank failed because of foreign exchange losses. Security National Bank of Long Island was closed because it had made too many insecure loans. These institutions were merged into relatively strong banks by the regulatory authorities.

The key question is whether a significant number of banks might fail again, and how adequate the safeguards will be. In 1974 and 1975, newspaper reports suggested that the Treasury and the Fed were keeping a close watch on several hundred banks. Some of the business and real estate loans made by these banks went sour during the recession. And the market value of the bonds held by these institutions plummeted with the sharp rise in interest rates. Technically, these institutions were bankrupt; the market value of their assets was less than their liabilities. The losses dwarfed the accumulated reserves of the FDIC.

The Fed faced a dilemma. Its tight money policy had caused the value of bank assets to decline and had forced the banks into technical bankruptcy. The rationale for setting up the Fed was to prevent the failure of banks. But the desire to break the double-digit inflation had driven the banks to the brink of failure. To prevent bank failure, the Fed was obliged to expand the economy—to float off the credit crisis. Monetary expansion could lead to inflation, which would lead to tight money, which would lead to increased bank failures. And so it goes.

creases differed so sharply among countries. And a third question asks how the severity of the inflation was related to the severity of the recession which followed.

Watergate Economics

In the United States, the year immediately preceding presidential elections is likely to be one of expansive financial policies. The party in power wants the economy prosperous when the voters go to the polls. If the economy is sluggish, the ins may soon be out. If inflation is soaring, the government may also be in trouble. So it wants to fine tune the economy and

147

somehow achieve full employment and stable prices—a neat trick.

Assume the economy is in recession. Initially, measures taken to expand the economy are likely to affect output and employment more than prices and costs as long as there remains substantial spare capacity. Increasingly, as the economy continues to expand, it will bump against more and more supply constraints, and prices will rise to ration scarce goods. At first, price increases will be selective, as scarcities develop in particular goods; then the price increases will become more widespread. Fine tuning suggests that the authorities try to time the expansion so that the maximum employment effects are felt on the Sunday before the election; someone else can begin to worry about subsequent price increases after the election.

In 1959 the prospects for a recession in the U.S. economy by November 1960 seemed strong. Arthur F. Burns, formerly chairman of the Council for Economic Advisers and an informal adviser to then-Vice-President Nixon, recommended an expansion of the economy to set the stage for a Nixon victory. Supposedly, President Eisenhower and William McChesney Martin, then chairman of the Federal Reserve Board, rejected the advice. The economy sputtered into 1960. John Kennedy ran his campaign on the slogan of "Getting the Economy Moving Again." Nixon made his move to California.

In 1969, President Nixon appointed Arthur R. Burns as a White House adviser; a year later Burns became chairman of the Federal Reserve Board. After continuing a monetary crunch designed to wring the inflationary excesses out of the U.S. economy in 1970, the Fed began to expand the rate of money supply growth in the spring of 1971 to stimulate the economy through increased expenditures. In August 1971, one element in Nixon's New Economic Policy was price and wage ceilings, which tilted the effect of increased expenditures toward increases in output and employment rather than increases in prices and wages. The U.S. economy began to boom—industrial production, employment, man-hours per week, and the stock market all went up.

As a recession recovery year, 1971 was unusual. The unemployment rate peaked at about 6 percent, but the consumer price level was still increasing at an annual rate of 3 percent. In previous recessions, in contrast, prices usually increased no more than 1 percent when unemployment peaked—and the unemployment rate peaked lower.

One interpretation is that the structure of U.S. economy had changed: an increase in the unemployment rate to perhaps 7 or 8 percent for several years would have been necessary to get the rate of price increase down to 1 percent. A second interpretation is that if monetary expansion hadn't begun in mid-1971, the economy wouldn't have been booming in November 1972. Nixon's margin in the 1972 election was the largest ever. Whether McGovern contributed as much as Burns is debatable.

The 1972 inflation began at a time when prices were increasing at a rate of 3 percent a year, rather than at the 1 percent rate of the 1950s and early 1960s. The public had recently seen the value of the dollar shrink by 30 percent in five years. So when prices resumed their rapid increase, the public began to anticipate further inflation; rather than risk holding money while its value declined, they began to reduce their money balances. They spent (and prices increased more rapidly than would have been predicted from the money supply changes alone), but spending only transferred the money to someone else.

Price increases were inevitable after the election; the uncertainty was the timing. The price ceilings of phase 1, phase 2, and phase N only delayed upward movements in prices. Nixon and Burns had a tiger by the tail, and they couldn't afford to let go.

Upward pressures on U.S. prices also resulted from the devaluations of the dollar at the end of 1971 and then in early 1973. In the late 1960s, U.S. consumption increased more rapidly than U.S. production, as imports increased more rapidly than exports. As long as foreign central banks were willing to add to their dollar holdings, it was not necessary for the dollar to be devalued, and the increase in U.S. imports relative to U.S. exports dampened upward pressure on the U.S. price level. The combination of the delayed devaluation and the price ceilings meant that the price increases which would have occurred in 1970 and 1971 instead were bunched in a much shorter interval. After the devaluation, the incomes of U.S. consumers increased more rapidly than the supply of goods available, so sharp price increases were inevitable to ration the reduced supply. Prior to the devaluations, the increase in imports relative to exports meant that domestic prices increased less rapidly than they otherwise might have; after the devaluation, the reverse was true. In 1973, dollar goods were cheaper to consumers in other industrial countries; U.S. exports soared, and U.S. consumers shifted to U.S. goods from more expensive foreign goods. The reduction in the supply of goods because of the decline in the trade balance, together with the higher price of imports, reinforced upward pressure on U.S. price levels from Burns's monetary expansion. The effect was delayed by price ceilings. But these ceilings were removed early in 1972—soon after the 1972 election, long before the 1976 election.

Governments rarely admit their mistakes. If their policies backfire, the problem is that unforeseen—and unforeseeable—events occurred. So the inflation was attributed to supply shortages. The anchovies disappeared from the west coast of Latin America, so there was a deficiency in the world supply of protein. The Russians had a bad wheat crop. The United States had a bad wheat crop. The Arabs raised the price of crude petroleum. These supply shortages did contribute to the increase in prices. But the prices of many other commodities were also increasing. In the absence of demand booms, the supply shortfalls would have had a much less severe impact on prices. The government had sailed too close to the wind; these supply shortfalls would have been far less troublesome if the government had followed a less risky policy.

Watergate was an exercise in overkill: Nixon would have won the 1972 election even without any possible information that might have been gathered illegally from Democratic National headquarters. Similarly, the Republicans would have won in 1972 even without the rapid monetary expansion of 1971. They chose not to take the risks. The costs fell elsewhere.

Comparative Shrinkage

Political leaders—at least U.S. political leaders—frequently suggest that if things aren't quite perfect at home, at least they're much worse abroad. President Nixon was fond of comparing the rate of U.S. inflation with that of other countries, as long as the U.S. rate was lower.

One of the factors which put upward pressure on U.S. prices during the early 1970s—the Fed's monetary policies—did not directly affect other countries: the Europeans and the Japanese couldn't vote in the 1972 election. Moreover, if the devaluations of the dollar are supposed to have led to a more rapid increase in U.S. prices, the converse—the revaluations of the yen, the guilder, the Swiss franc, and the mark—should have dampened upward pressure on price levels in these countries. For both reasons, price levels abroad should have increased less rapidly than in the United States. But in fact, prices in most foreign countries increased more rapidly than in the United States.

The simplest explanation for the differential movements in national price levels is that the market baskets of goods used in the comparison are not identical. Thus, the British price level might be heavily weighted with fish and chips, the American with hamburgers and French fries. This implies that if the components of the indexes are more or less the same, then the indexes should tend to move together. But this explanation is too simple, for while the indexes with similar components may tend to move together, they may not move by the same amount. Within the United States, prices for the same market basket of goods are higher in some cities than in others, and they may increase at a more or less rapid rate. While the goods markets in the various cities are linked by arbitrage, there are enough frictions so that modest differences in price level movements are possible. Similarly, the index in the countries with the most rapid increases in prices might contain relatively more of those goods whose prices are increasing most rapidly. The U.S. Department of State and the United Nations have calculated the cost of living in various national capitals; if Washington is 100, then Tokyo and Paris may be 150, New York 130, and Manila 60.

The rate of inflation in each country is measured by the increase in the consumer price index. The movements in the consumer price indexes in several countries may be quite dissimilar, even though the same countries' wholesale price indexes move together. The wholesale price indexes in various countries are more nearly similar to each other than the consumer price indexes, although the wholesale index is much more volatile than the retail index. The reason for this volatility is that the prices of many goods included in the wholesale index are set in competitive markets.

Two different approaches can be used to explain the differential price movements. The simplest is to assert that prices increase most rapidly in countries that follow the most expansive monetary policies. For years, prices in Argentina, Brazil, and Chile have increased more rapidly than those of other countries, and they have been obliged to devalue; the movements in exchange rates and in price levels should be largely offsetting. In Europe and Japan, the growth in the money supplies has been more rapid than in the United States, in part because their very large payments surpluses in 1971 led to a sharp increase in the rate of money supply growth. For example, Japan had money supply increases of 30 percent in 1971 and 25 percent in 1972; Germany's were 13 percent and 14 percent, marginally smaller than those for Europe. Their reluctance to revalue in 1971 had belated price consequences.

TABLE 9–1

Changes in Money and Prices
(percent Change in 12 Months)

	1971		1972		1973		1974	
	M	P	M	P	M	P	M	P
World	13.0	5.9	15.0	5.9	12.9	9.6	10.5	15.1
United States	6.2	4.3	7.6	3.3	7.3	6.2	2.8	11.6
Canada	27.8	2.9	15.5	4.8	13.8	7.6	11.7	10.9
Japan	29.7	6.3	24.7	4.8	16.7	11.8	11.5	22.7
Germany	12.8	5.3	13.9	5.5	.7	6.9	12.2	7.0
Netherlands	15.0	7.5	17.5	7.8	−.1	8.0	12.5	9.6
France	11.9	5.5	14.9	5.9	9.8	7.3	15.2	13.6
Switzerland	17.7	6.6	5.5	6.7	−.2	8.7	−3.5	9.8
United Kingdom	15.3	9.4	13.9	7.1	5.1	9.1	10.8	15.9

SOURCE: International Monetary Fund, *International Financial Statistics*, 1975.

Changes in exchange rates are almost automatically related to changes in price level movements. Thus, more rapid price increases have led to devaluations, less rapid price increases to revaluations. The relationship is reciprocal: if a country devalues, its price level is likely to rise, because the domestic price of both imports and exports increases. If it revalues, or if its currency appreciates, its price level should fall relative to that abroad.

The way out of the circle is straightforward. To the extent that prices increase more rapidly in Great Britain than in the United States, sterling should depreciate relative to the dollar. To the extent that independent factors, such as capital move-

153

ments or changes in tastes, induce changes in exchange rates, the changes should affect the price level.

Germany, for example, has generally followed a more restrictive monetary policy than has the United States. High German interest rates led investors to acquire mark-denominated assets, so the mark tended to appreciate. Because the mark appreciated, commodity prices increased less rapidly than in the United States.

Since 1973, prices in France, the Netherlands, Switzerland, and most other European countries have risen more rapidly than U.S. prices; at the same time, their currencies have also appreciated. The price-increasing effects of the rapid monetary expansion dominated the price-reducing impact of the appreciation of their currencies. And the appreciation of their currencies may reflect the fact that OPEC investors wanted to acquire various European assets.

The Waves Rule Britannia

Great Britain has been an extreme case of graceless economic aging. Britain was the first country to industrialize, and the resulting surge in income provided the economic base for expansion of the British imperial system. While colonization had started in the seventeenth century, it was not until the nineteenth century that the empire flourished. Britannia ruled the waves. London was the world's financial center.

Empires have their own built-in self-destruct systems; they become too large and too rigid to adjust to change. Rome flourished for centuries. In 1914 the sun was never supposed to set on the British empire. By 1975 the sun never appeared to shine on British economic performance. In 1950, British per capita income was twice that in West Germany; in 1975, German per capita income was twice that in Britain. Moreover,

British prices increased more rapidly than those in any other industrial country.

The British self-analysis is in terms of the sociological theory of inflation. The workers expect—and demand—a continual increase in their real standard of living. They expect that their demands can be met by taxing—or soaking—the rich, by redistribution rather than by productivity gains. And by raising the price at which they sell their labor services, they obtain a higher money income; for the most part, the higher wage costs are passed on to consumers as higher prices.

So taxes have been raised, especially on the middle and upper classes, and extensive subsidies have been given to the population at large. Medical services are free. Universities are free. Many services—local transports, electricity, the railroads—are priced below their production cost, with the losses financed from general taxation.

But because there are so few rich, leveling their wealth has had only a modest impact in raising the living standards of others. The time has long since passed when the living standards of the workers could be significantly raised by further taxing the rich. So the country has borrowed abroad. As the ability to borrow abroad declines, the demands of workers can only be satisfied if some workers—or retired workers—take a decline in real income.

The government and its sympathetic supporters suggest that the problem arises because of the aggressive behavior of the unions, not because of British government financial policies. Most sellers recognize that if they increase their prices, demand will fall and eventually they will be left with unsold goods or idle labor. If the government pursues a tight money policy, then the seller may be cautious about raising the price. In contrast, if the government is concerned that no resources be unemployed, then it in effect surrenders control of the price level to the aggressive unions; it governs in name but not in substance.

When prices and wages rise 10–15 percent a year, it is hard to determine whether wages are pushing up prices or prices are pulling up wages. And it is silly to try to disentangle the two. For regardless of the initial cause, the government is unwilling to bear the costs it believes are associated with measures that would lead to price stability. By exaggerating these costs, the government provides a rationale for doing nothing.

The rate of inflation in Britain was 7 percent in 1972, 9 percent in 1973, 16 percent in 1974, and as much as 25 percent in 1975. And the rate continues to increase. For until governments take measures to return their countries to relative price stability, inflation tends to accelerate. Some groups are always falling behind, since they have underestimated the rate of price increase; at the next negotiation, they seek to catch up, stay even, or get ahead.

The Tunnel at the End of the Light

What will be the level of U.S. prices in 1984? Will the United States follow the British model of a shrinking empire, an ever-increasing government sector, and more rapid price increases?

Monetary history shows periods of price stability followed by inflationary episodes. Not since the Great Depression has the commodity price level actually fallen. And at that time, the unemployment rate exceeded 20 percent. The British experience since World War II suggests that inflation may be inherent in the process of aging and slower growth.

Continuation of a succession of bouts of price increases interspersed with periods of price stability means that the value of money will decline, although not at a stable rate. Indeed, the record of the 1965–1975 decade suggests that inflation may get worse before it gets better. Contrast three episodes. In 1965 the economy began to expand after a period of price stability going back to 1959; during the 1959–1964 period the unemployment rate was in the range of 4 to 5 percent. Then expansion occurred when the rate of price increase was still around 3 percent; the unemployment rate reached 6 percent. Monetary contraction had had substantial business casualties —Penn Central failed, Lockheed teetered on the brink, and many long-established stock brokerage firms—Walston, Glore Forgan, Francis I Dupont—fell by the wayside.

When the authorities expanded the money supply, the economy boomed; then the 1965–1969 scenario was advanced to 1971–1975. The monetary contraction of 1974 was much more severe than that of 1970; business failures were more acute. Franklin National Bank and Security National Bank were closed, W. T. Grant failed, Pan Am, TWA, and Eastern Airlines were all on the ropes, and numerous real estate investment trusts were far behind in making scheduled payments to their bankers. The years of inflation had weakened the capital structure of numerous firms. The unemployment rate mounted; the automobile industry was shell-shocked.

Then, in late 1974, the monetary reins were relaxed and expansion resumed. Yet the rate of price increase was nearly 9 percent. In 1971 the expansion began when prices were increasing at the rate of 3 percent a year; the 1975 expansion began when they were already increasing at 8 percent a year. If history is any guide, prices will begin to rise still more rapidly in 1976, even while the unemployment rate remains above 6 percent. Attention will turn to reducing inflation. The central bank will apply the monetary brakes. Business failures will escalate. History also suggests that eventually the boom-bust cycle will be contained. The only uncertainty is how bad the inflation must become before the public concludes some other policy is preferable.

Monetary Reform—Where Do the Problems Go When They're Assumed Away?

A paradox of the 1960s was the glaring contrast between the problems of the system—the gold and exchange crises and the threat to the dollar—and all the good advice in the editorials of the *New York Times* and the *Economist*, in congressional testimony, in international conferences of economists and bankers, and in university lectures. Salvation was readily available. The system's problems would be solved if only the monetary price of gold were doubled or tripled, or if gold were eliminated altogether from the monetary system, or if the support limits around currency parities were widened or narrowed, or if currencies were allowed to float, or if a world central bank were established, or if national monetary policies were coordinated, or if national currencies were eliminated.

Each of these proposals had the support of eminent authorities. Nearly every expert left the impression that if only his favorite proposal were adopted, the system's problems would disappear, or at least become much less pressing. Since few of the proposals—other than that of floating rates—were adopted, the experts' convictions cannot be readily tested. The wide diversity of the "solutions" is surprising. Some proposals— raise the gold price or demonetize gold, widen the support limits or narrow these limits—were contradictory; some of the authorities had to be wrong if others were right.

The Flat-Earthers

Before Columbus, many people believed the earth was flat; it stood to reason that if it weren't, everyone on the underside would fall off. The flat-earthers prospered until Columbus sailed to the Indies in 1492 and Newton defined gravity in the *Principia* in 1687. The conclusions of the flat-earthers in other areas—business, language, and money—may be as incomplete as they were in physics; the commonsense, intuitive approach does not always come up with the right answer.

In business and economic life, it stands to reason that there will be savings if systems of weights and measures used in various countries are the same. It's inane that half the world uses gallons, miles, and inches while the other half uses liters, kilometers, and kilos—and that a U.S. gallon is one quart smaller than a Canadian gallon. It stands to reason that savings would be achieved by standardization on one system of weights and measures, road signs, electrical voltages, bottle sizes, and liquor proofs.

Less than 100 years ago, each local area in the United States was free to set its own time and to decide when noon occurred. In the 1880s, Congress legislated that the country be divided into four standard time zones. About the same time, international convention segmented the world into 24 time zones. Some areas were obliged to move the hands on their clocks ahead, but no area had to change its time-measuring devices or the units. It stands to reason there are inconveniences and costs in having London six or seven hours ahead of Chicago and in trying to remember whether one loses or gains a day when crossing the international dateline on a San Francisco-Tokyo flight. The flat-earthers favor one world time-zone, so that, when it is 12:00 in Washington, it will be 12:00 in London and Peking. But because bedtimes and milking hours would have to be rescheduled in much of the world, the change isn't imminent, since countries appear unlikely to agree on who incurs the costs and the inconveniences of rescheduling.

Money is a unit of measure or account. Each of the 126 members of the International Monetary Fund has its own money; most other nonmember countries also do. Multiple monies incur costs of exchange transactions, which is the monetary equivalent of translation of language. Moreover, the exchange of national monies leads to one problem that is not encountered in language translation, for future values are not known; the price of the yen or the mark a year from now—or even next week—is uncertain, largely because national central banks manage their own monetary policy to achieve domestic employment, growth, and financial objectives.

The flat-earthers favor one world money, just as they favor one world time, one world language, one set of measures; it stands to reason that the costs incurred in foreign exchange transactions would be saved if there were only one money. Money differs from distance, time, and language in that it is managed as an instrument of economic policy. The move to a worldwide money means that the flexibility inherent in national monies would be lost.

If these proposals were as attractive as their proponents suggested, why were so few adopted? Why was the adoption of floating exchange rates a choice of despair, not of conviction? The simple answer to the general question is that the politicians around the world were not convinced. But if not, why not? Perhaps the national political leaders were unable to understand the proposals. Perhaps vested interests in the various countries prevented their adoption. Or perhaps the proposals were ahead of their time—whatever that means.

One feature common to each of these diverse proposals was the belief that changes in the institutional framework of the international system would somehow resolve the problems associated with payments imbalances. However, old problems, unlike old soldiers, do not always fade away. Changes in the institutional framework may help countries reconcile some conflicts between their domestic and their external objectives and between their objectives and those of other countries. But some conflicts are inevitable as long as there are separate countries, each with its own economic structure, its own set of economic priorities, and its own national constituency. Changing the institutional arrangements for the exchange market or for producing international money may make it easier to resolve some conflicts. But such arrangements, by themselves, do not eliminate the conflicts of interest; rather, they alter the framework within which the conflict is reconciled.

Within each country, there are sharp conflicts of interest; this is what political parties, elections, revolutions, and coups are all about. If the existing rules seem inadequate to accommodate the desired changes, some groups may have a tea party and set up a new set of rules. For international conflicts, too, there are numerous parties to be heard from when a new set of rules is devised.

The major features of the new set of rules for international financial relations will almost inevitably be drawn from proposals that are already on the shelf. Most of these proposals can be placed in one of several categories. One set of proposals would have countries submerge their national interests and act as if they shared identical interests. The proposals for a common international currency, a world central bank, monetary unification, and the coordination and the harmonization of monetary policy are in this category. In contrast, a second set of proposals suggests that countries should concentrate on maximizing their domestic interests; exchange market arrangements should be organized so that any tendency toward payments imbalances would be anonymously adjusted by market forces. Under these proposals, the floating exchange rate system is retained and legitimatized. Someplace in between is a third set of proposals, which recognizes the conflict among domestic interests in various countries and seeks to find some optimum path between the desires for national monetary independence and for a free and open international economy.

Politicizing Economic Conflict:
An International Money

An increasingly frequent observation is that national monies are redundant, since the price of wine in terms of wheat is pretty much the same in each country, after conversion at the prevailing exchange rate. So the argument goes that since relative prices are stable across countries, no economic function is served by having separate national currencies. In fact, the observation is incorrect—or, more politely, insufficiently exact. The cost of virtually identical Holiday Inn rooms may vary from a low of $12 to a high of $36, depending on whether the room is in New York City or in a small town in Alabama. The United Nations calculates that with the costs for a particular standard of living set at an average of 100 for all the capital cities of the world, the specific cost may range from a low of 50 in Manila to 200 in Tokyo and Paris. And the cost of producing the standard Volkswagen "Beetle" also differs sharply, even though the price is the same. The prices of internationally traded goods are similar, but not the prices of goods which are less readily traded.

Those who believe that national currencies are redundant also sometimes argue that changes in exchange rates are ineffective, since relative prices do not change. Perhaps. But there seems considerable evidence that changes in exchange rates are effective for a while, for the relation between the prices of traded and nontraded goods changes.

Most changes in exchange rates result from differences in national rates of inflation. It might be argued that inflations change only absolute prices, not relative prices. But if that were the case, no one would be concerned with inflation, except for the minor inconveniences of having to carry more money around. In fact, inflations change relative prices, at least for a while—*which is why they occur*. In the early stages of inflation, farmers become better off, the city folks less well off; borrowers may do well and lenders poorly. In a deflation, or even when the rate of inflation declines, the tables are turned; lenders gain and borrowers lose.

The demand for separate national monies has an analogy in military security. During most years, most countries are at peace. If a country is at peace, then it has no need for military forces; indeed, the military forces might be disbanded or united. But military forces are needed when peaceful means of settling disputes between nations are not deemed satisfactory by at least one party. So, too, with separate national currencies.

Proposals for a common international money as a substitute for separate national monies are attractive. Exchange crises would disappear. There would no longer be a need to debate whether a surplus country should lend international money or its own currency to deficit countries, for there would be no measurable imbalances and no more bickering over which countries should take the initiative in adjusting to payments imbalances. But a common international money does not eliminate the problems of the existing system; it simply shifts their location. Problems of accommodating to divergent national interests would become centralized in the international money-producing institution. This institution would have a set of directors who would be ultimately responsive to the political authorities of the member countries. The institution's directors would have to determine how its managers are to be selected, how rapidly the institution should produce international money, and when countries might control payments to foreign areas.

The participating countries would also have to agree on the voting strength of each member country. Would the United States, the Netherlands, and Brazil each have the same number of votes; if not, what criteria should be used to determine the voting strength of each member country? Would the largest countries have veto power over any decisions of the institution's managers, or would they be obliged to follow its mandate? The

United Nations principle of one country, one vote would mean that the United States, a nation of 212 million, could readily be outvoted by Trinidad, Jamaica, and other Caribbean countries whose total population is less than that of Chicago. The costs of adjustment to payments imbalances might be shifted to the United States. At the other extreme, if votes of each country were in proportion to its population (on the principle of one person, one vote), then China and India together would come close to having a voting majority.

Clearly, some accommodation is necessary between these extremes. But what formula would be acceptable to countries with large and small populations, with high and low per capita incomes? Unless this issue can be resolved, an agreement is virtually impossible. Some countries would be more willing than others to compromise, not because the agreement fully satisfied their needs but because they know that if the costs of abiding by the agreement are too high, they can ignore their commitments; they might adopt exchange controls or refuse to lend their currencies to other countries. Some countries are substantially more cynical than others when signing international treaties.

Almost as soon as the international authority was established, a decision would have to be made about how fast the supply of the common international money should grow. Each country would have its own views: some might favor a growth rate of 5 percent a year, others 10 or 15 percent. This disagreement would reflect differences in national economic structures. Some countries grow more rapidly than others, perhaps because they have higher savings and investment rates, or because their labor force is growing more rapidly, or because they adapt better to the new technologies. Labor unions are much more militant in some countries than in others; these countries may favor a more rapid growth in the money supply to permit sustained full employment. Moreover, some countries are more tolerant about inflation and would be willing to risk more rapid price increases, in the belief that they might thus reduce their unemployment rates.

Thus, countries which formerly permitted their national money supplies to grow at a 15 percent annual rate probably would want the supply of common international currency to grow at a similar rate. Countries that had previously favored a slower growth for their own national money would probably also want the international money to grow at a slower rate. Japan, for example, would want a rapid rate of monetary growth, while Belgium would want a slower growth rate. But Japan and Belgium cannot each have their way.

Perhaps the directors from different countries could be shown that the differences among them were unimportant and that the rate of money supply growth could be determined randomly. Then each country could quickly adjust to the new rate, and the cost and inconvenience of forgoing the preferred rate for the community rate would be small. Perhaps. But it is unlikely.

The debates among directors from different countries about the preferred rates of money supply growth would be vigorous, just as they frequently are within individual countries. Countries with similar interests would form caucuses. The small countries would be concerned that their interests would be steamrollered by the large countries. Large industrial countries, on the other hand, would worry about being outvoted by the many small countries.

Some countries might devise numerous ad hoc means to limit their international payments—or their international receipts, even in defiance of the rules. A few might threaten to secede from the common currency union rather than accept a monetary policy deemed inappropriate to their needs. In the face of substantial diversity among nations, a unified monetary policy is a contradiction in terms. Those who advocate such a union are either blithely ignoring the real problem or else harboring secret knowledge about how diversity among nations can be readily reconciled—knowledge that is not generally available.

As long as basic structural differences in national economies remain, and as long as countries retain sovereignty, the likelihood that a common international currency might be adopted is small—and the likelihood that it would work if adopted is smaller still. Control over the production of national money is a large part of what sovereignty is all about. That countries would give up the flexibility and financial advantages of a national money—as well as the domestic political advantages—to avoid the costs and the newspaper headlines of exchange crises seems unlikely. Perhaps more importantly, such a move would be questionable on the grounds that as long as national economic structures and values are diverse, countries as a group may gain if this diversity of interests is recognized and accommodated, rather than suppressed.

In time, the differences in the national interests of participating countries may diminish and be eliminated; time tends to have a homogenizing impact. Eventually, business cycles will be in phase across countries, and rates of productivity growth—even attitudes toward inflation and the inflation-unemployment trade-off—will be similar. The nation-state as an efficient political unit will then be obsolete. However, the date at which interests are so alike that the nation-state can be shelved does not seem imminent.

The fact is that a move to a common worldwide currency is an extreme solution and a straw man, and relatively few experts favor the idea at this time. Yet the political problems associated with less ambitious reform proposals are similar to those encountered in the more extreme solution. The smaller the scope that individual countries have in setting their own monetary policies and their own exchange rates, the larger the energies they will inevitably direct to how the international system is managed. The politicians in each country are understandably reluctant to permit international civil servants to undertake measures whose costs they must bear; the civil servants are not obliged to run for office.

166

The U.S. suspension of gold transactions in August 1971 led to proposals for a new international monetary system to be built around Special Drawing Rights (SDRs) as the only international money; the international roles of the dollar and gold would both be phased out. National monies would be retained; each national currency would have a parity in terms of SDRs. Each country could devalue its currency in terms of SDRs if it had a large payments deficit, or it could revalue its currency —perhaps even be obliged to do so—if it had a large payments surplus.

The SDR-producing institution would become an international central bank. Member countries would jointly decide how much in SDRs to produce each year and how much in newly produced SDRs would be allocated to each country. Each country's interest in these decisions almost certainly would reflect its view of how best to advance its own interests. The rate at which the supply of SDRs would grow would not satisfy all of the participating countries, any more than all would be satisfied if there were a common international currency which grew at the rate of 3, 5, or 8 percent a year.

Proposing an SDR system, either by that name or by some other, is easier than getting it accepted, for countries are naturally concerned with the future value of SDRs. Gold was acceptable as an international money because of its underlying commodity value. Central banks held gold believing that if it were demonetized their losses would be minimal, since they could sell gold in the commodity market. Similarly, dollar assets and sterling assets were acceptable as international money because it seemed—once—that these monies could be used to buy gold from the U.S. Treasury and the Bank of England, or at least to buy American or British goods.

Every central bank recognizes that SDRs are useful only if they can be converted into a national currency. A few central banks must worry that some other countries might prove reluctant to sell their currencies for SDRs, as some countries have at times been reluctant to sell their currencies for gold when the future of gold as an international money was clouded.

U.S. participation is essential to the success of the SDR system; holders of SDRs would want assurance that they could convert SDRs into dollars to make payments for the purchase of U.S. goods or securities. The United States has the world's largest market in goods and the most comprehensive set of financial markets. Participation in the SDR arrangement by Australia and Zambia is insufficient for its success if the United States does not participate. Without U.S. involvement, the SDR arrangement would flounder, whereas it makes little difference if Australia and Zambia do not participate. The reason is that the supplies of goods available in the two countries are not so large that the various central banks would want to hold Australian dollars or Zambian kwacha as international money.

As it is, many countries would probably prefer U.S. dollars to SDRs as international money, for the dollar has greater "moneyness." Foreign central banks would hold SDRs because they could be used to buy dollars. Some countries fear that the United States might at some future date stop selling dollars in exchange for SDRs. In that case, holdings of SDR would become much less valuable. Few countries would accept SDRs if they were not acceptable at the U.S. Treasury. To minimize this concern, the United States could pledge to remain attached to the SDR standard. But this pledge could be broken. The United States could give a super-pledge; but the super-pledge could be broken, as was the U.S. commitment, and a succession of super-commitments, to maintain the $35 gold price. Many countries would remain reluctant to hold a substantial part of their reserve assets as SDRs, as long as they doubted the commitment of the U.S. authorities—currently and in the indefinite future—to buy SDRs in exchange for dollars.

A paper money or paper gold proposal can only succeed if

countries have confidence in the money—that is, in its future purchasing power in terms of goods. This confidence requirement is not likely to be satisfied simply because the members agree to a treaty. For any member might, when it suits its pressing national needs, walk away from the treaty. And every other member recognizes this reality—or at least most of them do.

The Nonpolitical Market Solution

Proposals for floating exchange rates recognize the divergent pulls of independent national monetary policies. The central bank in each country could produce the amount of money deemed appropriate for its domestic needs. In Japan the money supply could grow at 20 percent a year; in Belgium, at 10 percent. Hopefully, each country would choose the rate of money supply growth that might enable it to achieve price stability. If errors occurred (which is likely), no country would have to worry about its balance of payments, since market forces would ensure that the country's payments would always be in balance, even if it did not succeed in achieving relative price stability. Exchange rates would change continuously and smoothly, without the volatile movements associated with parity changes.

Developments since 1973 test these claims. Contrary to predictions, movements in exchange rates have been volatile. Countries have worried acutely about their trade position and about whether their currency was appreciating or depreciating. The central banks in many countries have had to intervene in the exchange market. Some countries have sought to achieve a payments surplus as a basis for growth in their own money supplies; not every country has wanted to follow an independent monetary policy. Others have found depreciating their currency the most convenient way to stimulate exports and increase employment; their central banks have bought foreign currency in order to reduce the prices of their goods in foreign markets. In fact, economic expansion through increased exports may be the preferred way of stimulating the economy. Some countries have a mercantilist preference for exporting goods and importing international money.

The assumption made by proponents of floating exchange rates—that once the rate is free to move in response to market forces, central banks will no longer be interested in the level of the exchange rate—has been proved invalid since 1973. Once the exchange rate is no longer subject to international rules, governments are likely to manipulate the rate as a useful instrument of policy and as a supplement to monetary and fiscal policy.

To the extent that central banks do intervene in the exchange market, most buy and sell U.S. dollars. For example, the Bank of Japan might depreciate the yen to increase exports to the United States. But Germany and France might not welcome this move, since their competitive position in the U.S. market, the Japanese market, and their own domestic markets would be threatened. So they might respond by depreciating *their* currencies in terms of the dollar; the Japanese threat to the German market would be neutralized. One result would be the flooding of the U.S. market with both Japanese and German goods— and U.S. exporters, in contrast, would find themselves at an increasing competitive disadvantage in the Japanese and German markets. And so, U.S. authorities would be under domestic pressure to depreciate the dollar.

The original objective behind the IMF rules of fixed exchange rates had been to prevent individual members from adopting such "beggar thy neighbor" policies. During the 1960s, when most countries were relatively successful in achieving full employment, this problem appeared unimportant. But it became significant in the worldwide recession of 1970 and 1971, when countries sought to import jobs. There is considerable evidence for the proposition that whenever countries find it difficult to attain domestic targets by manipulating domestic policies, they will manipulate their international transactions.

In 1974 many countries allowed their currencies to become undervalued; they simply did not borrow in the amounts necessary to finance the increase in their net oil imports. By not borrowing, they financed their oil imports on a pay-as-you-go basis, which meant their currencies depreciated—in effect, they increased their exports to earn the dollars to pay for their oil imports. The paradox was that exchange market intervention consisted of not intervening. The lesson of the period since 1973 is that few currencies float freely; most float subject to considerable intervention. Central bankers are not about to rely on market forces; they want constantly to nudge such forces. The temperament of central bankers—and of their constituents —makes them reluctant to accept the market's verdict about what the appropriate exchange rate is.

Even most of the minority of economists who favor pegged rates over floating rates would probably agree that a floating rate system is workable and feasible, except perhaps in the relatively few periods when individual countries are subject to highly intense uncertainty about the political and economic future. But the choice of exchange rate system is made by central bankers and government officials, not by economists. And judging by their behavior, most officials favor pegged exchange rates, with only a few exceptions. It is not an accident that the financial officials who do favor floating rates are in the larger countries, while those in the smaller countries favor pegged rates.

Rules might be negotiated to prevent or limit central bank intervention under a floating rate system. The problem, however, is complex—and complex international rules tend not to work. Like the U.S. commitment to the $35 gold parity, adherence to such rules would cease when the national interest was deemed overriding.

Whither the System?

Several themes stand out among the events subsequent to the suspension of gold transactions in mid-1971. First, central banks around the world want to stay in business; few central bankers are interested in phasing out their institutions in favor of an international central bank, although central banks in Europe may merge into a Europe-wide institution. Most central bankers, with the exception of those in Canada and Germany, abhor the uncertainties and the vagaries of floating exchange rates, except as an interim measure. They believe floating rates have worked far less smoothly than their academic proponents predicted. Second, recent events have reduced confidence in the national government commitments which are necessary in any type of international system—an international central bank, an SDR arrangement, even floating rates. Third, within many countries bureaucratic regulation of international payments is now accepted as a means of balancing international payments and receipts. Bureaucrats tend to distrust the market—that is their nature.

These factors limit the scope of reform. The difference between ambitious and modest proposals for reform centers on two variables. One is the size of payments imbalances that could occur before exchange rates changed or were changed, or before controls on international payments were altered to restore equilibrium or at least reduce imbalances. The size of imbalances is limited by the ability of deficit countries to finance them and by the willingness of surplus countries to export goods in exchange for international money. The second variable is how the inevitable changes in the exchange rates would occur: would they involve explicit changes in the rate, or would the changes be implicit, as bureaucrats tightened and loosened controls on international payments?

The unfavorable outcome, from the point of view of an

integrated or open international economy, is a system with small scope for payments imbalances, with international payments balanced by variations in controls on international payments rather than by variations in the exchange rate, and with countries competing with each other to earn export and payments surpluses. This outcome would be unfavorable in several ways. Trade and investment might be dampened because of investors' uncertainties about how the system will evolve. And the growth of controls would reduce economic efficiency, while the "beggar thy neighbor" trade policies would produce political discord.

Economic Expertise Cannot Solve Political Problems

Each of the systems discussed—an exclusive international money, floating exchange rates, pegged rates, and controls—involves the tug of the international market against the pull of national constituencies. Most politicians win or lose elections on domestic issues or on broad foreign policy issues, not on whether exchange rates float or the price of gold is raised or lowered. The first two sets of proposals involve a change in the way countries establish their policies and exchange rates; the third, in contrast, revamps the arrangements to accommodate the pressing needs of individual countries. The third approach is less ambitious, although it might be more successful because it acknowledges that the diverse interests and preferences of individual countries are relevant.

The international money problem reflects the fact that while communications technologies have unified the world of national monies, national economic structures and national values remain diverse. Changes in institutions may provide a more or a less favorable framework for reconciling these national differences, but they cannot eliminate the conflict posed by divergent national interests. The problem reappears again and again in determining the rate of growth of international money, in setting appropriate exchange rates, or in determining allocation and use of international money. The diversity of interests is real. As long as some national monetary authorities have monopoly power, domestic political forces will compel them to exploit this power. Crises result when the established rules of the game begin to limit domestic choices.

The historical record suggests that there will be a move back toward pegged exchange rates once inflation rates in the industrial countries decline. This conclusion is reinforced by the extensive intervention of various central banks while currencies have been free to float. The timing of the move back toward pegged rates depends on how quickly national price levels stabilize.

The move toward pegged rates is likely to more nearly resemble pegging under the gold standard than under the Bretton Woods System. Individual countries will peg their currencies when the movement in the exchange market is small; pegging may be the climax of increasing intervention to limit large swings in the rates. Some countries are likely to peg sooner than others. Moreover, countries are likely to differ in the width of the support limits around their parities or central rates. After currencies are pegged, an international agreement might be negotiated formalizing the exchange market arrangements as they exist, rather than forcing sharp changes from the practices then prevailing.

Similarly, arrangements about the future international monetary role of gold will be negotiated after central banks begin to trade gold with each other at or near the market price. The rules then will be developed to formalize the practices. These practices will result from the give-and-take of trading monies and gold.

PART II

Living with
the System

11

Bargains and the Money Game

One useful model of the world is that of the bazaar or market-place. People, firms, and even governments continually buy and sell, wheel and deal, seeking profits, wealth, and more elusive objectives, like power, esteem, and prestige. The chapters in Part I considered the evolution and operation of the international system and the costs and benefits of a national currency. The chapters in Part II, in contrast, consider some of the consequences of the division of the world into multiple-currency areas. Some of the consequences are direct and result from the advantage to a firm of being based in a country whose currency is at the top of the hit parade. Others are indirect and result from the division of the world into numerous currency areas roughly congruent with the numerous jurisdictions for the collection of taxes and the regulation of business and banking.

Differences in national tax structures, for example, are frequently said to be unfair; firms in nearly every country believe they are at a competitive disadvantage in the international marketplace because their tax burden is higher than those of their foreign competitors. Taxes, like wages and rents, are a cost, and unless they are avoided or evaded, the firm pays the cost and adjusts its selling price accordingly. Firms establish subsidiaries in low-tax jurisdictions to avoid the cost; where possible, they shift profits to these jurisdictions. As a result, the tax payments of these firms are reduced and their aftertax profits are higher. But most taxes *are* paid: government expenditures must be financed. The next chapter considers whether the differences among countries in the tax burdens they impose on firms and individuals might explain why firms in some countries have strong competitive positions in the international marketplace.

Chapter 13 considers the impact of impending changes in the technology of the monetary payments process on the competitive position of commercial banks in different countries. Each country has its own set of regulations for commercial banks. These regulations are more extensive and detailed in some countries than in others. And these regulations all have one common result: they raise the costs incurred by banks. Almost inevitably, the banks in the countries with the most extensive regulations are at a disadvantage in the international marketplace. If the transport costs of money are high, then this adverse cost differential has a negligible impact on the competitive positions of banks in different countries. But as transport costs for money decline, banks based in various countries can compete over a wider market area, so the cost differential will inevitably become more important. The buyers of the commercial banks' services will seek out low-cost producers of money, even if they are abroad. Chapter 13 focuses on the question of whether U.S., British, or Swiss banks are likely to have a competitive advantage as the market for bank services expands.

The fourfold increase in the price of crude petroleum in late 1973 was a most severe financial shock to the international monetary system. Virtually overnight, the annual payments by the oil-consuming countries soared to $100 billion from $25 billion, and the incomes of the oil producers went up accordingly. The change in the pattern of payments for oil affected both the standing of various Western currencies in the exchange market and the markets for investment assets. There was considerable fear that the Arab sheikhs would end up owning the world.

As the costs of economic distance decline, ideas and concepts developed in one country move rapidly to other countries. Because of the size and wealth of the United States, new ideas and concepts in finance are frequently developed there. Some entrepreneurs, colloquially known as "import transformers," take ideas developed in the United States and convert them for use abroad. Bernie Cornfeld adapted the hard-sell U.S. mutual fund to the need of savers in Europe and elsewhere to protect their fortunes against inflation. Chapter 14 traces both Cornfeld's success and his failure to the dependence of European financial markets on those in the United States. Cornfeld's idea succeeded brilliantly—for three or four years. His failure was triggered by the tight U.S. money policies of 1969 and the impact of the worldwide drop in share prices on the demand for his product. The financial aspects of the oil price increase—the threat of Western bankruptcy—are discussed in Chapter 15.

The combination of expansionary pressures of dynamic business firms, static national boundaries, and reduction in the costs of economic distance has facilitated the growth of multinational corporations—large, diversified firms with operating subsidiaries in many different countries. Production in these subsidiaries is often integrated across national borders; each plant produces components for its domestic market and for numerous foreign markets. Since most multinational firms are U.S.-based, many Europeans and Canadians fear an eventual American domination of their domestic economies. Whether this outcome is probable depends on the reasons why international companies flourish, a question discussed in Chapter 16. The consequences of their growth for the welfare of the relatively few countries in which multinational companies are based (and of the many other countries in which they establish subsidiaries) are also considered.

179

Part I and Chapters 12–16 in Part II implicitly assume that the world consists of market-oriented economies which have reasonably similar per capita incomes. But not all countries fall in this group. Many countries—many more than half of the world total—are developing or less developed, with per capita incomes which range from $100 to $800 or $1,000 or more a year. These countries are highly diverse. But with the exception of a few oil-producing countries, most of these countries have been substantial importers of capital from the developed countries; their foreign debts have escalated.

Chapter 17 discusses the financial relationships between the market-oriented industrial countries and the developing countries. Private foreign investment within the developing countries has been growing, and receipts of the developing countries from various forms of foreign aid—grants, technical assistance, export credits, and long-term development loans—have grown even more rapidly. These countries' debt to government agencies in the industrial countries and to international institutions has been growing at the rate of 15 percent a year, or about three to four times faster than their exports and national incomes. The sharp increase in the price of petroleum led to a sharp increase in their indebtedness. Annual payments of interest and loan reduction principal have already exceeded the repayment ability of many countries. However, none has gone bankrupt; instead, new loans are issued so that countries can repay the older debts. This pattern may continue indefinitely, for default would be costly to the lenders.

Finally, a substantial part of the economic world relies on planning rather than the market forces for answers to basic economic questions. The Soviet Union, Poland, Rumania, and other Eastern European countries are in this group, as is China. These countries participate in the international economy—they trade extensively both with each other and with the market economies. Since private firms cannot import and export for profit as in the market economies, other institutional mechanisms are necessary for arranging trade.

Chapter 18 discusses the financial relations between the planned economies of Eastern Europe and the market-oriented Western economies, as well as the relations between the Soviet and other Eastern European countries. Business is done and bargains are struck. Imbalances in trade are settled by payments of money, frequently dollars. Exchange rates are inevitable, although they are not used, as in the West, as a mechanism for balancing receipts and payments. Nevertheless, the question is whether the exchange rate is a fair price. In trade among Western countries, the fair price is the free market price. But since there are no free markets within Communist countries, some other mechanism is needed to determine both the prices at which goods are exchanged and the exchange rates. And some Eastern European countries believe that the prices used in their trade with the Soviet Union are not in their own best interests.

Several themes run through the chapters of Part II. The costs of economic distance are declining; market areas are expanding beyond national boundaries. Differences in business frameworks that were insignificant when the costs of distance were high are now becoming much more significant and are likely to be a cause of friction among nations. While pressures for harmonization and coordination will develop, counter-pressures for retaining the accidental or intended advantages of the costs of distance will also rise.

12

International Tax Avoidance—
A Game for the Rich

Elizabeth Taylor is a mobile factor of production who engages in tax avoidance. She lives in Switzerland and works elsewhere —Mexico, London, Rome, Budapest. Her dramatic abilities yield a magnificent income, nearly all from sources outside Switzerland. Swiss taxes on her income are much lower than U.S. taxes would be if she lived in Hollywood, or than British taxes would be if she lived in London.

Miss Taylor and the Swiss have struck a bargain. The Swiss sell Miss Taylor tax-avoidance services—the right to live in a low-tax jurisdiction. Miss Taylor buys this service because she likes the higher aftertax income; better to live where taxes are low than where they are high. The Swiss profit from the trans-action, for Miss Taylor's tax payments greatly exceed her de-mand on local public services. In effect, she subsidizes the Swiss, since their taxes would be higher if she lived in London —or in some other tax haven.

Switzerland is also a tax haven for other mobile factors of production, for Swiss taxes are substantially lower than taxes in most other developed countries. But Switzerland is only one among many tax havens. Liechtenstein, Panama, the Bahamas, the Netherlands Antilles, and the Cayman Islands offer similar services. Tax havens desire to attract income from foreign sources. Competition among tax havens keeps their tax rates on foreign-source income low.

Tax havens share several characteristics. Their geographic size is small. Their governments have minimal revenue needs: defense and welfare expenditures are low.

Tax havens are only one example of tax avoidance. England's richest lords leave London for low-tax jurisdictions to avoid the very high British death duties. U.S. and German firms issue bonds in Luxembourg because interest income there is not subject to tax withholding; buyers of the bonds want to avoid the tax, or the nuisance of getting a refund on the tax collected at source. U.S. professors teach in Canada for two years and avoid both U.S. and Canadian income taxes; residence outside the United States for more than eighteen months means they are not subject to U.S. taxes, and Canada does not tax foreign professors on their Canadian income during the first two years of residence. Most individuals, however, cannot move to low-tax jurisdictions without suffering a serious loss in income; their occupations tie them to a particular town or country. Only when the possible tax savings are large relative to the costs of shifting residences do individuals move.

One alternative to moving to a low-tax jurisdiction is to shift income there. Some London-based professors have their royalty and consulting incomes paid to their bank accounts in Zurich or Liechtenstein. When a firm uses an Antillian or a Zugian (Zug is a Swiss canton near Zurich, one of the busiest tax havens in Europe) tax haven, it may manipulate the transfer price—that is, the price at which it affiliates in several countries buy and sell goods and services from each other. For example, a U.S. firm may export goods to its German affiliate through a sales subsidiary in the Bahamas. The parent charges the subsidiary an artificially low price, thereby shifting income from the U.S. parent to the Bahamian subsidiary. The subsidiary charges a high price to the German affiliate, thereby shifting income from Germany to the Bahamas. So the firm's taxable income in the Bahamas increases, while its taxable income in the United States and Germany declines. The goods never get to the Bahamas; indeed, neither the documents nor money go there.

The U.S. tax collector and the German tax collector both know about tax havens. They scan the prices used in transactions between the Bahamian subsidiary and the domestic offices of the firm to forestall flagrant attempts to avoid taxes. But many intrafirm transactions have no commercial counterpart and no ready-reference market price, so firms must necessarily be arbitrary. Similarly, they must be arbitrary in their allocation of common overhead costs of the firm among its branches and subsidiaries in various countries.

Tax havens are profitable despite the ever watchful eyes of the tax collector; sales subsidiaries based in tax havens are not usually created unless the probable saving in taxes more than compensates for the legal fees charged by high-priced lawyers —lawyers, incidentally, who received their most valuable legal education about taxation of foreign income while working for the tax collector. But if the use—or abuse—of tax havens were so extensive that governments felt a serious loss from runaway income and forgone taxes, transfer pricing would be examined more closely.

Even without tax havens, differences among national tax systems might be important for the pattern of international transactions. All governments tax, but in different ways and at different rates. They tax income, both personal and corporate, and assets, including real property like houses, land, machinery, and clothing. They tax interest, dividends, and capital gains on financial assets. They tax transactions—sales, purchases, imports and exports, births and deaths. Most governments have a virtually unlimited need for tax revenues; more revenues mean larger expenditures, and larger expenditures enhance political support.

184

But taxes have a cost, for they diminish political support. So each government seeks to increase its tax revenue at minimal cost in terms of political support. Ideally, governments would like to tax foreigners to subsidize domestic residents, which is essentially what tax havens are all about.

Not unexpectedly, the tax rates and the tax base—the types of incomes and transactions which are taxed—differ sharply among countries. These differences are frequently offered as an explanation as to why some nations grow slowly and others grow rapidly, why the exports of some countries grow more rapidly than those of others, or why money flows from some countries to others. In nearly every country, businessmen allege that they are at a competitive disadvantage in international trade because they are taxed more heavily than foreign firms. This is another way of saying that they would be better off if their tax burden were smaller. Like wages, interest rates, and the cost of electricity, taxes obviously have an economic impact; the firm is obliged to raise its selling price to cover these costs. The question is whether differences among countries in tax structures and tax rates have a significant economic impact.

Do Differences in Taxes Make a Difference?

The revenue needs of nations differ because the sizes of their public sectors differ. Where the government's role is extensive, tax rates are necessarily high. The larger a nation's fiscal needs, the higher its tax rates and the larger the range of incomes and transactions which are taxed to generate the required revenue.

Everyone agrees that taxes should be fair. Fairness, after all, is like motherhood. The disagreement arises over what is fair —over whether the government should or should not be involved in particular activities, and how these activities, as well as the total cost of all government activities, should be financed.

Governments differ from private businesses in one important aspect: governments generally offer certain goods and services (except alcohol) below their cost of production. Many of these goods and services are given away; some are sold, but at substantially below cost. But while particular goods and services can be sold below cost, the total supply of goods and services cannot be, unless a country continues to borrow abroad. In general, to the extent that some goods and services are available below cost, the prices of other goods and services must exceed their costs of production, and the subsidy on the first group must match the tax on the second group.

To the extent that a tax—say, a sales tax or a value-added tax—is indirect, that tax has a direct and obvious impact in raising the final selling price. Similarly, a corporate income tax almost certainly raises the price at which the corporate sector sells its output. Even personal income taxes might be considered taxes on the sale of labor; the aftertax income of the individual is below his pretax income. Many individuals are primarily interested in their aftertax income; if the tax bite is too large, they may work less, or not at all, or fiddle with their returns.

One thing is clear: someone in the society must pay for the activities of the government. Not surprisingly, one reason for having government provide certain goods and services is that it may be possible to get someone else to pay most or all of the cost. A free lunch at school is cheaper than a cash lunch; attractive as a free lunch may be, however, *someone* has to pay for it at some point.

The size of government is a good measure of the amount of goods and services that individuals have chosen to consume collectively. In Western societies, the amount of goods and services supplied by the government ranges from 20 to 60 percent of the total goods and services supplied to the economy.

The cliché has it that the amount of goods and services supplied by the government is determined in response to the demands of the society. The cliché is too easy. Most of the benefits of government-produced goods and services go to selected groups—farmers receive agricultural extension services, students get free milk for school lunches, and professors receive research stipends from organizations like the National Science Foundation—while the costs fall broadly on the taxpayers. For on margin, as long as the choice is biased and production of additional goods and services by the government can be dissociated from their costs, advantages may accrue to the government and to those members of the bureaucracy associated with the extension of new services.

A glance at the data in Table 12–1 might suggest that U.S. corporations are subject to a heavier tax burden than are foreign firms, since corporate taxes constitute a higher proportion of total taxes (column 1) in the United States than in certain other countries. Similarly, taxes on households (column 2) account for a higher percentage of total taxes in the United States than elsewhere. But it would be a mistake to infer that the burden on the U.S. Corporate and personal taxpayer is greater than that on taxpayers in Great Britain, Germany, and the

TABLE 12–1
Comparative National Taxes, 1970

	PERCENTAGE OF TOTAL TAXES FROM:				TAXES AS PERCENTAGE OF GNP	CORPORATE TAXES AS PERCENTAGE OF GNP
	CORPORATIONS	HOUSEHOLDS	SALES AND OTHER INDIRECT	SOCIAL SECURITY		
United States	11	34	32	22	33	3.5
Great Britain	7	36	41	17	35	2.3
Netherlands	6	29	28	38	49	3.0
Germany	14	23	33	30	47	6.4
France	6	12	43	39	39	2.4

SOURCE: United Nations, *Yearbook of National Income Statistics* (New York, 1975). Copyright, United Nations (1975). Reproduced by permission.

Netherlands. One cannot draw conclusions about tax rates on corporate income and personal income from the share of government receipts from each type of tax.

One reason why the ratio of tax receipts to GNP is higher in the United States than abroad is that foreign governments spend a higher proportion of the national income than does the United States (column 5). Their revenue needs are greater. A second is that corporate incomes—the tax base—are lower abroad. If, for example, corporate tax rates were identical around the world, then revenue realized from the corporate profits tax would be smaller abroad than in the United States because the corporate sector is so much smaller abroad. Many of the types of firms that are in the private sector in the United States, including utilities, transportation companies, and even some manufacturing companies, are in the government sector abroad. Moreover, the tax base for personal incomes is smaller abroad; a much larger proportion of taxpayers have incomes so low that they are exempted from personal income taxes. Thus, tax rates on personal incomes are much higher in Great Britain than in the United States, but because personal incomes are lower, taxes on personal income constitute a smaller share of both total taxes and GNP.

Comparison of national tax rates is a necessary first step in determining the impact of taxes on the competitive position of a country. The U.S. corporate tax rate is 48 percent, while corporate tax rates in most other developed countries are in the 40–50 percent range. Italy has a lower rate, and Switzerland has a much lower rate. Moreover, definitions of taxable income differ, largely because some countries permit firms to depreciate their plant and equipment more rapidly than others. When depreciation is more rapid, expenses are higher, profits are smaller, and tax liability and tax payments are lower. However, even if depreciation practices were standardized among countries, the tax payments by the same firm in the several countries would not change greatly.

188

Taxes can be avoided, evaded, or paid. Avoidance is legal, although there are costs. Subsidiaries in tax havens have to be established, and lawyers have to be paid. Evasion of taxes, which is not legal, incurs costs and risks; in some countries, a payment to the tax collector in his personal capacity may obviate the need for a larger payment to the collector in his official capacity. Still, evaders are caught and fined or jailed and ostracized.

One factor that should remain clear despite the variations in the national mix of tax revenues is that only individuals pay taxes. Corporations may have an infinite life, but they do not feel, suffer, breed, or smile; only people do. Corporations do not "pay" taxes—they collect them from their customers, their shareholders, their employees, or their suppliers. Similarly, firms do not "pay" social security taxes—they collect them from their employees. And social security taxes and sales taxes are simply alternative ways of taxing individuals. The large variety of taxes is a stratagem to befuddle the taxpayers: if they were aware that 30 or 40 percent of their income was taxed, they might be more cautious about further increases in government expenditures. And if all of their taxes were collected in the same manner, they would have greater incentive to calculate the payoffs from avoidance or evasion.

Most taxes are paid. But even though the corporations pay the tax, the burden may fall not on its owners (as a decline in their aftertax income) but on the customers, who pay higher prices, or on the suppliers, who receive lower prices. Thus, General Motors pays a tax of 48 percent on its corporate profits; until 1971 it also paid a sales tax of 7 percent on its sales of automobiles. Ostensibly, the corporate tax falls on the profits, while the excise tax fell on the consumer.

But the legal basis and form of these taxes should be distinguished from their economic impact. Both taxes fall directly on the consumer if the demand for the product is sufficiently strong. Then GM raises its selling price to offset both the

189

corporate and sales taxes, so that the aftertax return to the GM stockholders remains pretty much the same. Similarly, the depletion allowance, which allowed oil companies to reduce their tax payments, almost certainly meant a lower price for gasoline; when the allowance was reduced in 1975, the gasoline price went up very modestly.

However, a simple example demonstrates that taxes on corporate profits are not likely to have a major impact on selling prices. Assume that the profits for firm X are 10 percent of its sales. Suddenly the government levies a corporate tax of 50 percent; previously there had been no corporate tax. If all the tax is passed forward to consumers, then the pretax profits-to-sales ratio must rise to 20 percent to cover the tax liability; the firm's selling price will increase by 10 percent. If, instead, the profits-to-sales ratio is 20 percent, then the selling price rises by 20 percent; if the ratio is 5 percent, then the selling price rises by 5 percent. And so on. Note that the imposition of a high corporate tax has only a modest impact on the selling prices, except when the profits-to-sales ratio is high. The profits-to-sales ratios vary by industry; within the United States, the average for many industries falls within the range of 2–6 percent. For films with a 4 percent ratio, the impact of the introduction of a 50 percent tax, would raise the selling price (again assuming all of the tax is passed forward to the consumer) by 4 percent.

Changing the corporate income tax rate thus is likely to have an effect—probably modest—on the competitive position of firms in different industries. Assume another extreme example—the corporate income tax rate goes to zero. Eventually, after a period of adjustment, firms would reduce the price at which they sell their products, so aftertax profits would be the same after the tax is eliminated as before. One consequence is that price reductions in industries with high profit-to-sales ratios would be larger than those in the industries in which these ratios are low, so the first group of industries would probably expand relative to the second. A second consequence is that the ability of the most profitable firms in industry to cut prices would be enhanced relative to the ability of the less profitable firms, and the failure rate of the marginal firms in each industry would probably increase.

But taxes are only part of the story. Governments tax in order to spend. And while taxes raise costs to firms, government expenditures (or at least some of them) may lower their costs. Public expenditures can reduce the need for private expenditures, reducing a firm's costs. Thus, government expenditures on roads lower transportation costs for manufacturers. Expenditures on fire departments reduce the need to purchase similar protection privately, while expenditures on education reduce the need for firms to train their own employees. If government expenditures finance the deficits of nationalized corporations, their selling prices are lower and their customers are subsidized.

Thus, the impact of tax changes on the prices of goods produced by corporations depends on how much of the tax is passed on in the form of higher prices and on whether there is any cost-reducing impact of associated government expenditures. Most economists believe that most or all of the corporate tax is shifted forward to consumers, except for a brief interval after the tax rate is changed. Very few economists have attemped to analyze the impact of government expenditures on selling prices.

Corporate tax rates are likely to have a significant impact on international trade only if the tax rates differ significantly. The differences in corporate tax rates among industrial countries are generally smaller than 10 percentage points. For most industries, differences in tax rates can explain only a very small part of the differences in selling prices among countries, except for a few industries in which the profit-to-sales ratio is much higher than average.

Much of the pattern of international trade and investment

reflects differences in real costs: bananas can be produced in Ecuador at a lower cost than in Chicago because nature in Ecuador has been more generous with the requisite climate and soil. But steel can be produced at a lower cost in Chicago, since the iron ore is at one end of Lake Michigan and the coal is at the other. The differentials in real cost attributable to the uneven beneficence of nature and the variations in capital accumulation are much more significant in explaining price differentials than the differences in national tax systems.

An increase in taxes in a country, like an increase in wages, may affect its international competitive position in the short run; its economic position in the long run will be unaffected, for the exchange rate will change to offset the price-raising impact of higher taxes on the demand for domestic products. The competitive positions of some firms may improve and those of other firms may worsen, but the overall impact on the country is not likely to be economically significant.

True, if national cost structures become more nearly similar, then differences among the national tax systems will become increasingly important. The reduction of any barrier to mobility of goods and capital would make the differences in tax systems more significant. Then the search for low-tax jurisdictions would increase. And increased attention would undoubtedly be given to tax harmonization and tax coordination among governments, so as to minimize shifts in productive activities among jurisdictions. Inevitably, international arrangements would be established to harmonize national tax structures and to prevent competitive tax practices.

Taxes on Foreign Income

Tax collectors have a voracious appetite. They are continually hunting for new sources of revenue. So they tax firms and individuals on a wide range of their domestic activities. In some countries, they even tax firms and individuals on their foreign income.

Here we must distinguish among three different kinds of taxes: those levied on the domestic incomes of nonresident firms and individuals by the domestic government, those levied on the foreign incomes of nonresident firms and individuals by the domestic government, and those levied on the foreign incomes of domestic firms and individuals. The U.S. government taxes the U.S. income of foreign firms and individuals as if they were domestic residents; most foreign governments follow the same approach. No government attempts to tax the foreign income of nonresidents, except insofar as they buy domestically produced products and pay the tax component that is implicit in the price.

Governments differ significantly in the way they tax the foreign income of residents—income which has almost certainly been taxed in the country in which it was earned. The U.S. government taxes the foreign income of U.S. residents as if it were domestic income. The taxpayer calculates his tax liability to Uncle Sam using the U.S. definition of income and the U.S. tax rate. He can then receive a credit against his U.S. tax liability for foreign income taxes paid, as long as the foreign tax rate is not above the U.S. tax rate.

If a foreign affiliate is organized as a branch, the tax payments due the U.S. Treasury must be paid when the income is earned; if the affiliate is organized as a subsidiary—that is, if it is incorporated abroad—U.S. taxes are due when the income is repatriated. The opportunity to delay the tax payments on foreign income, known as tax deferral, is like an interest-free loan; in effect, the right to delay the tax payment means that the effective tax rate on foreign income is below the posted tax rate. At an interest rate of 10 percent, a tax liability of $100 has a value of $50 if the payment can be delayed 8 years.

Tax deferrals and tax havens provide firms with an attractive and flexible opportunity. Thus, the profitable foreign subsidiaries of a U.S. firm might be tiered—organized as the subsidiaries of a Swiss or Bahamian subsidiary. Profits in high-tax countries could be diverted to the tax haven, and the funds could in turn be invested in another subsidiary which is rapidly growing and needs an additional investment from the parent. Transfer pricing can be used to divert profits to the tax haven; the taxes on these profits are then deferred.

A perennial issue is how to tax domestic residents with foreign income relative to domestic residents with domestic income. The equity approach is that domestic taxpayers should be taxed on the same basis, regardless of the source or type of their income. Domestic income and foreign income, earned income and unearned income, interest income on state and local securities and corporate dividends would all be taxed at the same rate.

It's hard to disagree with the general equity principle. But practical problems arise when the taxable foreign income must be defined. Is it foreign income before taxes are paid the foreign tax collector, or is it aftertax income? If it is foreign income after taxes, what recognition should be given for foreign income taxes paid? One approach is to give a domestic taxpayer a credit against domestic tax liability for foreign income taxes paid: foreign tax payments reduce domestic payments on a dollar-for-dollar basis. An alternative is to treat foreign taxes paid as a deduction or cost in computing domestic tax liability: foreign tax payments of a dollar reduces domestic tax liability by about 50 cents. In this case, the total taxes paid to the two tax authorities would be higher than if the credit approach were used. Foreign investment would thus be discouraged for two reasons. First, income on foreign investments would be taxed more heavily than income on domestic investments; and second, income earned by U.S. investors in various foreign countries would be taxed more heavily than if the same incomes were earned by a foreigner.

From the U.S. point of view, it might seem desirable to discourage foreign investment, since the income accrues to the United States—both to the owners of the investment and to the U.S. tax authorities—only after taxes have been paid abroad. In some cases the aftertax return to the United States might be larger than if the same funds had been earned in the United States; in most cases, however, the reverse must be true.

The firms that undertake overseas investments aren't impressed with this logic; their own interests are best served by maximizing their profits. From their point of view, once you've seen one tax collector, you've seen them all. Given that they must pay a given amount of tax, they're largely indifferent to whether they pay taxes to Uncle Sam or to his foreign competitors. So the firms engage in a marketing campaign, stressing the favorable effect of their foreign investments on the U.S. balance of payments and U.S. foreign policy.

Thus, there is an inevitable conflict in the design of tax policy, depending on whose interest is to be served. The cosmopolitan or world economic welfare is served if investment funds are allocated between domestic and foreign alternatives on the basis of their pretax rates of return; the implication is that taxes on foreign income should be the same as those on domestic income. The national economic welfare is served only if the rates of return to the economy on foreign investment after payment of foreign taxes exceeds the pretax return on domestic investment. From the firm's point of view, it should be sufficient that it pay taxes to the countries in which it operates; there should be no residual tax liability to U.S. authorities. From the point of view of U.S. taxpayers, the taxes on foreign income should be the same as on domestic income; if foreign tax rates are lower than U.S. rates, then an additional tax is due the U.S. Treasury.

Taxes on Money

Medieval kings had a simple technique for raising money. They filled a leather bag with gold coins and shook the bag vigorously. The edges of the coins began to wear away, and gold dust began to collect in the bag. The gold dust was then sent to the mint for manufacture into new coins—and the coins which had been in the bag circulated at their face value. In effect, the king was taxing the holders of gold coins by shaving their commodity value. Sovereigns have been taxing the holders of money ever since.

Currently, however, sovereigns are more sophisticated in their approach to taxing banks: they provide banks with a monopoly position by limiting entry, and then they tax the monopoly profits. (See Chapter 13 for the discussion of competition among banks.) As a consequence, borrowers pay higher interest rates on their loans than if competition were more extensive. Similarly, depositors receive lower interest rates and a smaller supply of "free" services than if banks competed more aggressively for deposits. Bank profits are higher than they would be if banking were a competitive industry with unimpeded entry of new firms.

The "excess" profits resulting from barriers to entry are "taxed" by requirements that banks hold certain assets which offer a smaller yield than they would in a free market. For example, U.S. commercial banks must hold from 3 to 18 percent of their assets as deposits in the Federal Reserve System; they earn interest on these deposits. Without such a requirement, these commercial banks would almost certainly hold more income-earning assets, and the banks' revenues would be greater. And higher revenues would permit the bank to pay higher interest rates on deposits. So the banks would gain, in the first instance, but most of these gains would then be competed away.

The significance of this implicit tax on banks' earnings depends on the proportion of bank assets invested in non-interest-bearing forms and on the interest rates on various assets. For example, assume central bank A requires that its domestic banks hold 14 percent of their assets in non-interest-bearing reserves, while central bank B has a similar requirement of 4 percent; assume also that the average interest rate in both A and B on bank assets is 10 percent. The revenues of commercial banks in B are 9 percent higher than those in A—so the interest rates paid depositors might rise, while the interest rates charged by banks might fall. If banks in A pay an average interest rate of 6 percent to their depositors, those in B can pay 6.6 percent and still be no worse off.

If banks hold non-interest-paying deposits in the central bank, the central bank in effect receives a loan on which it pays no interest. And so the central bank can then lend to the government at a low rate, since it has no need for interest income.

The system has some of the characteristics of a Rube Goldberg device. Restrictions on entry into banking produce monopoly profits for the commercial banks; the central bank then taxes these producers of money. In the U.S. system, commercial banks increase their reserves or deposits at the Federal Reserve by selling U.S. government securities. And the Federal Reserve in effect buys these securities. So the interest rates that the Treasury pays on its debt is lower. The public is taxed again.

Differences among countries in the way producers of money are taxed might have a significant impact on the competitive strength of banks in different countries. These differences in the taxes on the producers of money appear more significant than differences in corporate income tax. What remains to be determined is their impact in intensifying or neutralizing the competitive advantages of banks in different countries in the international marketplace. This topic is the subject of the next chapter.

Banking on the Wire

"Why are Swiss bankers rich?"
"They compete against Swiss bankers."

A revolution is about to hit commercial banks. The technology of money payments is about to change. The geographic scope of the market will increase, and the effectiveness of national cartels in limiting competition among banks will decline.

Traditionally, to the extent they have competed at all, banks have competed only within their domestic markets. Domestic markets have been protected from foreigners by the prohibitive cost of establishing and managing overseas branches. Moreover, the difficulty of operating in a foreign currency has deterred expansion abroad. And regulation, informal as well as formal, has limited expansion.

Banking is a highly regulated industry. Banks are required to hold reserves in the central banks. Ceilings are placed on the interest rates they can pay on deposits. They are required to hold certain types of assets and are prohibited from holding other assets. Their loans to any one customer are limited to a small fraction of their capital; their loans to all customers are limited to some multiple of their capital.

Regulation is intended to protect the small saver from losses that might occur if the bank in which he holds his deposits were to fail, and to protect the economy from the collapse of the banking system in a depression. By limiting bank failures, regulation has helped the inefficient banks to be more profitable than they otherwise would have been. The efficient banks probably also are more profitable, even though regulation constrains their growth. Competition has also been limited by regulation.

Competition among banks based in different countries takes several forms: U.S. banks have set up branches in London and Zurich, while British and Swiss banks have opened offices in New York, Chicago, and San Francisco. Lloyd's Bank has bought a small California bank, while European-American Bank, owned by a consortium of banks in various European countries, acquired the remains of Franklin National Bank. U.S. banks have also purchased shares in foreign banks. And when the establishment of branch offices or the purchase of shares is prohibited or constrained, foreign customers have been invited to do business in the bank's home office or in a convenient regional office. Thus Canadian nationalism may prevent U.S. banks from developing branches in Canada, but those Canadian firms which desire less costly banking services than are available in Montreal and Toronto are welcome in New York and Chicago.

Entry into foreign markets by branching or acquisition enables aggressive banks to circumvent the regulations of the national authorities that limit their growth. Many commercial banks want to grow rapidly, for their profits depend on their size. Every central bank, however, directly limits the expansion of commercial bank liabilities denominated in its currency—and hence the growth in commercial bank assets—to prevent inflation. The upper limit to monetary expansion may be 6, 10, or 20 percent a year, but at each moment every central bank *has* a limit. So individual banks within a country can grow more rapidly than banks as a whole only if they can increase their share of the domestic market, which may be at the expense of some other banks. The aggressive banks can expand into new or ancillary businesses—travel agencies, insurance, leasing, and computer services agencies. Or they can penetrate the domestic banking market in some foreign country and offer services similar to those offered at home, either by setting up branches nearer the foreign customers or by attracting customers to their home offices. But a large aggressive bank is almost certain to expand abroad, for the costs of obtaining customers in a market which it has not previously entered are likely to be smaller than the costs of increasing its share of the domestic market.

Expanding into foreign markets, moreover, will become progressively easier as changes in the technology of the payments process reduce the economic distance between the banking office and the customer. In the future, more and more payments will be made by electronic transfer. The market area in which banks compete will be enlarged because the transport costs for money will decline sharply. Changes in the technology of banking are almost certain to affect the structure of the banking industry, just as the shift from propeller craft to jets altered the structure of the airline industry. For banks in some countries are probably more efficient or have other competitive advantages, and thus are likely to be in a position to increase their share of the world market.

What Banks Are All About

Most firms have a highly visible product—General Motors produces Cadillacs and Chevrolets, AT&T produces telephone services, IBM producers computers. But confusion surrounds what banks actually produce, partly because the product is not visible and partly because the banks, when they sell their products, "pay" their customers in toasters, TV sets, and interest.

Basically, commercial banks produce money in the form

of demand and time deposits. The receipts from the sale of these deposits enable them to buy loans, mortgages, bonds, and other assets, each of which carries an interest income. Banks also have numerous other activities for which they receive fixed-fee payments: they rent safe-deposit boxes, sell lottery tickets, and manage trusts. But the bread-and-butter activity of banking—and much of the jam—involves selling demand and time deposits and buying loans.

Banks deal essentially with two groups of customers, depositors and borrowers. While these roles overlap—most borrowers are also depositors, and some depositors are also borrowers—in practice the roles are sharply different. Business firms tend to be predominantly borrowers, while households tend to be primarily savers. Banks are intermediaries or brokers between lenders, who want a safe, secure, and convenient place to store some of their wealth, and borrowers, who want to expand their current production or consumption more rapidly than they can on the basis of current wealth and income. The spread or markup between the interest rates that banks pay lenders and the interest rates they charge borrowers covers their costs and is the source of their profits.

Profits in banking depend on three factors: marketing skills in selling deposits, investment skills in buying loans, and management skills. Since marketing deposits by raising interest rates—that is, through price competition—is usually limited by the authorities or by a cartel arrangement among the banks, banks compete by offering free fountain pens and frying pans and by giving assurances about their safety and stability. Their skill in selling deposits determines how successfully they can increase their share of the market.

Investment skills involve matching the yields on loans, mortgages, and other assets with their risks. Within each economy, the riskier loans carry higher yields. Banks—at least the successful ones—seek out those assets which offer the highest return for the risk. The banks that are best able to determine which assets are underpriced relative to their risks earn the highest profits. Management skills involve minimizing the costs of selling deposits and buying loans and operating a complex institution.

In many ways, commercial banks are like other financial intermediaries: mutual savings banks, savings and loan associations, even life insurance companies. Each sells its liabilities to the public and uses the receipts to buy loans, securities, and other income-earning assets. From the point of view of the customers of these institutions, owning these liabilities is one way to store wealth. A life insurance policy, a pension, or deposit shares in a savings and loan association are the symbolic form of wealth; the wealth is the liability of the institution. Thus, the loss of the policy or shares does not lead to any loss in wealth, for the institution will issue a replacement policy or shares.

Commercial banks differ from other financial intermediaries in one important way: their demand deposit or checking account liabilities are used as money. As a group, banks operate the payments mechanism. A check is a message or signal from a depositor to his bank to transfer ownership of bank liabilities to whoever's name follows the phrase "Pay to the Order of." The check is the symbolic form of money, but not the money itself; the money is the bank liability.

One pervasive worldwide tendency is for banks to pay virtually no interest on their demand deposits but to pay interest on time deposits. Selling demand deposits thus would appear to be more profitable than selling time deposits. In fact, however, banks incur substantially higher costs in managing their demand deposit business, for they must process billions of checks and shift money from the payers' to the payees' banks; these costs are so high that sale of demand deposits is only marginally more profitable than the sale of time deposits, despite the sharp difference in interest rates.

The Payments Mechanism

In the early nineteenth century, the major product of banks was bank notes—promises to pay the bearer in lawful money. Each bank produced its distinctive notes; the countryside was full of competing bits of paper. The several states chartered banks to finance the building of roads, canals, railroads, and other desired improvements. The payment process involved the transfer of bank notes in hand-to-hand circulation. Then the market area for each bank was largely limited to its immediate vicinity, largely because individuals lacked confidence in the value of notes issued by banks in distant locations. Firms and individuals in Chicago were reluctant to accept New York bank notes, because they were wary about the credit standing of banks 700 miles away. Banks in New York were even more reluctant to accept notes issued by Chicago banks. Indeed, bank notes frequently sold below their face value in distant cities; thus, a $1 note issued by a New York bank might sell for 95 cents in the Chicago market, while $1 bank notes issued by banks in Chicago might sell for only 80 or 90 cents in New York. Since the transport costs of money were relatively high, the price of the notes was likely to vary inversely with the distance from the issuing institution. The discount below the face value reflected the risk that buyers were taking both about the legitimacy of the note and the financial standing of the bank that issued it.

The extent of the market area of each bank was limited by the costs that potential borrowers and lenders incurred in dealing with banks: the time and financial inconvenience of dealing with a bank located in a distant city were higher than those in dealing with a nearby bank. Some banks, especially in the smaller cities and country towns, had a neighborhood monopoly; no other bank was within convenient walking—or horseback riding—distance.

When checks began to replace bank notes as a means of

payment in the latter part of the nineteenth century, the market area of banks expanded. Checks had a number of advantages over bank notes. One piece of paper could be used for large payments and for payments of odd amounts. The money transfer process was much less risky; the theft of checks, unlike notes, involved little risk, for payment on the check could be stopped. And checks, unlike notes, could be safely sent through the mail. Thus, the use of checks facilitated transactions between buyers and sellers separated by great distance; the transport costs for checks were lower than for bank notes. Indeed, the increased use of checks coincided with the development of a comprehensive railroad system and the resulting improvement in the postal system. The fall in transport costs associated with the railroad also enlarged the size of the market area for most goods, so individuals had much greater occasion to pay firms and individuals located at great distances.

By bringing depositors and borrowers within the expanding market area of a larger number of more distant banks, the change in the technology of payments reduced the monopoly position of the neighborhood banks. Then the size of the market was limited only by the speed and efficiency of the check transfer process and by the costs of acquiring information about distant banks. Of course, borrowers still found personal contact with their banks a necessity, for loans had to be negotiated in person, and so bankers found it convenient to stay in their offices to meet borrowers. But even then, the loan negotiations could occur elsewhere—in the borrower's office or on the golf course.

Banks began to develop branches as checks replaced notes. Large banks are more efficient than small banks in that there are economies of scale in the basic functions—selling deposits, managing assets, and operating the payments mechanism. Processing the flow of checks within one institution is less costly than among numerous institutions. And branching enables banks to marry offices located in areas which primarily serve depositors with those in areas which primarily serve borrowers. As business firms expanded rapidly and became concentrated in fewer and fewer centers, the demand for large loans from banks increased sharply. In the growing industrial centers, business firms wanted to borrow much more money than the banks in the vicinity of their offices could lend on the basis of local deposits. Banks located near these firms found that business demand for loans exceeded their lending capacity. Households, in contrast, were spread over a larger residential area. Banks within the residential areas frequently found that they were receiving more money in deposits from households than they could readily lend in their local area. A mechanism was needed so that the deposits of banks in residental neighborhoods could be available for loans in the business areas. Banks in the residential areas could simply lend to banks in the business areas, or banks from each area might merge in order to internalize the transfer of funds within one firm. The growth of branch banks suggests that internalization was more efficient.

With the technological revolution in the offing, the move to electronic banking promises to displace checks—and paper—in the money transfer process. Under such a system, when John Doe wishes to pay his electric utility bill or his taxes, he will simply signal his bank by inserting a coded card in a small device attached to his telephone. This device will have a few keys, like those on the new push-button phones or the hand-held calculators. Suppose John Doe wishes to pay $100 to Richard Roe. He punches the keys accordingly, entering his social security number, his bank account number, and a secret number to prevent the misuse of his account by someone else; the coded number serves the same function as the signature on a check. A special card inserted into the device would reduce the likelihood that some thief could draw funds from Doe's bank account. The signal would then go to the computer in Doe's bank and from there to the computer in Roe's bank; these computers would be tied together. Roe's computer in turn might send a message to the device attached to Roe's phone, which would print a slip indicating that his balance had increased—indeed, Roe's computer might call Roe on the phone, indicating that his balance had increased.

The electronic banking system has several advantages. Postage costs are avoided. The transfer process is instantaneous; there is no delay between sending and receiving the funds. The monthly or weekly balancing of checkbooks is redundant; Roe and Doe could determine their balances continuously, simply by pushing a predetermined key. And there is no equivalent of a bad check; if Doe wants to pay Roe $100 and has only $50 in his account, the computer balks. The printing, transfer, and identification of billions of pieces of paper becomes outmoded.

Wire transfers mean that credit cards will become obsolete. When John Doe fills up his car at the corner gas station or checks out of his motel room, he will type a message to his computer-bank; payment will be made immediately, regardless of the time of day or the day of the week. The bankers may work from 9 to 3, but the computers work around the clock. If his intended payment exceeds his deposit balance, he may be able to draw on his credit line with the bank.

Individuals who make relatively few payments will continue to use checks. And notes and coin will still be used for small payments. But those who make a large number of payments are almost certain to find the electronic system the least costly.

The move to electronic banking has already begun. Many banks now have robot electronic banks alongside their teller's windows as a way of reducing waiting time; such robots, placed in the outer lobby, are now used at any time of day or night. Similar consoles are being installed in grocery stores and gas stations. The next step is to develop a simplified model for homes and offices.

Most importantly, electronic banking will further enlarge the market area for deposits beyond national boundaries. The distance between the customer and the bank will be irrelevant.

The neighborhood becomes the world. Chicago banks will advertise in Frankfurt for mark deposits and loans, while Frankfurt banks will compete for Chicago deposits and loans. Banks will be able to attract foreign customers without the cost of establishing offices abroad. Canadians will be able to bank as easily in Chicago or New York as in Toronto.

International Banking Competition

Banking has been an international industry for centuries. The Rothschilds and the Fuggers were extended families with banking offices spread across countries; however, they were essentially investors rather than producers of money. In the latter part of the nineteenth century, British banks established foreign branches to help finance the overseas trade and investment of firms based in London and Liverpool. But these branches were largely limited to areas in the outposts of the empire which were poorly served by domestic banks. Thus, relatively few branches were set up in the United States, for British firms could use established U.S. banks. Similarly, U.S. banks, when they began to go overseas in the early years of this century, followed U.S. business overseas largely to areas that were not adequately served by existing banks.

In recent years, the motive for overseas expansion has shifted. Initially, a relatively few New York and San Francisco banks followed U.S. firms to Europe, competing for these firms' foreign business in the hope of gaining some of their U.S. business. The expansion of the overseas branch networks of the four or five largest U.S. banks has been especially rapid. The sudden increase in the number of U.S. banks with branches abroad was partly a defensive response to meet the competitive thrust of the first U.S. banks to go overseas; the Chicago banks moved abroad to protect their established relationships from the competitive threat posed by the New York banks already operating abroad. In 1960 about eight U.S. banks had 130 foreign branches. By 1974, 130 U.S. banks had nearly 750 foreign branches. Over the same period, over fifty foreign banks have set up branches in the United States, nearly all in New York. These banks wanted to participate directly in the largest financial market in the world. Their direct interest was in retaining the U.S. business of their domestic customers—and in attracting some U.S. customers.

U.S. banks operating abroad and foreign banks operating in the United States share a common problem: they lack the deposit base essential to provide them with the funds to make loans. They can borrow from the home office, they can borrow in the interbank money market, and they can borrow from the external currency market. And they do all three.

Many countries are reluctant to admit foreign competitors. Thus, Norway and Canada do not permit foreign banks to establish branches. Peru and Chile have closed the local branches of foreign banks. Venezuela applies discriminatory legislation to foreign banks. U.S. banks find it virtually impossible to establish branches in Mexico. And although some twenty-five U.S. banks would like to establish branches in Japan, only a handful have been allowed to. Even when a U.S. bank establishes a branch abroad, the price is often a commitment that the bank will not compete actively for domestic business.

Such attempts by governments to protect their own banks from having to compete with the local branches of foreign banks will become increasingly irrelevant. For the move to electronic banking, by reducing the importance of national boundaries as a limit to the size of the market, will diminish the need to establish foreign branches. With electronic banking, instructions to make payments can be handled over the wire. Thus, banks outside Switzerland, for example, can deal in Swiss francs on the same terms as banks inside Switzerland—

perhaps on even more favorable terms. Transactions can be negotiated in the Zurich Airport, at the Intercontinental Hotel in Geneva, or in Paris.

Money havens will follow the tax havens. The computer may be placed in the Cayman Islands. If a face-to-face contact is necessary, the local office can concentrate on generating loan and deposit business and information for the home office; it need not deal in money. Once the effective size of the market becomes the world—or at least the major industrial countries—some banks whose domestic sanctuaries had been protected will find themselves subject to intense pressure from foreign banks. Competitive skills will become increasingly important in the enlarged market area.

The Competitive Edge

The speed of the shift to electronic banking on an international scale is unpredictable. Assume, however, that the system will be in place next Monday morning and that banks then begin to compete vigorously to maintain or enhance their market share. Some will succeed, others will fail; whether particular banks are in one group or the other will depend on how efficient they have been in the domestic context.

In this new international market, U.S. banks will have three advantages: size, efficiency, and association with a currency at the top of the hit parade. Not only is size important in making very large loans, but it also confers a competitive marketing advantage, for depositors often equate safety with size. In the credit crunch of 1974, the competitive positions of the largest U.S. banks improved relative to those of smaller ones; investors reasoned that the Federal Reserve might permit the twentieth-largest U.S. bank to fail, but they could not permit the largest ones to go bankrupt. And the largest U.S. banks are much bigger than their foreign competitors. The five largest banks in the world are based in the United States, and so are six of the top ten, eight of the top twenty, nine of the top thirty, eleven of the top forty, and fourteen of the top fifty. The deposits of the largest U.S. banks are nearly twice the size of their nearest foreign competitor.

European and Japanese banks have responded to the competitive threat posed by the size of U.S. banks by merging. In Great Britain, Barclays, the largest bank, merged with Martin's Bank while Westminster and National Provincial merged also. In Belgium, Banque Lambert, the fourth in size, merged with Banque de Bruxelles, the second largest. In the Netherlands, the number two and number three banks have merged. Yet, by international standards, the largest banks in many European countries are still quite small; the largest Swiss bank, for example, is no bigger than the fourteenth-largest U.S. bank, and the largest Swedish, Dutch, and Belgian banks are only one-fifth the size of the largest U.S. bank. The entire Belgian banking system is smaller than First National City Bank of New York.

If, therefore, European banks want to be as large as one of the three or four leading U.S. banks, they will almost certainly have to merge across national borders. But national differences in the ownership and regulatory structures will make this difficult. French banks, for example, are owned by the government, those in Italy are indirectly government-owned, and those in other European countries are largely private. One alternative to a merger is an association: Crédit Lyonnais, the second largest French bank, Banco di Roma, the fourth largest Italian bank, and Commerzbank, the fourth largest German bank, have formed an association, as have Société Générale de Banque in Brussels, Amsterdam-Rotterdam Bank of the Netherlands, Midland Bank of England, and Deutsche Bank of Germany. The banks participating in these associations have agreed to coordinate the worldwide activities of their subsidiaries, to assist each other in providing funds to meet customer needs, and to cooperate in reducing costs and improving their services.

U.S. banks are probably more efficient than those abroad—a result of the much larger number of U.S. banks. There are 4,000 banks in the United States, more than in the rest of the world combined. The very large number of U.S. banks reflects the nineteenth-century populist fear of centralized monetary trusts, which led to prohibitions against branching across state lines, branching across county lines in Indiana, and branching across the street in Chicago. The reason U.S. banks are both numerous and larger is that the U.S. economy is such a large part of the financial world. There are more financial assets in the United States per capita than in any other country. Demand deposits in Chicago alone exceed those in France.

Since restrictions on branching constrain U.S. banks from expanding geographically and setting up branches in other states, other means must be used to attract customers. The contrast between the relatively uninhibited growth of U.S. business, both nationally and internationally, and the severe restrictions on the domestic expansion of U.S. banks has forced the banks to become innovative and adaptive. Many of the large U.S. banks attract deposits from, and make loans to, firms in cities 3,000 miles away. As a consequence, the market for bank loans and deposits in New York includes more than the New York banks; banks with home offices in Newark, Boston, Philadelphia, and Chicago participate in this market. Similarly, New York banks participate in the Chicago market. Competition has prevailed, despite the regulations.

The result is that U.S. banks in the major cities have been more fully subject to competitive pressures than banks based abroad. One measure of bank efficiency is provided by the spread between the average price the banks pay on their deposit liabilities and the average price they receive on their loans— that is, by the markup between the interest rates the banks pay and the interest rates they receive. Within a country, competition ensures that spreads among banks are similar; differences in markups are not sustainable. Otherwise, the banks with larger spreads would lose deposits or loans, since less efficient banks lose their share of the market to more efficient banks. Among countries, however, spreads tend to differ: they tend to be larger, in some cases substantially larger, in continental Europe than in the United States. The differences among countries are sustainable only as long as national markets are largely protected from external competition; gradually, banks in the countries with the higher markups would lose their share of the market.

TABLE 13–1
Comparative Markups in Banking

	BANK PRIME RATE (1)	BANK DEMAND DEPOSITS (2)	BANK TIME DEPOSITS, 90 DAY (3)	TYPICAL MARKUPS	
				(1–2)	(1–3)
United States	7.00	zero	5.38	7.00	1.62
Great Britain	11.00	zero	4.88	11.00	6.12
Germany	9.50	0.50*	4.55*	9.00	4.95
Switzerland	8.50	1.00*	4.00*	7.50	4.50
Netherlands	9.00	1.50*	3.75*	7.50	5.25
France	12.35	zero	6.38	12.35	5.97
Canada	9.00	zero	6.75	9.00	2.25

* Residents only.

Table 13–1 shows that the spread between the prime rate and the demand deposit rate is lower for U.S. banks than for those in any other country listed. And the spread between the prime rate and the time deposit rate is lower than for banks in any other country. So in the new worldwide market, banks based in countries where larger spreads prevail will be under sharp competitive pressure. If, in order to hold deposits, they offer higher interest rates to depositors while their spread remains unchanged, their minimal lending rate will be so high that the least risky domestic borrowers will seek funds at foreign banks, which will be charging a lower interest rate. If, instead, they set rates on loans competitive with those charged by foreign banks, then their deposit rates must decline, assuming their spreads remain unchanged. They may try to reduce their spreads, but to do so they must pay lower wages, induce their employees to work harder, or find some magical approach to become more efficient.

Some banks will attempt to discriminate by charging a different set of interest rates to those customers who have more attractive opportunities abroad. But such price shading can only be a partial response to the problems raised by the apparently higher costs in European banks. In the final analysis, either costs will be cut or the least efficient banks will fold.

The third advantage of U.S. banks in the new international market is that their domestic currency, the dollar, is likely to remain the preferred currency brand name. Indeed, the share of banking business denominated in dollars (and perhaps marks) may increase relative to other currencies. This gives a clear advantage to U.S. banks, for if depositors prefer dollar-denominated deposits, they will also prefer that these deposits be issued by U.S. banks. Combined with their lower costs, this suggests that U.S.-owned banks are likely to end up with a larger share of the world market for deposits.

Banking is generally viewed as a sensitive industry, because banks both produce the financial wealth and operate the money payments mechanism. Governments will therefore be wary of allowing a substantial part of the banking services demanded by their residents to be supplied by foreign banks. If banks in a country are largely foreign-owned, or even if the larger customers of the banks have ready access to foreign banks, then the effectiveness of national regulation and of national monetary policies is threatened.

Some countries may decide to nationalize their banking industry outright, rather than allow foreign firms to supply most of their banking needs. Others will pay to keep the domestic banks' prices competitive. Efforts will undoubtedly be made to limit the access of foreign banks to domestic borrowers and lenders, measures which will counter the thrust toward an open international economy.

14

The Rise of the House of Cornfeld—
And the Fall

Bernie Cornfeld provides a contemporary twist to the traditional immigrant saga. Many poor Jewish boys traveled from Europe to Brooklyn in search of riches; Cornfeld went from the United States to Europe and made $100 million—for a while. The Cornfeld saga begins in 1955, when Cornfeld, then a social worker in Philadelphia, went to Paris for a vacation. To stay in Paris, he began to sell U.S. mutual funds, both to U.S. troops in Germany and France and to the expatriate American professional community—diplomats and oil drillers. Then, in 1958, he shifted his operations to Geneva. He prospered, and in 1960 he set up Investors Overseas Services, Ltd., his own investment fund. Then he broadened his clientele to include Europeans, Latin Americans—indeed, anyone with money to invest.

At the peak of his success in 1969, Cornfeld had the largest financial sales organization in the world, an empire of selling offices in fifty countries, with salesmen in 100 countries, 30,000 employees, and more than a third of a million shareholders. The assets of the IOS empire were $2.5 billion. In 1968, sales of new shares in IOS funds totaled $800 million.

At first, the European financial establishment looked upon Cornfeld as a hard-sell con artist from Brooklyn. But as IOS grew and Cornfeld acquired hundreds of millions of dollars to invest, the establishment became respectful. Cornfeld was hailed, for a while at least, as "the greatest force in Western capitalism"—probably by his public relations flack.

His success was no fluke. Cornfeld capitalized on a short-coming in the financial markets and institutions of Europe; he developed the right product at the right time. Savers in Europe wanted attractive investments that would provide protection against inflation and devaluation and would at the same time be readily convertible into cash. Cornfeld provided an answer through offshore mutual funds.

Mutual funds collect money from savers and invest the pro-ceeds in a diversified group of securities, thereby spreading the market risks of the individual securities. In their most popular form, mutual funds are open-ended—that is, the numbers of shares and shareholders are variable and change in response to investor demand. Any would-be investor can buy into an open-end fund by paying the net asset value and a sales charge, usually in the range of 4 to 8 percent; the net asset value is computed once or twice a day by dividing the total assets owned by the fund by the number of its shares outstanding. In addi-tion, any shareholder can sell his shares back to the fund and be immediately repaid on the basis of the net asset value.

The essential feature of offshore funds is that they invest in the companies and real estate of developed countries, princi-pally in U.S. companies and U.S. real estate, while their buyers are located outside the United States. Most are incorporated in low-tax, minimal-regulation jurisdictions like the Bahamas, Panama, and the Cayman Islands.

Buyers of shares in offshore funds are attracted by the con-cept of having the underlying value of their investments located in the politically secure and wealthy United States. That the mutual funds are designed to minimize taxes on incomes and capital gains provides sales appeal. In some instances, the funds help their shareholders to circumvent domestic exchange con-trols on the purchase of foreign securities.

216

The promoters of offshore funds are not running a charity. They receive income from the buyers of funds in several ways, some direct, some indirect. First, when the funds are sold, there are commissions, which are sometimes 8 or 10 percent of the total value. The funds require a variety of technical services; these are provided by a management company, owned by the promoters, which receives investment fees from the funds for managing their assets and brokerage fees for buying assets for the funds. The management company can buy these assets from friends, and so share in the commission income. The management company might own a bank and provide financial services to a fund or its shareholders—for a fee. The lists of shareowners are salable to other promoters. And as the profits of the management company grow rapidly, the promoters capitalize anticipated profits by selling shares in the management company to the public.

Under these arrangements, the profits of the management company depend almost entirely on the number of shares outstanding, which in turn depends on how hard the funds are sold. Mutual funds are sold, not bought—and the energy given to selling depends on the profit and income orientation of the sales force. Many IOS salesmen sold contractual saving plans, whereby the buyer became committed to making a series of periodic payments, monthly or quarterly, over a ten- or fifteen-year period, much as if he were buying a life insurance policy. Most of the salesman's commission was taken out of the payments made by the buyer in the first year. The salesman, in other words, received immediate income against payments that the buyer was committed to make over a ten- or fifteen-year future. The buyer might withdraw from his plan, but the sales commission was nonrefundable.

Certain aspects of IOS activities provoked a hostile reaction. Some authorities objected to the hard-selling effort, others to the self-serving investment practices, while still others objected to the tax avoidance and violations of exchange controls. The

Swiss had strict rules about work permits for nonresidents; IOS evaded the rules by having its foreign employees register as students at the University of Geneva. The Bank of England had strict controls regulating the purchase of dollar securities by residents; the British subsidiary of IOS adhered to the letter of the regulation while avoiding its spirit. Thus, British residents were sold insurance policies through the IOS-owned Dover Plan, and premiums were siphoned into an IOS subsidiary in Luxembourg. The U.S. Securities and Exchange Commission (SEC) required—and still requires—that funds furnish lists of their shareholders; IOS refused. While the financial establishment around the world became more respectful as IOS prospered, the bureaucrats became more hostile.

By the middle of 1970, Cornfeld's empire was broken, but not because of the hostile reaction of national governments. There were two principal causes. First, tight money in the United States led to a collapse in U.S. equity prices, so selling shares became much more difficult. Cornfeld and Co. got caught in the bear market. Second, the funds had been extravagantly managed, and the accelerating costs eventually came home to roost. The assets of IOS-managed funds declined rapidly. Shareholders in the management company sold its stock; initially offered at $10 a share, the stock sold for less than $1 after having reached a peak of $19.

Then, when IOS was down and the support of the financial establishment had dried up, the governments began to step in. The Swiss government forbade sales of IOS funds; the Italian government forced the sale of the Italian subsidiary of IOS to a government subsidiary. In Germany the sales force fell by two-thirds. IOS and other offshore funds were subject to heavy withdrawals as shareholders cashed in. Several funds were forced to cease redeeming their shares for cash. Finally, Cornfeld himself was benched—removed from all responsibility of IOS.

Several morals, usually variants of the Puritan ethic, have been drawn from Cornfeld's rise and fall. His unqualified success highlighted the inadequacies of Europe's financial markets. And his downfall indicated the curious dependence of these markets on those in the United States.

The Elements of Cornfeld's Success

Making $1 million in a tough, competitive world is an achievement; making $100 million is a heroic accomplishment. Cornfeld's success invited imitation. The result was the offshore fund industry, with assets that reached a total of $6 billion in 1969. For several years, the European editions of *Time* and *Newsweek* appeared to be largely supported by the advertisements of Cornfeld and his imitators.

Three factors contributed to Cornfeld's success. One was the inability of European financial markets to supply savers with the types of assets they preferred. The second was Cornfeld's personal ability to motivate salesmen. The third was the economic miracle in Germany. All three elements were necessary to the phenomenal growth of IOS.

Cornfeld's genius was to perceive that the European middle class needed liquid financial assets that would offer protection against domestic inflation, which was precisely what a mutual fund with a portfolio of dollar-denominated shares could provide. At the time he began, most European investors had few attractive financial investment opportunities in their own currencies; basically, they could put the money in the bank or buy land. But interest rates on bank deposits were kept deliberately low, partly because banks were inefficient and partly because the banking systems were rigged to subsidize borrowers, including the government. In some countries, the interest rates were below the annual increase in the price level, so the real value of the purchasing power of savings deposits declined over time. Land is a highly illiquid investment; besides, land owner-

219

ship attracts the attention of tax authorities. Land ownership, moreover, is like musical chairs; X can buy land only if Y sells land, and then Y must decide how to invest the proceeds. Everyone cannot buy land at the same time.

The European investor could also look to the European stock markets. But the volume of shares in most European countries was much smaller than in the United States, for nationalization of the utilities, steel, and other industries had reduced the supply of equities; so, incidentally, had the take-overs of European firms by U.S. firms. In every European country except Great Britain, equities were a lower percentage of GNP than in the United States (see Table 14–1). Buying shares in European companies, moreover, was frequently like blindman's buff, for the correct factual information released by many companies was small, and there were no equivalents of

TABLE 14–1

Market Value of Listed Domestic Equities, 1970
(billions of dollars, current exchange rates)

	MARKET VALUE OF EQUITIES	EQUITIES AS A PERCENTAGE OF NATIONAL INCOME
United States	$515	53
Great Britain	212	72
Germany	22	12
France	20	13
Italy	10	11
Netherlands	11	34
Belgium	3	14

SOURCES: Organisation for Economic Co-operation and Development, *Capital Markets Study: General Report* (Paris, 1967); International Monetary Fund, *International Financial Statistics* (Washington, D.C., 1972); "Interest and Dividends upon Securities Quoted on the Stock Exchange" (London, 1968).

Note: Data for market value of equities are 1966 values reported in OECD's *Capital Markets Study* adjusted to 1970 using stock price indexes reported in *International Financial Statistics* for all countries except Great Britain. Data for Great Britain are from "Interest and Dividends upon Securities Quoted on the Stock Exchange" (London, 1968).

Data for the United States and Great Britain include both domestic and foreign securities.

the SEC. Besides, shares in European companies were riskier than shares in U.S. companies, for the day-to-day and week-to-week movements in equity prices were more volatile.

In the long run, share ownership in one country is probably not much better or worse than in most other countries. Certain proportional relationships dominate financial variables. Thus, stock prices in every country grow about as rapidly as its national income, largely because profits within every country grow about as rapidly as national income. Otherwise, the share of profits in national income would become very large or very small, and the price that investors would pay for profits would become very high or very low. Moreover, in the long run, national income in most developed countries tends to grow at roughly the same rate. (Differences in per capita income among countries reflect the dates when they began to industrialize.) Consequently, the price of shares should grow about as rapidly as profits.

Of course, in the short run, share prices may grow at different rates in various countries. And Cornfeld benefited greatly from just such a short-run discrepancy between the changes in U.S. and European stock prices. The European financial establishment was as familiar as Cornfeld with the advantages of dollar equities. But it was largely geared to satisfying the needs of the wealthy, sophisticated European investor who might otherwise deal with a U.S. broker; the middle-class investor was ignored.

Dollar mutual funds were very attractive in the early 1960s, and their value appeared to be constantly increasing. During the 1950s, their performance had been impressive because stock prices in the United States had risen rapidly—more rapidly than GNP and corporate profits—and mutual funds reflected this gain. In the 1940s, stock prices were unusually low by historical standards; their rapid rise in the 1950s represented an adjustment. In effect, U.S. investors were making a belated adjustment to the Great Depression and to wartime pessimism about the future of capitalism.

In contrast, in the early 1960s, European stock prices were declining or moving sideways, even though GNP was rising. Paradoxically, the unimpressive performance of European shares in the early 1960s reflected the legacy of the U.S. securities analysts' discovery of Europe, the Common Market, and the German boom in the late 1950s. (See Figure 14–1 for the comparative movement of stock price indexes.) U.S. investors had

FIGURE 14–1

Comparative Stock Price Indexes, 1951–1971 (1963=100)

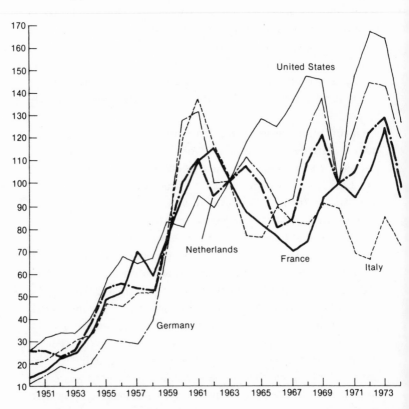

SOURCE: International Monetary Fund, *International Financial Statistics* (Washington, D.C., 1975).

bought European stock in amounts sufficiently large to push their prices up sharply to peak values in 1961. But this passion for European stocks quickly faded, and their prices then fell almost as rapidly as they had risen. In Germany stock prices more or less fell between 1961 and 1967; only in 1969 did they again reach 1961 levels. Similarly, stock prices in Italy fell during most years after 1961, as they did in the Netherlands. A similar pattern is observable in France, with the difference that prices peaked in 1962. In contrast, U.S. stock price indexes were generally rising during this period; the 1968 values were 50 percent higher than the 1960 values.

In some respects, the mutual fund industry is like the soda pop, soap, breakfast cereal, and cigarette industries; there are a large number of products which are barely distinguishable from each other. Clearly, there are some differences in the products, but many of these differences are largely created to facilitate sales. Firms compete in figuring out what the consumer really wants and then design the product accordingly. There are several types of mutual funds: funds are designed for high income, rapid appreciation, or a combination of income and appreciation. But there is one important difference between funds and soaps. Each fund has a performance record indicating year-by-year changes in its net asset value. Investors seek those funds with the most successful investment skills. Certainly the investment performance of IOS cannot explain why it did so much better than its competitors; the Salvation Army probably had a more swinging portfolio.

The personal element in Cornfeld's success was his great marketing genius. He established the Fund of Funds. The name had resonance—and the concept was magnificent. Since the basic idea of a mutual fund is to offer an investor greater diversification in his assets than he can obtain by direct purchases of shares of various companies, a fund which owns other funds appears even better diversified—and therefore less risky —than one which only owns shares. In fact, once a fund has forty or fifty securities, there is no significant reduction in risk through further diversification. The real advantage of layering the funds was that Cornfeld and Co. did not need to engage in investment research about individual securities; he could simply choose funds on the basis of their performance. The managers of the funds whose shares he purchased provided him with research, since his purchases enhanced their incomes, and with other valuable services. Moreover, some of the funds purchased by the Fund of Funds would also be IOS-managed funds, so the IOS management companies obtained two sales commissions.

Cornfeld had a special genius for motivating salesmen. Sales commissions increased as annual sales increased. Large annual sales qualified a salesman to become a super-salesman, or the boss of other salesmen; a super-salesman got a share of the commissions on the sales of those under his supervision. If the sales of the super-salesman and the group of salesmen under his supervision were sufficiently large, he in turn qualified to become a superduper-salesman. And *his* salesmen became super-salesmen, who could in turn hire salesmen if the sales volume of the superduper-salesman's sales force was sufficiently large, and so forth. Moreover, as the salesman advanced higher in the hierarchy, he qualified to buy shares in the IOS management companies at favorable terms. The prices of these shares were expected to rise forever. And he could borrow from an IOS bank on favorable terms to buy the shares.

The primary motivation for energetic selling by most salesmen was therefore not current income but the prospect of future income from both the commissions generated by salesmen in the lower stages of the hierarchy and from capital gains on holdings of stock in the management company.

This sales structure has a direct analogy in pyramid club or chain letter schemes, where an individual receives a letter with five names and addresses and is told to send a dollar to the name at the top of the list, add his name to the bottom of the

224

list, and mail the list on to five friends. Each individual is promised that if he follows the instructions and everyone else does too, then he should receive $625 in fifteen days—provided the mail service works. Chain letters work well for those who are initially at the top of the list. But eventually the supply of would-be participants is exhausted. (A chain letter with twelve successive stages, for example, would involve nearly 200 million people.)

Whether Cornfeld and Co. recognized that what they were involved in was essentially like the chain letter is irrelevant, although most people in IOS presumably did not. What is relevant is that the forces which led to strong sales motivation were bound to weaken eventually. And any weakening in turn would have a multiplier effect in dampening the drive of the sales force.

Finally, Cornfeld's success was helped enormously by Germany's economic miracle. The base of the IOS empire, especially in the latter part of the 1960s, was in Germany at a time when savers were becoming richer. But memories of the German financial collapses in 1923, 1930, and 1948 induced prudent investors to seek safety in foreign investments. Germany was a virtually unregulated economy—the largest market economy in Europe—so there was far less regulation of IOS activities in Germany than elsewhere. Moreover, the German government was continually embarrassed by its large balance-of-payments surplus, and therefore it initially welcomed Cornfeld's venture in the hope that importing dollar securities would reduce its payments surplus.

Acting together, these three factors—the inadequacy of European financial markets, Cornfeld's ability to motivate salesmen, and the German boom—developed a momentum of their own. As long as U.S. stock prices were rising, selling dollar shares in IOS funds was relatively easy. As long as sales were easy, recruiting and motivating the sales force was easy. As long as Germany had a large balance-of-payments surplus,

Germans appreciated the efforts of Bernie's army of salesmen. Cornfeld had a veritable money machine as long as the momentum continued.

Cornfeld's success was such that relatively little attention was paid to the high administrative costs of IOS, its lackluster investment record, or the hanky-panky of its management. Continued rapid growth meant that these factors were irrelevant; rising net asset values dominated these shortcomings. The shareholders were happy.

The withdrawal of one of these elements would inevitably dampen the momentum. Once U.S. stock prices stopped rising —or fell—selling shares would be hard. The profits of the management company would falter, and the incentives for the sales force would decline. And so would its selling efforts. The customers would be unhappy, and the governments would begin to crack down. And that is what happened to the House of Cornfeld.

The Fall of the House of Cornfeld

The first crack in Bernie's house appeared in the spring of 1969 when, as a result of the very tight U.S. monetary policies designed to dampen inflation, U.S. equity prices began to fall in what proved to be the worst decline in the New York Stock Exchange since the Great Depression. Selling mutual funds when the net asset value is declining sharply is more difficult than when these prices are rising. Some holders of the funds began to voice their dissatisfaction with the hard sell, now that they were no longer protected from their hasty investment decisions by rising net asset values. The German government began to make anxious noises about IOS. But the sales pitch hadn't changed—the direction of stock price movements had.

At the same time, the high administrative costs incurred by

the management company in expectation of future sales led to profits much lower than expected when these sales failed to materialize. So the price of the management company's shares fell sharply.

Even under the best of circumstances, maintaining IOS's growth rate over an extended period would have become progressively more difficult. Once it became clear that not all salesmen could become super-salesmen, and relatively few could become superdupers, motivating the sales force was bound to be more difficult, since the salesmen could no longer be "paid" with the promise of high future incomes.

Most firms—even those with skillful management—find it hard to adjust to a reduction in their growth rate. Adjustment from an annual growth rate of 40 percent to 10 percent is inevitably traumatic. Budgets have to be cut; pretty secretaries have to be laid off.

In an attempt to maintain the momentum, the IOS managers engaged in some colossal hanky-panky: they sought to disguise their lousy investment results by revaluing underdevolped Canadian land from $17 to $119 million. The shareholders were accordingly "richer" by $100 million; the management company was richer by $10 million. Nevertheless, its earnings were still far below expectations, with the result that the price of its shares also fell. When these shenanigans became public knowledge, new customers became wary of the "water" in the net asset value.

As the shares of the management company plummeted, some of the IOS employees who had borrowed greatly from IOS banks to buy these shares were forced to sell them to repay the banks. Distress selling depressed the share prices further, and the salesmen lost their enthusiasm.

In retrospect, the failure of IOS was inevitable and predictable. The villain was not, as Cornfeld thought, envious competitors or hostile government regulators. Rather, the mechanism of his success provided the basis for his failure. Systems based on the chain letter principle cannot maintain their growth rate forever; they necessarily falter when the momentum weakens. The IOS system was designed to deal with success; it was poorly equipped to handle difficulties.

The collapse of IOS should not obscure Cornfeld's insight about the inadequacies of the options for investors in Europe. The lack of information about European equities and the absence of a broad base of investors are reinforcing; European equity prices are more volatile than U.S. equity prices.

Cornfeld's purchases of U.S. shares had a marginal impact on the United States and a major impact on Europe. Even without his operation, European firms had been at a financial disadvantage in relation to U.S. firms. Directing European savings to U.S. investments increased the handicap.

There is another lesson. The U.S. equity market is so large that Europe cannot escape the U.S. impact. Europe is also affected by its own forces—by student riots in France, inflation, and Russian pressure on Berlin. But European financial markets are so small relative to U.S. markets that these factors make little difference to the U.S. market. So Europe combines its relatively inadequate financial structures with a substantial dependence on the United States. And as Chapter 16 suggests, the factors which made it possible for Cornfeld to establish an army of salesmen in fourteen years may help to explain why U.S. firms have had such a great advantage in buying up European industry.

15

And Now for Something Completely Different

The quadrupling in the price of crude petroleum in 1973 led to visions of financial disaster for the West. The World Bank, headed by Robert McNamara, remembered at Ford for the Edsel and at the Pentagon for the McNamara Line, projected that the financial wealth of oil producers would climb to $300 billion by 1980 and $650 billion by 1985. The specter was that the West would lose all its money with the OPEC countries (the common abbreviation for the Organization of Petroleum Exporting Countries) stuffing dollars into the wells almost as fast as they pumped the oil out. Since their wealth would grow more rapidly than world wealth, it was only a matter of time before they would own the world.

The Western industrial countries were squeezed; the OPEC countries sat on their lifeline. Prices were higher and employment lower as a result of the fourfold price hike. The sharp price increase did not cause the inflation—indeed, it probably could not have been possible in the absence of inflation. Yet the inflation rate in the Western industrial countries in 1974 was several percentage points higher because of it. While the OPEC action did not cause the recession in the industrial countries, it intensified unemployment, especially in the automobile industry.

The financial collapse of the West seemed imminent. Italy seemed about to go bankrupt, with the rise in oil prices the straw that tripped the boot. Japan seemed alone and defenseless, since all of its petroleum and most of its energy were imported. Great Britain was threatened because the OPEC members eventually would shift from holding sterling funds in London to dollar funds in New York and Swiss franc funds in Zurich, with sterling depreciating sharply as a result. Western capitalism was supposed to be in serious danger, for the OPEC members would buy up the shares of the major industrial companies and run them to suit their own (largely Arab) political aspirations.

Worse, the example was contagious. Some observers saw cartels of raw material producers under every bed. Bauxite producers threatened large price increases. Venezuela bankrolled the Latin American coffee producers so they could withhold output. The Algerians were pointing toward a new economic order; they wanted an increased share of the world's income to go to the developing countries.

Newspaper headlines gave content to the threat. Iran bought 25 percent of Krupp, the major German conglomerate. Kuwait bought a large bloc of shares of Mercedes Benz, perhaps the most prestigious Western car firm. The Iranians showed interest in Pan Am and offered to become bankers for Grumman Aircraft. One unidentified group of Arabian investors tried to buy a small town in the northwestern United States—George, Washington. All the major symbols of Western industrial success seemed to be on the block. The Arabs would buy General Motors, the Bank of America, and the Bank of England.

The view that the OPEC members would eventually own the world depended on extrapolation—the $10 a barrel price of crude petroleum was multiplied by 30 million barrels a day of OPEC production and exports. But extrapolation of long-term trends on the basis of a few observations over a relatively short period can be misleading.

Take, for example, the case of Charlie Ponzi, who ran a bank in Boston in the early 1920s which paid 30 percent interest a month. Supposedly Ponzi earned the money to pay the

interest by buying International Postal Reply coupons with depreciated European currencies; he would exchange the coupons
for U.S. stamps, and then cash the stamps—much as if they
were checks—for U.S. currency. He would then buy more
sterling, francs, and lira to buy more International Postal Reply
coupons, and so on. Once in business, Ponzi used the money
received by depositors in February to pay interest to January's
depositors; the money received from March depositors was
used to pay off February depositors. Many depositors were
content to let their investments compound; where else could
they get 30 percent a month? So Ponzi could readily meet the
cash withdrawals from the inflow of new deposits. Other
financiers—Billie Sol Estes, Tino de Angeles—also developed
modest business empires using today's receipts to pay yester-
day's interest. They too succeeded for a while.

Unless these financiers are able to attract new funds at a
constant rate, their system falters, for then the inflow of new
money is inadequate to meet cash withdrawals. But deposits
can't grow more rapidly than the system forever, anymore than
IBM's sales or profits can continuously grow more rapidly than
total corporate sales and total profits; if they could, IBM eventually would become larger than the economy. Ponzi and Co.
forgot the principle that no element in the system can grow
more rapidly than the system without fostering restraints to its
more rapid growth.

The implication is that OPEC wealth may grow more rapidly
than world wealth for a short interval, but thereafter it can
grow no more rapidly than world wealth. The economic system
has its checks and balances, even if it doesn't have a written
constitution. The check to the growth in OPEC wealth might
arise, paradoxically, if OPEC countries became increasingly
reluctant lenders as their wealth increased; they might feel that
the supply of safe investments wasn't large enough to justify
pumping more oil: better to keep their wealth in the ground
than to acquire high-risk investments. More likely, the check

to the growth of OPEC wealth will arise because the borrowers prove unwilling to increase their debts as rapidly as McNamara suggested they would.

Recycling Money

If the OPEC members spend less than their total receipts, they must acquire financial wealth in the industrial countries. While they might be able to bury the checkbooks in the desert sands, they can't bury the money: it remains as deposit balances in the banks in the petroleum-importing countries (hereafter PICs.) The early common view was that the money paid the sheikhs for the oil had to be recycled, or else it would somehow disappear from the system. But this view was incorrect: money paid for oil imports is recycled automatically. The oil exporters are paid for oil with checks. They deposit these checks in their banks, and their bank deposit balances increase. Then they can spend the money, give it away, or lend it—and they may simply produce less oil if the investment opportunities do not appear sufficiently attractive. Unless they spend, lend, or give the money away, the banks will be in a position to increase their loans— for example, to importers of oil and to developers of new energy sources.

The rich have one problem the poor don't: they must decide how to invest their wealth. OPEC members have the same problem. They have to choose between securities issued by primary borrowers, such as firms and governments, and securities issued by banks and other financial intermediaries; between securities denominated in dollars and those denominated in Swiss francs or German marks or sterling or many other currencies; between fixed-price assets, such as bank deposits and bonds, and variable-price real assets, such as land and equities. And if investments are made in equities, they have to decide whether they want a controlling interest or a minority interest and, if the latter, whether it should be large or small.

There was immediate concern over whether there was a sufficient volume of the "right" securities—securities that would appeal to OPEC members—among the PICs. The fear was that the rapid growth in oil wealth meant that OPEC members could quickly buy all the available PIC securities. Then they would reduce their oil production.

The $50 billion annual projected increase in OPEC financial wealth was favorably compared with the value of all the listed equities in the United States, Great Britain, and continental Europe. At the end of 1974, the market value of IBM—the product of its shares outstanding and their price—was $8 billion. The implication was that if OPEC countries invested all of their savings in IBM shares, they could buy the company—lock, stock, and barrel—in two months. Ponzi calculated that it would take only ten years for OPEC to buy all U.S. equities, three years to buy all of British equities, and a year to buy all of the equities in continental Europe. But the extrapolators fell into the Ponzian trap, for the prices of these shares and all other shares would rise as OPEC members bought them. The rumor that the Kuwaitis would buy some IBM shares led to a 10 percent increase in the price of the shares in one day—even before the Kuwaitis had bought any shares. Relatively small OPEC purchases of shares would lead to increases in their price, so that the same dollar volume of purchases would buy fewer and fewer shares.

Long before OPEC countries could buy up IBM or Shell, the governments of their countries of origin would apply limits on these purchases; they would be concerned about loss of control. So total foreign ownership of "security sensitive" industries might be limited to 25 percent—or perhaps even less. Such limits would deflect OPEC demand to other assets, and might induce some OPEC members to reduce output.

Matching the $50 billion annual increase in OPEC wealth

233

with the increase in the supply of PIC equities, or even with the total supply of equities, is a straw man argument; equities are only a small part of total financial wealth. The more effective comparison is between the increase in OPEC financial wealth and both total PIC financial wealth and the annual increase in that total. The increase in financial wealth covers a very wide range of financial instruments—bank deposits, stocks, equities, mortgages, and so on. Total financial wealth in the United States is about $5,000 billion, and the annual increase in U.S. financial wealth is about $200 billion; comparable numbers for other PICs are $7,000 billion and $300 billion. So $50 billion of OPEC purchases is about 10 percent of the annual increase in the supply. The OPEC countries would buy more than 10 percent of some assets, relatively less of others. If they develop large appetites for some assets, prices of these assets would rise, and more of them would be produced.

True, $50 billion a year is a large number, even when compared with $500 billion. But the PICs have a wide array of investment alternatives—if OPEC has the money to invest, the PICs have the securities to sell.

Who Lends to the Poor?

Saudi Arabia, Libya, Kuwait, and the United Arab Emirates have to deal with this question: Is it worthwhile to sell one more barrel of oil for $10 or $15 and then to invest the proceeds, or is it better to delay production until some future date? Investing the receipts in one or another PIC means that wealth will grow at about the interest rates in these countries; at an interest rate of 7 percent a year, the investment would double every decade. Delaying production is profitable only if the price of oil will increase as rapidly as the investment will grow.

234

Projecting the future price of oil is risky; much depends on whether the cartel succeeds in holding up the price and on how rapidly new energy sources become available. The less attractive are the investment assets available to the producers, either because of low interest rates or high risks, the more likely they are to restrict production.

The asset preferences of OPEC members are similar to those of investors in other countries in one important respect: they like diversification. Their preferences may differ from those of money managers in New York, London, and Zurich. To the extent that the oil producers prefer assets denominated in a particular PIC currency, the price of this currency will rise in the foreign exchange market. The greater their demand for assets denominated in the Swiss francs, the greater the appreciation of the Swiss franc. Then, as the Swiss franc becomes more expensive to the mark, the dollar, and other currencies, Switzerland's ability to export cheese and chocolate bars will decline. However, the Swiss will find it relatively easy to finance their oil imports.

A preference for assets denominated in some currencies means that assets denominated in other currencies are disfavored. Some PICs may not be able to borrow to finance their oil imports. Bangladesh and India are in this group; for a while, Italy and Britain appeared likely to join them. If these countries can't borrow, they may have to curtail their imports, if not of oil, then of other products. The analogy with the household is useful: if John Doe loses his job and can't borrow to finance his consumption of Cadillacs and corn muffins, he must consume less. Charity from the Salvation Army and income from the unemployment insurance bureau (or the welfare department) set an upper limit to his consumption. If he consumes only essentials and their prices rise, then he must tighten his belt and consume fewer essentials. Similarly, if a country can't borrow to finance its imports of petroleum and other essentials, it too is obliged to reduce imports. So OPEC exports will decline, unless its least credit-worthy customers can finance their imports.

It would be in the interests of OPEC countries to extend credit to Bangladesh, Ethiopia, and Paraguay; subsidized or cheap credit is a sales supplement for high-priced oils. As long as the effective price of oil exceeds the cost of production— and it does by a factor of 50 or 100—then such sales are desirable. If the cost of production is 20 cents a barrel, the posted price is $10 and the discounted price is $3, the profit is $2.80. OPEC members have sold some oil to the developing countries at reduced prices or at subsidized credit terms; these discounts and credits have been small relative to their total sales to the developing countries. If the OPEC members aren't willing to recycle to the least credit-worthy borrowers, then the rate at which their foreign investment grows will be smaller than McNamara's estimates. Unless, of course, the World Bank and other international institutions lend to the borrowers that OPEC won't lend to—so OPEC can continue to sell them $10 oil.

The International Monetary Fund has developed a credit arrangement under which the IMF borrows from OPEC members and in turn lends to its poorer members. While the OPEC members could have lent directly to the oil importers, the international institutions provided much more attractive guarantees. And they can still sell the oil at the $10 price. Bangladesh may fail to repay OPEC and not go out of business, but the IMF is not about to fail to repay OPEC.

All countries want the best possible deal in selling their exports; the OPEC members are no exception. They want the best possible price for their oil; if there hadn't been a Yom Kippur War, they would have invented one. Nevertheless, most OPEC members face a dilemma. They know the price of petroleum is more likely to fall than rise; and even if it does increase, the price certainly will not double in a decade. Hence, the future price is likely to be below the current price plus added interest. So the self-interest of each individual OPEC member is served by increasing production now and putting the export receipts in the bank. If several members of OPEC do increase production, or if the largest—Saudi Arabia—does, the price of petroleum will fall, perhaps as sharply as it rose.

So the OPEC members are in a tenuous situation. As a group, they must restrict output to maintain the high price. Individually, however, they want to take advantage of the high price as long as it lasts.

Lenders Without Borrowers Are Neuters

If OPEC members as a group are to lend $50 billion a year, then PICs as a group must borrow $50 billion a year. Some countries which had been international lenders must become borrowers; others, which had been small borrowers, must become large borrowers. Unless PICs as a group are willing to borrow $50 billion a year, then OPEC cannot lend $50 billion, even if it is willing to.

The $50 billion of PIC borrowings must be distributed among the oil-importing countries. One approach toward distribution of this $50 billion is that each PIC increase its annual borrowing by the increase in its oil import payments, less any increase in its commodity exports to OPEC members. For example, the oil import bill for Japan and Germany would increase by $10 billion given the volume of their oil imports. To the extent that they are successful in increasing their commodity exports to various OPEC members, their need to borrow would decline. If each PIC increased its exports to OPEC members by its share of increased payments for oil imports, then the position of one PIC would not change relative to others; its currency would neither appreciate or depreciate. The difference between the increase in oil import payments and the increase in exports would be borrowed from OPEC countries or, indirectly, from other international lenders.

This approach toward distribution of PIC borrowings can be called standstill, since the payments position of each PIC do not change relative to any other PIC. If the exchange rates are pegged, then the deficits and surpluses of individual PICs do not change. If currencies float, then exchange rates are not affected; no PIC currencies either appreciate or depreciate. The foreign indebtedness of some PICs—those which are large importers of petroleum—would increase more rapidly than that of others, but this would be a matter of no concern.

The alternative way to distribute the $50 billion among PICs is that many or most PIC countries choose to pay for oil on a pay-as-you-go basis because of their reluctance to incur the international indebtedness implied by the standstill approach. These countries adjust to the increase in the cost of oil imports by allowing their currencies to depreciate; thus, while their exports increase to help finance the increase in their oil import payments, their non-oil imports decline. The combination of the increase in export earnings and the reduction of import payments equals the increase in oil import payments and their sales of domestic assets to foreigners.

At the extreme, the currencies of all PICs except one might depreciate in the foreign exchange market; this country—the Nth—would incur the indebtedness which would be the mirror of the increase in OPEC investments. While any country might be the Nth—or several together might be—it seems plausible that the United States might take on this role, at least initially. Just as the U.S. payments deficits in the 1950s and early 1960s were determined by the reserve demands of other countries, so the post-OPEC change in U.S. indebtedness would equal the difference between the increase in OPEC wealth and the increase in foreign indebtedness of all other PICs. At most, the United States would increase its indebtedness by $50 billion annually. Germany, Japan, and other PICs would increase their exports of autos, steel, and chemicals to the United States to earn the dollars to pay for their oil; their foreign indebtedness would remain unchanged.

Both standstill and pay-as-you-go are concepts, representing ends of a spectrum; and so the question becomes whether the system is likely to move toward one end of the spectrum or another. If countries are to move toward standstill, then they must take the initiative and borrow abroad. If they are reluctant or unwilling to borrow, their currencies will automatically depreciate, and they will—willy-nilly—move toward the pay-as-you-go end of the spectrum.

The more individual PICs borrow abroad—that is, the more they export their securities—the less their currencies will depreciate. Increased exports of securities are a substitute for increased exports of goods. But there is a difference—if a PIC borrows, then it must repay. To get the foreign exchange necessary to repay the credit, the country must increase its exports in the future.

So the choice for the authorities in each PIC is not whether its currency will depreciate to pay for oil, since the currency will depreciate anyway—in the immediate future if the country follows the pay-as-you-go approach, in the distant future if it follows the standstill approach. If the line of least resistance is to do nothing, the automatic and instantaneous depreciation of the currency will ensure that oil imports can be paid for currently without any initiative toward borrowing.

Whenever a PIC permits its currency to depreciate, the domestic price of oil increases; the amount spent on its oil imports will decline. Domestic production of coal, petroleum, and other types of energy will be encouraged. Some countries have taken nonmarket measures to limit their oil imports; they have placed ceilings or quotas on oil imports. Others have raised tariffs to reduce oil imports. Several have engaged in barter deals with individual OPEC members, exchanging tanks and trucks for oil. Some might place a ceiling on the rate at which they will allow their foreign indebtedness to increase. Taken together, these various measures determine the upper limit of PIC borrowings—and OPEC lendings.

If PICs are willing to borrow less than OPEC members are prepared to lend, then the indebtedness will increase by the smaller total. Each PIC must then adjust to the reduced availability of petroleum. And OPEC members must allocate reduction in petroleum exports among themselves.

The Exchange Rate Implications of OPEC Money

The oil price increase, like any major shock to the system, led to realignments in the values of currencies in the exchange market. The increase in oil payments by the PICs caused their currencies to depreciate. The increase in PIC exports of goods and securities caused their currencies to appreciate. Both depreciation and appreciation are measured relative to the U.S. dollar, because most payments for oil have traditionally been made in terms of the dollar. Whether an individual PIC currency appreciated or depreciated depended on whether the increase in its payments for oil was smaller or larger than the increase in its exports of goods and securities.

Shortly after the oil price was increased, the common view was that the Western European currencies and the Japanese yen would weaken relative to the dollar, because these countries were such larger importers of oil than the United States. Subsequently, the European currencies and the yen appreciated, for the increase in their exports of goods, services, and securities to OPEC members dominated the increase in their oil payments. For example, Germany's oil import bill increased by $10 billion as a result of higher oil prices; yet in 1974, German exports increased several billion dollars more than

German imports. And the Germans borrowed several billion dollars abroad. Similarly, the Japanese trade surplus in 1974 decreased by much less than the increase in oil payments. While U.S. payments for imported oil went up by $25 billion, U.S. imports rose by only $10 billion. Germany overcompensated; it was too successful in increasing its exports.

Thus, Germany and Japan, two of the three largest countries in the system, were following the pay-as-you-go approach, and the third, the United States, was leaning in this direction. The major PIC borrowers were Great Britain, Italy, and to a lesser extent, France. More than half of the increase in OPEC financial wealth represented borrowings by developing countries, or the reduction in their reserves.

It is striking that those countries with the weakest economies and the least ability to borrow did most of the borrowing. Perhaps they have done so again in 1975. Yet there must be a limit to their ability to borrow. As the limit is approached, they will be forced to pay-as-you-go. Unless the big three countries are willing to borrow, OPEC members will find themselves with money to lend and no borrowers.

16

Why Are Large, Multinational Firms Mostly American?

In the late 1960s one of Europe's best-selling books was *Le Défi Americain—The American Challenge*. The author was Jean-Jacques Servan-Schreiber, publisher of *L'Express,* the French imitation of *Time*; *L'Expansion*, the French version of *Fortune*; and for a while, *European Business*, the French counterpart of the *Harvard Business Review*. He was energetic, if not original.

The central thesis of *Le Défi Americain* was dramatic: after the United States and the Soviet Union, the third economic power in the world was U.S. business firms in Europe. As evidence, JJ-SS cited the increasingly important position of U.S. subsidiaries in European industry, especially is such technologically advanced fields as computers and electronics.

These U.S. firms, moreover, were at that time well ahead of their British, French, and German competitors in integrating their production and marketing across European borders. International Harvester's French plant produced tractor transmissions, and its German plant produced the motors; each exported its product to the other. And IBM-Europe produced its computers using components made in various plants across the continent; indeed, its production line in Europe was at least seven countries long.

Servan-Schreiber advocated numerous changes to help Europe

meet the U.S. challenge. In effect, European business should become more like American business—more graduate business schools like Harvard, more professional management like that of Exxon, greater decentralization of corporation decision making as in ITT, and more expenditures on research and development like IBM. To meet the American invasion, Europeans should become more nearly American—as had JJ-SS himself.

One of the not so best-selling books in London in 1902 was *The American Invaders* by F. A. McKenzie, a modest Englishman worried by the American threat to British industry. Americans, he wrote, were "succeeding in Europe because of advantages in education, their willingness to accept new ideas, and their freedom from hampering tradition." In part this supremacy was reflected in U.S. exports, in part by the growth of subsidiaries of U.S. firms in Europe. McKenzie especially noted the dominance of Americans in the new industries: "applications of electricity to traction, the typewriter, the automobile, and the machine tools."

Servan-Schreiber does not acknowledge McKenzie or *The American Invaders*. But if he did, he then would have to explain why sixty-five years and two world wars later, U.S. firms account for no more than 5 percent of corporate assets in Europe and 10 percent of European imports. And he would also have to explain why the ratio of U.S. foreign investment to U.S. national income in the early 1970s was about the same as in 1913.

McKenzie was somewhat premature in predicting the invasion. While a very few U.S. firms had set up branches in Europe as early as 1850, U.S. direct foreign investment until the 1920s was modest, and was largely confined to firms engaged in mining and producing crude petroleum. Only in the 1920s did U.S. investment in manufacturing abroad jump sharply. From the 1930s through most of the 1950s, new outflows of investment were modest because of the Great Depression and World War II; many U.S. firms sold their European subsidiaries. But beginning in the late 1950s, direct U.S. foreign investment soared; U.S. firms purchased foreign firms or set up new plants of their own.

By 1970 a substantial part of total manufacturing in Canada and several other countries was foreign-owned, especially by U.S. firms. In some Canadian industries more than three-fourths of the local plants were foreign-owned; however, in many industries, such as public utilities and retailing, foreign ownership was minimal. The industry mix is varied. U.S. firms in the "new" industries continue to invest abroad extensively, much as they did in McKenzie's day; the major difference is that the names of the new industries have changed. But U.S. firms are well established abroad in traditional industries like hotel keeping and food processing, automobiles and tires, soaps and toothpaste. London has a Playboy Club, and the number of Hilton Hotels and Holiday Inns outside the United States is growing very rapidly.

Altogether, direct foreign investment for firms in all countries totaled about $180 billion in 1974, of which about $120 billion was undertaken by U.S. firms and $20 billion by British firms. Foreign investment by German and Japanese firms is small, although it has been increasing rapidly (one cost of losing wars is that the foreign subsidiaries of domestic firms tend to be expropriated). Forty percent of U.S. foreign investment is in manufacturing, 30 percent in petroleum, and nearly 10 percent in mining. These numbers are only ballpark estimates, but that does not make them any less significant.

U.S. firms and firms based in small number of foreign countries—Great Britain, the Netherlands, and Switzerland—account for nearly all of direct foreign investment. Foreign investment is extensive in some industries (aluminum, petroleum) and minimal in others (textiles and steel). Dutch firms (Unilever, Shell, Philips) are large investors abroad, while Belgian firms are not. Although U.S. firms remain strong as international competitors, foreign firms have set up U.S. subsidiaries to compete in the U.S. firms' backyard. British Petroleum bought up Sinclair Oil; Imperial Chemical, the leading British chemical firm, acquired Atlas Chemical, which ranks about twentieth in the United States in sales; BASF (a German chemical company) has acquired Wyandotte Chemical. Panasonic, one of the top three Japanese electronics firms, bought Motorola; a subsidiary of Nestlés, a Swiss firm, successfully bid for Libby, McNeill & Libby. Several of the major drug suppliers in the United States are Swiss, CIBA and Hoffmann-La Roche among them. Petrofina, the Belgian petroleum firm, is beginning to refine and distribute in the United States. Sony has set up a TV production line in the United States. The European penetration of the U.S. market has gone so far that the Good Humor Company is part of the Liverpool-based Thomas Lipton Tea empire. Still, the list of foreign firms investing in the United States is much shorter than the list of U.S. firms abroad; U.S. direct investment abroad is six or seven times as large as direct foreign investment in the United States.

U.S. foreign investment surged in the late 1950s and the 1960s not in response to any plan, but rather in response to market forces. A few firms were undoubtedly playing follow the leader, but the game was expensive if market opportunities were inappropriate. Fortunately, the economic growth of Western Europe during this period was rapid, partly because of the bounce-back from World War II and partly because of the optimistic expectations generated by the formation and development of the Common Market.

Then, in the late 1960s, the growing overvaluation of the U.S. dollar because of more rapid inflation in the United States than in Europe further stimulated U.S. firms to invest abroad, if only to protect their markets. Earlier, these firms had supplied foreign markets from U.S. plants. But as U.S. costs and prices increased, these U.S. plants lost their competitive edge— in the U.S. market as well as in the foreign market—and the firms felt obliged to invest abroad. Some U.S. firms began to invest abroad to protect their position in the U.S. market; perhaps the best examples of this are the U.S. electronic firms which set up manufacturing and assembly plants in the Far East to protect their position in the U.S. market relative to Japanese firms.

The depreciation of the dollar relative to European currencies in the 1970s reduced the incentive for U.S. firms to invest abroad. German and Japanese firms began to invest more extensively in the United States; as Volkswagen's market share and profits in the United States plummeted, it considered whether to establish a U.S. assembly or production line. Volvo committed itself to a $100 million assembly plant in Tidewater, Virginia. Just as U.S. firms increased their foreign investment as the dollar became overvalued, so foreign firms began to increase their investment in the United States once the dollar appeared undervalued.

The relation between foreign investment and the national interests of the host countries—and of the source countries—came under critical attack as nationalist pressures increased. By the late 1960s, when Servan-Schreiber's book came out, ownership of domestic factories and resources by foreign firms —especially by U.S. firms—had become a sensitive political issue. Is Canada worse off because such a large part of Canadian production occurs within U.S.-owned firms? Many Canadians think so. Canada and other host countries fear that the activities of the giant multinational firms, especially those based in the United States, are a new form of imperialism, more insidious than the gunboats of the late nineteenth century. Nationalists in many countries—primarily in developing countries, but also in industrial countries like France and Canada— complain about a loss of sovereignty to the large international companies. Nationalist pressures have been specially directed against firms engaged in extracting resources in developing countries. Peru has expropriated International Petroleum, the local subsidiary of Standard Oil of New Jersey, and also some of the local properties of W. R. Grace. Bolivia has taken over the local operations of Gulf Oil. Venezuela has expropriated the properties of foreign oil companies. In Chile, the Christian Democratic government of Eduardo Frei purchased 50 percent of Anaconda mines; subsequently, the Marxist government of Salvador Allende nationalized the rest of Anaconda's share as well as the mines of most other companies. Mexico has restricted foreign ownership to participation in joint ventures with Mexican partners; the share owned by foreign firms, once limited to 50 percent, is being further reduced.

The source countries are also concerned about foreign investment, especially about its possibly harmful effects on the balance of payments, on unemployment, and on tax revenues. Firms that wish to invest abroad may find it increasingly difficult to obtain approval from the governments of their own countries as well as from the would-be host countries.

Patterns of Market Penetration

By almost any measure, the foreign investments of U.S. firms are nearly twice as large as the foreign investments of all foreign-based firms combined. And if anything, this statistic underestimates the situation, since part of the "overseas investment" of British, French, and Dutch firms originated as domestic investment. For example, French companies held extensive assets in Algeria in the late 1950s; Algeria was then one of the geographical components of metropolitan France. When Algeria became independent, these investments were counted as part of French foreign investment. British foreign investment is extensive in what were formerly colonies or outposts of Empire —Australia, South Africa, and Canada.

The question of why U.S. firms invest extensively abroad cannot be answered without first considering the unique qualities of each firm. A firm consists of individuals whose activities are coordinated by central managment. The managers buy certain inputs to produce a variety of outputs. Most of the activities conducted within the firm *could* be purchased, in modular fashion, from other firms. The managers might hire one company to develop new products, a second to produce them, a third to market them. The choice of whether to conduct an activity within the firm or to acquire the product of the same activity in the market is usually made on the basis of cost; competition forces the firm to choose the low-cost alternative. Some magazines—for example, *Playboy* and *Penthouse*—are primarily cut-and-paste jobs in that a very small editorial staff buys most of the stories and photos from outsiders. *Time* and *Newsweek*, in contrast, maintain much larger staffs which write most of the stories.

Each firm has certain advantages—managerial and financial skills, marketing and engineering know-how, customer loyalties, and so forth. Firms are identifiable as repositories of marketing skills, financial skills, or organizational skills; these tags denote their advantages in relation to their competitors. Each firm continually seeks to exploit its advantages in the most efficient way. Since competitors are constantly trying to erode its advantages, the firm must continually strive to maintain its market position by developing new advantages and exploiting its established advantages in new markets, either in other industries or in more distant markets, including those abroad. A firm may exploit its advantages directly, through sale to other firms, or indirectly, by selling goods which embody the advantages.

When a firm considers expansion into foreign markets, it must decide on the most efficient way of exploiting its advantages: by exporting from domestic production, producing in the foreign market, or selling its advantages. If the firm decides to produce abroad, it must consider whether to enter into a partnership relationship with a host-country firm. The choice will depend on a variety of economic—and perhaps political—considerations.

Initially, the firm may satisfy the foreign market by exporting the output of its domestic plants. Then, after the foreign market has become sufficiently large, a plant may be established abroad. At first, the production in the foreign country may involve only the assembly of imported components, so as to save on transport costs and tariffs. The drug companies, for example, repackage drugs from large containers into smaller bottles; the auto companies may assemble cars and trucks from imported components. As the host-country market expands, more of the inputs in the product—and of the management—may be locally produced, although the parent may continue to supply senior management, technical knowledge, and some financial assistance. As the scale of output in the host-country plant increases, production costs are likely to decline; the output of this subsidiary may supplement and ultimately perhaps supplant exports from the home-country plants.

At some point, costs in the subsidiary may fall below those in domestic plants, and the firm may begin to supply part or all of the domestic market from foreign subsidiaries. Ford imports motors for Pintos for the U.S. market from its English and Belgian subsidiaries. And some U.S. electronics firms produce part or all of the inputs for particular products in Taiwan, South Korea, Singapore, and Malaysia; these components may be shipped to the United States for assembly into the final product.

The extensive integration of manufacturing activities in different countries is a relatively recent innovation. Initially the market for many products was local or regional; most of the local needs were satisfied from nearby production. Imports were minimal. Every town had its butcher, baker, and candlestick maker, as well as its cobbler, tailor, and tobacconist. The potential for cost reductions associated with large-scale production was small. And even where savings in production costs were possible, the extra costs of controlling a large-scale operation with activities in widely separated locations dominated the savings. The change in the last 150 years is that technological developments have both greatly increased the savings associated with large-scale production and reduced the costs of coordinating distant activities. Thus, bauxite mined in Jamaica is shipped to eastern Venezuela for refining to take advantage of extremely low-cost electricity. Some U.S. electronics companies fly partially assembled radio receivers to South Korea for further processing by skilled, relatively inexpensive labor. The combination of increasingly sophisticated products—higher unit values—and declining transportation and communications costs has reduced the pressure on firms to locate the productive activity near either the market or the source of raw materials. As in banking, these changes in technology have increased the size of the market; regional markets are grouped into national markets, and national markets into the international market.

Enlargement of the market has encouraged firms to integrate their activities in different countries. In some countries a firm may both produce and market, in others it may only market, and in still others it may only produce. Thus, it is necessary to distinguish between the share of the world's market for a product held by U.S. firms, British firms, and Swiss firms, and the share of total production in each country undertaken by domestic firms and by foreign firms. The factors which explain where particular goods are produced are likely to differ from those which explain market shares, and both may differ from those which explain output shares. Servan-Schreiber focused on output shares, which is what U.S. industry in Europe is all about. Whereas U.S. firms produce largely in Europe to satisfy the European market, European firms traditionally satisfied the U.S. market by exporting European output. General Motors and

Ford have major subsidiaries in Britain and Germany, while the British and German auto companies supply the U.S. market from their domestic plants.

Why Firms Invest Abroad

Some reasons for overseas investments are noneconomic. General Leonard Wood established Sears, Roebuck stores in Mexico and elsewhere in Central America because he wanted to plant the U.S. flag in Latin America. A few firms may invest abroad because the corporation president likes semiannual trips to Madrid or Florence. Some firms invest abroad because of the bandwagon effect; their competitors are investing abroad, and they fear being left behind. The list of ad hoc explanations is long, and some investments may indeed be explained by one or several of these factors. But since the patterns of foreign investment do not appear to be random, there is probably a systematic explanation for most—but not necessarily all—foreign investments.

U.S. firms competing in the European market are usually at a disadvantage in relation to their host-country competitors, since they incur costs their host-country competitors do not. Thus, the activities of European subsidiaries must be managed from New York or Des Moines if they are to be integrated with those of the parent; the costs of plane travel across the Atlantic and international phone calls mount up. And the salaries and expenses of U.S. managers in Europe may be three or four times higher than those of comparable European managers. Because of this cost disadvantage, firms with foreign subsidiaries must possess some offsetting advantages if their profit rates are to be comparable to those of their host-country competitors. Similar statements might be made about foreign firms which have set up (or bought) U.S. subsidiaries. These firms believe that it is more profitable to satisfy the U.S. market by producing in the United States than by exporting.

Three possible and nonexclusive advantages are attributed to the source-country firms. According to Servan-Schreiber, the U.S. advantage is a product of the combination of managerial know-how and a flexible business system. The United States often has superior businessmen; each manager may combine an undergraduate degree in engineering from MIT with a graduate degree in business from Harvard.

Superiority theories imply that Mother Nature plays favorites in the distribution of talent. If this is true, and if Americans are indeed superior, the low-cost response for European firms is clear: they should hire more American managers. Few do. (The success of U.S. management consultants in Europe might be deemed a proxy for hiring American managers.) Other objections to the superiority hypothesis include its failure to provide insights about why foreign investment is so large in some industries and so small in others—and its failure to explain why the Dutch and Swiss invest extensively abroad. Indeed, this "theory" is really a tautology. All it really says is that firms based in source countries are superior, and the evidence of their superiority is that they invest abroad.

A second explanation is that the source-country firms have an advantage in the form of a patent or technical know-how or marketing skills; these could be called firm-specific advantages. In a few industries, these advantages may derive from large U.S. government programs on defense and space; however, this doesn't explain Playboy Clubs, Holiday Inns, Coke, or Pepsi. Of course, the advantages might reflect the fact that relatively high U.S. wages compel U.S. firms to give greater attention to reducing their costs by developing new laborsaving processes, while intense competition forces U.S. firms to develop new products for both old needs and newly created needs. So U.S. firms tend to develop "advantages" more rapidly than firms in

252

other countries do. Once these new products and processes are available, U.S. firms then exploit them to satisfy demands in foreign markets. So this explanation is directed to the market share question.

Presumably, the factors which explain why U.S. firms develop these advantages might also explain why firms in the Netherlands, Switzerland, and other countries also develop advantages. So the question of what source-country firms have in common becomes transformed into a question of which common characteristics of source countries lead firms to develop advantages that have value abroad.

The trouble with an explanation based on firm-specific advantages is its incompleteness. For one thing, the explanation is vague about why firms in some countries develop more of these advantages than firms in other countries. Moreover, U.S. firms could sell their patent, know-how, and product advantages to foreign firms. Indeed, many U.S. firms do exactly that, by licensing their advantages. Coca-Cola sells franchises and its concentrate to foreign producers. If the sale price is sufficiently high, the U.S. firms would never incur the cost of establishing subsidiaries.

So the reluctance to sell the advantage to host-country firms must be explained. One suggestion is that firms fear that such sales might facilitate the growth of foreign firms which would later become their competitors. A competing suggestion is that firms may find it difficult to sell the advantages, perhaps because they are ill-defined, especially if research and development leads to continuing changes in the advantages or if they involve marketing know-how. The more general reason for their reluctance to sell their advantages is that the firms believe their income will be higher if they exploit them through a subsidiary, although it is curious that host-country firms will not pay a sufficiently high price to equal that income.

A third explanation is that a firm invests abroad when further expansion within its traditional industry in the domestic market becomes difficult or expensive. One reason might be that demand for its product is growing more slowly, perhaps because the domestic market is saturated. In this situation, the firm might expand into other industries in the domestic market —that is, it might cross the borders between industries. Alternatively, the firm might cross national borders, expanding abroad with its traditional product. For many firms, crossing national borders may be easier than crossing industry borders, since the unique advantage of the firm is its expertise in producing or marketing a particular product. This view explains why firms seek foreign markets, but not why they produce abroad. It may explain market shares, but it does not explain output shares.

A fourth explanation of the dominance of U.S. firms—the capital market view—is that U.S. firms (and those based in other source countries) have an advantage in the world capital market: they can borrow at lower interest rates and sell their shares at higher prices than firms in other countries can. These firms benefit from country-specific advantages which are available to all the firms within a country.

Interest rates on dollar bonds are lower than those on debts denominated in nearly every other currency. And since the dollar is their domestic currency, U.S. firms are able to borrow on more advantageous terms than their foreign competitors. Similarly, interest rates on bonds issued by firms in other source countries tend to be lower than those in most countries. By and large, the source countries are the low interest rate countries; the host countries, the high interest rate countries. Canadian and European firms have come to New York to borrow, not because they want to spend the funds in the United States but because U.S. interest rates are sufficiently below domestic rates to justify incurring the exchange risk.

One consequence of the general preference of investors for dollar securities is that U.S. firms are willing to pay more for an advantage—for an income stream—than non-U.S. firms. In Wall Street argot, everything else being equal, the price-earnings ratio is higher for U.S. firms than for non-U.S. firms. And given an opportunity to increase its income by undertaking a new project, a U.S. firm will generally pay a higher price for the same future income than a non-U.S. firm will. The other side of the coin is that if a U.S. firm buys a French firm, even though the earnings of the French subsidiary remain unchanged, investors will pay more for the equities because of their preferences for dollar-denominated assets.

This suggests that the advantages of U.S. firms are inherent in investor preferences for assets denominated in dollars, just as the advantages of Swiss firms are inherent in investor preferences for assets denominated in Swiss francs. U.S. firms are *identified* with dollar equities, just as Swiss firms are identified with Swiss franc equities, and Dutch firms with guilder equities. A firm cannot change the currency denomination of its equities without changing its national identity. And firms almost never change their nationality. As long as interest rates on dollar assets are low relative to those on assets in other currencies, U.S. firms will maintain an advantage over their foreign competitors, an advantage that foreign firms cannot buy since it is inherent in the system rather than in the behavior of individual firms.

The implication of the capital market view is that the source countries for foreign investment are those with relatively low interest rates. Casual observation suggests that the countries other than the United States which are large exporters of direct foreign investment—Switzerland, the Netherlands, and Great Britain—have traditionally been low interest rate countries. The Netherlands was the low interest rate country in the eighteenth century, when the Dutch empire was expanding abroad and Dutch trading firms were setting up overseas offices. In the nineteenth century, British firms followed the growth of empire. Even though both political empires have shrunk decisively since then, the large international businesses have continued to flourish.

The capital market view also has implications for changes in the pattern of ownership in different countries. As long as the dollar is the preferred currency, U.S. firms will establish foreign branches and buy up foreign firms. Foreign ownership of plants in the United States and foreign takeovers of U.S. firms may increase, but the implication of the capital market explanation is that the growth of U.S. investment abroad will be substantially larger; more importantly, the output shares of U.S. firms will increase.

The test of any theory is its ability to explain reality. And the most demanding test of these explanations of direct investment is their ability to explain cross-hauling, the direct investment in the United States by Swiss, Dutch, British, and other non-U.S. firms. If, as Servan-Schreiber suggests, Americans are the supermen of the business world, why do European firms compete with U.S. firms in their own backyard? Servan-Schreiber has no answer. The product know-how explanation is that the European firms wish to exploit in the U.S. market the advantages developed in their home countries. A plausible extension of this view is that they invest in the United States because they want to participate in the largest, most competitive market; they fear that without such participation they will become technologically backward. Lessons learned in the U.S. market, morever, help them compete against U.S. firms in other markets, including their home markets.

A further implication of the capital market view is that foreign firms invest in the United States to reduce their borrowing costs in dollars and to secure a higher price for their equities once a larger proportion of their earnings is in a preferred currency like the dollar. Thus, British Petroleum purchased a part of Sinclair and also invested extensively in oil fields in Alaska's North Slope to be able to borrow dollars on more equal terms with Exxon, Gulf, and Mobil. Moreover, British Petroleum also anticipated that investors would pay a higher price for its shares if a larger part of its total earnings were in dollars. Note that this view also assumes that investors will pay a higher price if the dollar income stream results from production in the U.S. market than if it results from exports to the U.S. market from Europe and Japan.

These competing explanations for foreign investment are tentative, not conclusive. None has been subjected to rigorous testing. Direct foreign investment is a complex process. In the absence of an accepted theory, predicting changes in national investment patterns that might result from economic factors is risky. And the issue may become increasingly academic if political factors begin to dominate economic factors.

The Costs of Direct Foreign Investment

One of the paradoxes of the mid-1970s is that both source-country governments and host-country governments have questioned the economic advantages attached to the activities of multinational firms. That these firms have grown and expanded suggests efficiencies greater than those of the smaller domestic firms they supplant. Their efficiencies must be distributed among their employees as higher wages and salaries, or to their customers as lower prices, or to their shareholders as higher profits and dividends. All three groups may gain. Either the source country or the host country may gain as a result of their activities, and both may gain; it is implausible that both source and host countries could be worse off.

The source countries have several major criticisms of multinationals. One involves runaway jobs; unions often find that international firms circumvent their national monopoly over the supply of labor. Belatedly—fifty years belatedly—the unions

257

are becoming interested in the international labor situation. Hence, the choice for the unions in the source country is whether to merge with unions in the host countries or to develop some other fraternal relationship with these unions.

A second criticism involves taxes: the foreign income of the domestic firm is taxed initially by the foreign government, and in most cases there is little left over for the domestic tax collector. For example, the United States has double-taxation agreements with many other countries. These agreements provide that the income is first taxable in the country in which it is earned, and that the combined tax rate of the foreign host and the U.S. government cannot exceed the higher of the two national rates. Assume the British tax rate is 40 percent and the U.S. rate is 50 percent. If a U.S. firm invests at home, each dollar of profit generates 50 cents for the U.S. tax collector. If the firm invests in Britain, each dollar of profit generates 40 cents for the British tax collector and only 10 cents for the U.S. collector.

A third concern involves the adverse balance-of-payments consequences. Foreign investments mean that exports decline and imports increase more rapidly than might otherwise occur. While the payment of dividends may counter the loss of exports, the offset may be partial rather than complete.

These criticisms imply that the source country firm faces the choice between producing at home or producing abroad, when the effective choice for some firms may be producing abroad or not producing at all. The shift in the production of many electronics products to Southeast Asia occurred because productions costs there were much lower than in the United States; if U.S. firms had not participated with German, Dutch, and Japanese firms in this move, they would have lost both their export markets and the domestic market. The loss of U.S. jobs, the shortfall in U.S. tax revenues, and the adverse impact on the U.S. balance of payments would have been even sharper. Even when U.S. firms might have retained the domestic

market, at least for a while, without shifting to offshore production, their long-run competitive position would have been
weaker.

There are other criticisms. During the dollar crises, the multinationals moved funds to avoid losses from the changes in
exchange rates; some may also have sought to profit. Some
critics even suggest that the crises resulted from the behavior
of the firms, and not from the mismanagement of the system.
More likely, the firms simply felt the need to protect and
advance their interests.

An even more sensitive issue involves the alleged political
involvement of the multinationals in the host countries. Multinationals may contribute to political parties, much as host-
country firms do. ITT tried to forestall the election of Allende
in Chile. Again, the firms say they are just protecting their
interests. The criticism is that the interests of the firm may be
identical neither with U.S. national interests nor with the interests of the host countries.

Source-country governments—or at least the U.S. government—may be embarrassed and inconvenienced by disclosure
of the political activities of the multinationals. But the managers
of the firms are paid to protect the firm's interests. And they
have on ocassion found themselves in the dilemma that the
methods of decision making and persuasion that are typical or
at least not uncommon in the host country would not be en-
dearing in a New England town meeting.

Host-country attitudes toward multinational firms are ambivalent. Many countries compete to attract these firms, for
they bring employment, on-the-job training, and tax revenues.
In many products, these firms provide access to world markets.
Yet foreign investment has been much criticized within the
host countries. Some of these criticisms are vague and reflect
simpleminded xenophobia, equating foreign investment with
imperialism. Having nationals work for foreigners or having
foreigners own domestic resources is said to demean the nation.

259

Other criticisms are specific: the foreign firm exploits the nations' patrimony of nonreproducible petroleum or copper or bauxite or tin, or reduces employment, or evades taxes, or stifles domestic entrepreneurship. The host-country government may feel that foreign-owned firms diminish its sovereignty and may resent that these firms' involvement in the domestic political process.

Appraisal of these criticisms requires a benchmark, a view of what would have happened to growth, income, employment, and corporate development had foreign investment not taken place. Assume that the Canadian government had progressively restricted the operation of foreign firms in Canada. More of the Canadian market would be supplied by the domestic production of Canadian firms. And Canadian imports from the same U.S. firms which now have Canadian subsidiaries would increase. Canadian incomes would be lower, or at least would have grown more slowly, since the supply of capital and knowledge would be smaller or more expensive. But determining the relative size of each of these adjustments is virtually impossible on an a priori basis. The Canadian firms that replaced the U.S. firms would import some of the resources that the Canadian subsidiaries of U.S. firms now get from their parents, and they might pay higher prices. As a group, Canadians would be worse off. But whether they would be worse off by 1 percent or 5 percent is difficult to estimate. Perhaps they might gain more control over their destiny—or their culture might remain purer—but these factors too are difficult (probably because they are too small) to measure.

One of the major concerns of small countries is that they might become technological backwaters; these countries fear that because their own science and technology and industry do not offer attractive careers, highly educated and trained nationals will migrate to the larger countries. Multinational companies often centralize their research and development activities in a relatively few locations, which is why government officials sometimes view the large international firm as impeding the development of a viable local scientific community. The underlying presumption is that in the absence of the multinational company, domestic firms would undertake research and development comparable to that done abroad by the foreign firm. Perhaps. But it is equally possible that the domestic firm might import its research and development because the import cost would be less than domestic production costs.

Host-country governments worry that multinational firms diminish their sovereignty. Occasionally the head office of a firm may, in response to pressures from its own government, direct the subsidiary to cease exporting to certain markets or to shift funds to the home office. Host countries fear that the power and influence of the state may be used directly against a foreign firm, perhaps because it enjoys the backing of its more powerful government. The host-country government would like to be able to rely on foreign as well as domestic firms to increase exports or boost employment, or to take other measures that may not be in the firm's interests. Foreign firms may be less amenable to such measures than domestic firms would be. Perhaps. But foreign firms know they can be asked—or forced—to leave the country. For this reason, they may be less able than domestic firms to withstand the pressures of the government.

To the extent that firms offer access to the world market, they are likely to be the "pawns" of competing national governments. For example, when Canada adopted a set of measures to induce U.S. auto companies to produce more cars in Canada, U.S. employment and U.S. tax revenues declined. When Malaysia adopted a set of measures to attract foreign electronics firms, Singapore and Taiwan began to worry, much more than did the United States and Japan.

Foreign firms are sometimes accused of making excessively high profits, especially in the extraction of nonreproducible resources. Host-country governments know that mines or wells will eventually be exhausted, so they want to maximize national gains from these resources. Typically, the host-country governments have auctioned concessions to exploit the resources; they may receive a lump-sum payment or a contingent payment based on the prospective profits. If a concession proves attractive and profitable, then a host country may seek to revise the contract in its own favor. But the game is asymmetrical; if the firm fails to discover oil or the concession proves unprofitable, the company never gets a refund. In some cases, of course, the arguments for reopening the contract may be strong; perhaps the state issued the concession under duress. Or a minister may have been bribed and thus have betrayed the national interests. Since most resource-owning countries manage to attract foreign firms to exploit their resources, the threat of contract renegotiation cannot be too severe. And increasingly, the firms may recognize the likelihood of expropriation or contract renegotiation as they determine how much—or how little—to bid.

In manufacturing, the profits earned by a foreign company reflect its efficiency. High profits mean that the firm can satisfy the market demands more efficiently than its domestic competitors. High profits also mean higher taxes to the host-country government. And higher efficiency allows the firm to use fewer domestic resources, which are thus preserved for other uses. Most governments, of course, would like to get the taxes and the efficiency, but at a lower cost in terms of profits to foreign firms.

The arguments are inconclusive. At various times (like nearly every year), the Canadians have set up study groups to determine whether Canadian interests have been served by the presence of multinationals. There is a supply of anecdotes about the misbehavior of the multinationals; the critics have a point or two, if not a case. The virulence of the criticism is more evidence of the increasing nationalist sentiment so evident in monetary policies.

Various governments have set up foreign investment review

boards to screen desirable foreign investments from less desirable proposals. Even the expansion of existing subsidiaries may require government permission. So firms may act cautiously, if only because the criteria for acceptable behavior are so vague.

Whither the Conflict?

The conflict between governments and multinationals is likely to become more intense. Problems arise because the firms are dynamic organizations and respond to developments in technology and markets, while political organizations—states— remain largely static. Firms grow and consolidate and expand their activities around the world, while the states are locked into a more or less fixed set of boundaries. Reductions in the cost of transportation and communications increase the mobility of business firms, but this increased mobility may be viewed as a threat by the governments of host countries.

In many industries the growth and expansion of multinationals has increased competition and reduced the monopoly power of the dominant domestic firms. The U.S. automobile industry is much more competitive because of the eargerness of foreign firms to export to the U.S. market, and the German automobile industry is more competitive because of the presence of General Motors line of Opels and the Ford line of Taunus. Sony and Panasonic have greatly increased competition in the electronics industry. In drugs, chemicals, and numerous other industries, trade and investment have substantially increased the number of participants. And evidence of unusually attractive profits would be expected to induce other firms to enter the market. Forming cartels where the national backgrounds of firms are so diverse is much more complex than in any national economy, largely because it is more difficult to develop trust across national boundaries.

263

Inevitably, pressures to regulate the multinational corporations—and to regulate the capacity of states to regulate these corporations—will develop. Because the issues are complex and the interests of various states and corporations highly diverse, ambitious efforts at a regulatory code are not likely to succeed.

Three changes are possible. The first is an agreement among governments to limit their reach into the foreign activities of firms which they identify as "their corporate citizens"—or into the extraterritorial span of national control. This change would be directed primarily to the United States. The second, a set of rules governing the entrance of foreign firms into manufacturing, would be much like the rules governing the access of foreign goods into the domestic markets. These rules might specify when access should be unimpaired and when the firm might be required to join with a local partner. The third is a set of rules about compensation for foreign firms when their property is expropriated or when they are othewise deprived of the full value of their advantages.

Yet the likelihood of meaningful rules is small, at least in the near future. And the reason is that governments in both the source and host countries appear to find more political support in what is effectively an ad hoc approach to regulation. In other words, the economic issues interest them less than the domestic votes.

Optimal Bankrupts: Deadbeats on
an International Treadmill

Deadbeat—someone who deliberately avoids paying his debts.

If history is a guide, then sometime in 1984 the structure of public international credits will collapse. The developing countries will default on a substantial part of their debts to government agencies in the developed countries and to international institutions. New York bankers will propose an international financial conference. The World Bank will call for borrowers and lenders to meet and sort out their problems amicably.

At the end of the conference, the terms on the $400 billion (remember the date) owed by the governments of developing countries will be renegotiated. A new international agency, Development Refinance International, will be established to help the debtors consolidate their debts. In a few cases, some of the debt will be forgiven—converted into a grant or a gift. In others, the annual debt service burden of the borrowers will be eased; the maturities on these debts will be extended and the interest rates reduced. Yet the debt obligations held by the lenders will continue to be listed in the annual reports of the national treasuries and international agencies at the same face value as before the renegotiation. Face will be saved all around. The economic statesmanship of the ministers of finance of the lending countries will be applauded. The international institutions will appear to have emerged unscathed. The credit standing of borrowers will remain intact.

Then the borrowers will increase their credit-financed imports. Six years later, the external public debts of the developing countries will again be in default. A new conference will be held, and the debts will again be renegotiated. And so it goes.

Within domestic economies, bankers shy away from deadbeats. Lending money when the probability of repayment is low is an inefficient form of charity. Nevertheless, loans are sometimes defaulted. Businesses fail. Some borrowers are incompetent, some untruthful; some are incompetent *and* untruthful. Credit bureaus run an elaborate intelligence operation on the habits of borrowers—who repays promptly, who repays slowly, who rarely repays. Lenders pay for this information, although they recover the costs by raising the interest rates charged borrowers; they scale interest rates to the riskiness of borrowers. To further protect themselves against loss, the lenders frequently require that the borrowers pledge real property—houses, land, cars, and rings—as surety for the loans. If the borrowers do not repay according to schedule, the lenders may take title to the property, the borrower's car is repossessed, his rings go to the pawnshop, and the sheriff arranges a foreclosure sale on his house. His income may be garnisheed—that is, the courts may direct the borrower's employer to make a direct payment to the lender.

Lending among nations is an altogehter different proposition. Most such loans are either public loans or publicly guaranteed loans, where those making the loan use someone else's money, usually the taxpayers'. (The careers of the lenders are not likely to be directly affected by whether the loan is repaid. The glory is in making the loan, not in securing its repayment.) Some of the loans may be politically inspired: the lender may want something from the borrower, like an air base or support in a UN vote. There are no credit checks, for diplomacy rules out an analysis which might suggest that Haiti is not so good a credit risk as Finland. When Finland borrows from an international institution at 6.5 percent, so does Haiti. The income of kings cannot be readily garnisheed. Kings no longer mortgage their castles—and even if they did, the marines are no longer used for evictions.

Perhaps the most important distinction between domestic and international loans is that governments may abrogate contracts with foreigners; this is the essence of sovereignty. A government cannot be sued, except with its permission. Failure to repay, a legal problem within a country, becomes a political problem internationally. Domestically, the law specifies the options open to the lender; if the borrower defaults, there are bankruptcy proceedings that operate in accordance with established rules. But no such rules are available internationally.

Moreover, borrower and lender governments are usually also involved in a web of other relationships—trade issues, airline landing rights, military alliances—and the lenders cannot demand repayment on overdue loans without endangering the whole skein of the two countries' relationships. Thus, the U.S. government may be reluctant to be hard-nosed about a country's failure to repay, perhaps because some U.S. firms are negotiating for oil concessions or because the U.S. Air Force has valuable air bases there. Borrowers and lenders within the domestic economy are rarely involved in such a complex set of relationships with each other.

Fifty years ago, international credits were primarily commercial; since then, they have become increasingly governmental, with political overtones. Yet the terms of commercial credits are retained. Commercial loans are supposed to be repaid. The lenders, and to a lesser extent, the borrowers, kid themselves that much of the postwar government-to-government credit is commercial. The lending exercise has become a charade.

International Lending—The Background

Lenders have long been fascinated by foreign securities, partly because the yields have been higher than on domestic securities. But these higher yields are matched by greater risks. During the nineteenth century, British investors were severely burned on their U.S. loans—first when the canal companies failed in the 1840s, then when state and local governments defaulted in the 1870s. Similarly, French investors lent extensively to the Russian czars and the Austro-Hungarian Empire; these debts became worthless after World War I.

By 1920 the risks of international lending were increasingly obvious; in an era of nationalism the political risks were compounding the commercial risks. The European demand for foreign securities declined, partly because of defaults on prewar loans to Eastern European countries and partly because Great Britain retained exchange controls on the purchase of foreign securities by domestic residents. So the center of the international capital market shifted to New York. Americans paid little recognition to European experience as they became the new international lenders. During the 1920s the U.S. public acquired billions of dollars of foreign securities. Some were issued by reputable borrowers. Many were issued by German cities and minor rather than major governments; most of these securities became worthless during the Great Depression. With the principal exception of purchases of Canadian securities by U.S. lenders, the international bond market remained dormant for thirty years.

The principal change since World War II is that today the lenders to the developing countries are largely public institutions, both national and international, rather than private parties. During the Great Depression, most national governments established export loan or loan guarantee agencies to stimulate exports and promote domestic employment. Today, loans and loan guarantees are often tied to the purchase of domestic products by foreigners. In effect, subsidized credit is used to stimulate export sales. If buyers are short of cash or if they have domestic money and lack foreign exchange because of exchange controls, the availability of credit may be the crucial factor in the choice of suppliers. Indeed, the advantage of easy credit terms may often compensate for the disadvantage of a higher sales price. Suppliers—the export firms within each country, and their employees—are subsidized by these credits, since the larger the line of credit, the larger their sales and the higher their profits. Consequently, exporters lean on their governments to ease credit terms. The process is competitive. Firms in countries with relatively high prices request their governments to provide attractive credit terms to offset the price disadvantage. Their competitors in low-cost countries then lean on their own government to match these eased credit terms.

One consequence of these export credit arrangements is that foreign customers can frequently obtain loans at a lower rate than domestic customers. Thus, in the summer of 1975, the U.S. Export-Import Bank in Washington would finance the export sales of Boeing 747 jets at an interest rate of about 6 percent, or about 0.5 percent above the interest rates on medium-term U.S. Treasury securities. The interest rates paid by U.S. commercial airlines was probably 1 or 1.5 percentage points higher, since they are denied the advantage of guaranteed government credit.

The postwar period has also seen the establishment of multilateral agencies designed to facilitate the financing of economic development. First came the International Bank for Reconstruction and Development (IBRD), or World Bank, which was set up in the mid-1940s to finance postwar reconstruction in Europe. After the defaults of the 1930s and the exhaustion of the war, European countries were poor credit risks and could only borrow if some other country cosigned the note.

The World Bank is an international financial intermediary: it borrows money by issuing its own securities to private parties and to national governments, and it then lends these funds to its members. The major reason why the Bank's securities have proved so attractive to private lenders is that the United States and other governments are the effective residual cosigners. If the lenders fail to repay the World Bank and the World Bank proves unable to repay its debts as they mature, then the creditors have ultimate recourse to the United States.

The World Bank was set up to help finance both post–World War II reconstruction and economic development. Relatively few reconstruction loans were made, largely because the Marshall Plan placed the financial needs of the European countries on a grant basis. In the 1950s the Bank turned increasingly to development financing as part of a worldwide effort to stimulate economic growth in nonindustrial, low-income countries. The development needs of these countries were legitimate; besides, it was only natural—for a bureaucracy—to find another client.

Regional multinational lending institutions, such as the Inter-American Development Bank, the Asian Development Bank, and the African Development Bank, have been modeled after the World Bank. These institutions are also international financial intermediaries: they sell their own bonds in the world's capital markets and lend the funds to their members. Their success reflects the fact that the credit standing of each institution is higher than that of the individual borrowers; most borrowers from these institutions would find it virtually impossible to sell their securities directly to private borrowers in the world market. Increasingly, the major industrial countries participate in each of these regional institutions as lenders, while the borrowers are grouped regionally.

During the early 1950s, much of the financial assistance to the developing countries was on a grant basis, a carryover from the Marshall Plan. But in the later 1950s, there was increasing pressure within the United States to place assistance on a businesslike basis. And the synonym for "businesslike" was loans. The idea was that the borrowers would use the funds only for productive projects—projects which would earn rates of return higher than the interest rates on the loans issued to finance the project. If aid is extended on a grant basis, so ran the argument, then the recipients have no strong incentive to use the funds efficiently. A loan, on the other hand, would force the recipients to pay much more attention to efficiency and costs. In fact, the developing countries have borrowed extensively. But whether they have used the loan funds more wisely than if they were grant funds is not at all clear.

A few countries have successfully made the transition from borrowing from international institutions to borrowing from the private market. Some of these private loans have been long-term bonds. Some countries borrowed from the banks in the Eurocurrency market. Perhaps in time, other countries will be able to borrow from private sources. Much will depend on their ability to restrict their public indebtedness. Much will also depend on whether private lenders retain confidence in the general idea of extending credits to the developing countries, or whether the defaults of a few sour the lenders, much as in the 1930s.

*

The Current Imbroglio

From 1955 to 1972 the external public debt of the developing countries increased from $10 billion to 100 billion. The annual growth rate was above 15 percent, or about three times faster than the growth in these countries' foreign exchange earnings. India's external public debt was the largest, at about $12 billion; other large borrowers included Brazil, $8 billion; Iran, $6 billion; and Indonesia and Mexico, $5 billion. These five countries accounted for more than a third of the total; 16 of the 86 borrowers accounted for more than 70 percent of the total. Since 1972, the quadrupling of oil prices has eased the problem for the oil producers, including Iran and Indonesia, but has greatly intensified the problem for the poorer developing countries.

The explosive increase in the size of the external public debt reflects a convergence of several factors. Governments in the lending countries, especially in the United States, wanted to stay in the foreign aid business. But since their citizens were reluctant to engage in "giveaway" programs, aid had to be shifted to a loan basis. Whereas in the late 1950s as much as 50 percent of aid was in the form of grants, by the end of the 1960s the grant component was down to 10 percent. Moreover, in their scramble for balance-of-payments surpluses, the developed countries frequently resorted to subsidizing credit on exports. But these export credits were on hard terms— short maturities and relatively high interest rates. (Nevertheless, the interest rates, while high, were below those that lenders would charge if they didn't want to subsidize exports.) Besides, interest rates throughout the world rose sharply in the 1960s and 1970s, so that the repayment burden was greater for loans of any size.

The developing countries borrowed in the hope that economic growth would resolve many of their domestic and external problems. And the 1960s was a decade of grandiose expectations about the development process; borrowers incurred substantial external debts because they believed that they would soon be on a self-sustaining growth path. In a few cases, national leaders with imperial ambitions—Sukarno of Indonesia, Nkrumah of Ghana, and Nasser of Egypt—greatly mortgaged the future export earnings of their countries.

The economics of debt service is straightforward. Assume that a country needs an excess of imports over exports of $100 million per year for ten years if it is to achieve its growth target; the import surplus will provide resources to build dams, factories, and schools. The import surplus can be financed in a variety of ways, including grants, soft loans at long maturities and low interest rates, and hard loans at short maturities and higher interest rates. In this example, an annual grant of $100 million per year will enable the country to finance the import surplus. If the country borrows $100 million in year 1 to finance the desired import surplus, then it will be obliged to make interest and loan-reduction payments in each subsequent year until the loan is repaid. These payments are a charge against its export earnings. So if it wishes an import surplus of $100 million in year 2, then it must borrow somewhat more than $100 million in year 2; the year 2 loan must be greater than $100 million by the amount of the interest and loan-reduction payments on the year 1 loan. Similarly, in year 3 the loan must be greater than $100 million by the amount of the interest and loan-reduction payments on the loans arranged in years 1 and 2. And so it goes.

The simple proposition is that the harder the loan terms, the larger the size of the new loan required each year so that the country can have the same import surplus. The harder the terms of the loans, the more rapidly total indebtedness rises, and the more rapidly the country becomes vulnerable to a credit crunch.

The combination of a larger volume of external debt and harder terms meant that a crunch in debt service was inevitable; the major uncertainties involved which country would be the first to fall into the position of being unable or unwilling to repay. Argentina provided the answer in 1955—and so its external debts were renegotiated. Over the next twelve years, eight countries found themselves in the same predicament of being unable or unwilling to make the interest and loan-reduction payments on schedule. This meant, of course, that they were unwilling to cut imports or to take measures to increase exports in order to obtain the foreign exchange for these

TABLE 17–1

International Debt Rescheduling Exercises

COUNTRY	YEAR	TOTAL AMOUNT RESCHEDULED (IN MILLIONS)
Argentina	1955	$ 500
	1962	240
	1963	72
	1965	76
Brazil	1961	605
	1964	200
Chile	1965	96
	1972	160
	1974	367
	1975	236
Egypt	1971	145
Ghana	1956	170
	1968	100
	1970	25
	1974	290
Indonesia	1966	247
	1967	95
	1968	85
	1970	2,100
India	1968	300
	1971	92
	1972	153
	1973	187
	1974	144
Pakistan	1972	234
	1973	103
	1974	650
Peru	1968	58
	1969	70
Poland	1973	32
Turkey	1959	400
	1965	220
	1972	114
Yugoslavia	1971	59

SOURCE: U.S. Congress, House Committee on Appropriations.

payments. Rather than incur the domestic political costs of these Draconian measures, they threw the ball to the lenders. The lenders had several options: they could cancel all or part

of the loans, or they could reschedule the loans. One consequence of the measure to reduce the annual debt-service payments of the borrowers was, paradoxically, to make them more
attractive recipients for additional loans.

Some of these debt relief activities were short-sighted; Argentina's debts were rescheduled four times in a ten-year
period (see Table 17–1) and will almost certainly have been
rescheduled again in 1975 or 1976. Once the debt burden was
rearranged for one borrower, other borrowers wanted their
own debts rescheduled to, since they would then be able to
obtain a larger volume of new loans. India's debts were renegotiated four times in four successive years, while Pakistan's
debt was rescheduled in 1972, 1973, and 1974. The creditors
are reluctant to be too liberal in the reduction of the debt-
service burden: they want the borrowers on a short string. But
if the string is too short, then the borrowers are not reluctant
to demand a new rearrangement.

The sharp increase in oil prices eased the problems of the oil-
exporting countries, at the cost of intensifying the problems of
the oil-importing countries. However, world inflation has eased
the problem for developing countries as a group, since the rate
of increase in prices of their exports was substantially greater
than the interest rates on their credits. The real burden of their
external debt was declining sharply, even while the nominal
value was increasing. In effect, they were floating off part of
their debt. But what was true for these countries as a group
was not true for each member of the group, and some were
still candidates for write-offs.

The Optimal Bankrupt

A country's debt-service payments cannot increase forever in
relation to export earnings; if they did, eventually all export
earnings would be required to service the debt. At some point,

the volume of the borrower's external debt must reach a ceiling relative to its export earnings. When this stage is reached, the value of the annual flow of new loans is about the same size as the debt-service payments. In effect, the receipts on the new loans are being used to finance interest and loan-reduction payments on the outstanding loans; these new loans do not bring additional commodity imports or real resources to the country. At this stage, the borrowers have an incentive to default.

The principal reason for the borrower to repay outstanding loans is to continue to be eligible for new loans. When the funds available under new loans are smaller than the debt-service payments on the existing loans, the incentive to default is high. By defaulting, the borrower reduces the debt-service payments; export earnings are now available to buy imports. And the borrower may be able to sell more new loans to eager exporters in the industrial countries.

Some of these borrowing countries are practicing the art of optimal bankruptcy. The optimal bankrupt lives well by borrowing. First the country borrows as much as it can from low-cost lenders; when that source is exhausted, the country borrows as much as possible from high-cost lenders. The borrower uses funds from new loans to pay the interest and amortization charges on outstanding loans. The only reason the country desires to service the debt at all is to protect its credit rating—its ability to borrow more. So it will continue to make payments on outstanding loans only if the flow of new loans is rising. If the country's export earnings decline sharply or if the new loan seems too small, the borrower will threaten to default. At that point, the lenders will usually offer a debt renegotiation to save themselves the embarassment of being caught with worthless loans; the borrower may demand new funds before agreeing to the renegotiation.

Of course, the optimal bankrupt knows that creditors are reluctant to throw good money after bad. But the borrower also knows the injury it might do them by defaulting. The larger the possible damage, the larger the amount of new credits the borrower can probably secure. But the larger the volume of new credits the lenders extend today, the more severe will be the borrower's debt-service problems in the future.

Some lenders might seek to avoid the embarrassment of a default by placing all future aid on a grant basis. But in that case, many of the developing countries would borrow as much as they could on subsidized export credits and loans extended for political objectives; the debt would still rise and the process would be repeated. The only constraint on the amount they *do* borrow is the amount they *can* borrow.

The irony is that attempts to make U.S. financial assistance more businesslike have made it less businesslike. And the efforts to gain an advantage for U.S. exports and the balance of payments have been largely self-defeating, since other countries have adopted similar measures. If both lender and borrowers act under the presumption that a loan is on hard terms, less can be demanded of the borrower. Stricter conditions may be attached to the use of grants.

But it is naïve to believe that changing the terms of aid could now make any great difference. The fact is that politicians in the aid-receiving countries do not have the same interests as the development planners in the donor countries and the international agencies; nor do they have the same constituencies. And so, even if the borrowers should promise—and keep their commitments—to use the external assistance wisely and frugally, domestic and other non-tied resources would still have to be used to accomplish their political interests. Why, then, do the lenders continue to be manipulated by the borrowers? The answer is that, on margin, continuing the game seems attractive: the cost of new loans always appears lower than the losses that would occur if the borrowers defaulted, for the point of no return has already been passed.

As the external debts of the developing countries mount, the obvious question is whether the debts will be repaid at all. A few countries have succeeded in repaying their international debts—France after the war with Germany in 1870 and Finland after World War I. And the reconstruction loans of various European countries after World War II have been repaid. But these repayments were all from the relatively wealthy countries. Many of the developing countries are now so poor compared to the developed countries that refinancing—and eventually some form of cancellation or forgiveness—seems inevitable. And thus the loans in all probability will eventually convert to de facto grants.

Zlotys, Rubles, and Leks

Hjalmar Schacht was Hitler's chief financial adviser, a veritable wizard of money. Indeed, the term "Schachtian policies" has become a synonym for the kind of economic polices used by a large country to exploit its smaller neighbors. Under Schacht, the Eastern European (née Balkan) countries paid above-market prices for their imports from Germany and received below-market prices for their exports to Germany.

Schacht is dead, but Schachtian policies live on. Once again, the Eastern European countries are exploited; now, however, the Soviet Union does the exploiting. And planned economies can more effectively exploit their smaller neighbors than can market economies.

Market Prices and the Planned Economy

Marxist doctrine predicts that Socialist societies will one day function without money. That day does not appear imminent. Stocks and bonds went out with the czars, and most productive assets—and many nonproductive assets—are owned by the state. But government-owned banks in the Soviet Union and in Eastern Europe produce money, workers receive part of their incomes in money payments, and most of their consumption expenditures are financed by money payments.

279

Within the West, with a few exceptions—postal services, railroad passenger services, and other government-provided goods and services—prices are set to cover costs. The heart of a market economy is the belief that a good should be produced only if the public will pay a price sufficiently high to cover its production costs. And in competitive industries, profit-maximizing firms expand output until prices fall to the level of costs. The managers of the firms make the decisions about which goods to produce and in what amounts, in response to their estimates of consumer demand.

Within planned economies, in contrast, the planners determine which goods will be produced. Then they make an independent decision about the prices at which these goods will be sold. If they set the prices too high, then the goods will pile up on the store shelves. If they set the prices too low, then queues may develop and a large number of customers will remain unsatisfied. In planned economies, selling prices cover production costs on a much smaller range of goods than in the market economies; there are more loss leaders. The planners recognize the needs of the public, although they believe that they know what the public wants better than the public does.

So many goods and services are sold at nominal prices—at prices much below their production costs. Thus housing, medical services, university education, and air transport are cheap in the Soviet Union. But not all goods can be sold at prices below their costs. Indeed, for the economy as a whole, the excess of costs over revenues in some industries must be matched by the excess of revenues over costs in other industries.

These differences in the approach to setting prices become important when the planned economies trade with market economies. Within the West, international trade reflects the decentralized decisions of numerous firms in different countries. Firms export if their costs are low enough for them to be able to undersell the domestic producers in foreign markets. And they import if foreign prices are sufficiently below the prices of domestic producers. The planned economies import and export for the same reason the market economies do—it is cheaper to import some goods and to pay for them with exports than to produce these goods domestically. So the planned economies import industrial products, raw materials, machinery, wheat, coffee, and tea, as well as goods which may be temporarily in short supply. Their exports consist largely of raw materials, a few industrial products, and securities. Like good capitalists, they are eager to borrow to finance; they need more imports than they can pay for from their current export earnings.

In the planned economies, prices are less useful as guidelines for which goods to import and which to export. If prices were used as guidelines, then the goods exported would tend to be those which are priced far below their costs, while the imported goods would be those which are sold at prices much above costs. Instead, the planners decide which goods to import and which to export. Trade decisions are centralized to fit the plan—and the breakdowns in the plan.

The Communist countries conduct their foreign trade through state trading organizations. When these countries trade with market economies, they deal at world prices, more or less; their exports must sell at or below prices of comparable Western goods, regardless of the cost of producing them. When the oil price was increased in late 1973, the Russians had little hesitation in raising the price of their oil exports, even to their friendly allies in Eastern Europe. Similarly, the planned economies must pay world prices for imports, unless they are successful in obtaining special deals, as they did with the purchase of U.S. wheat in the summer of 1972.

In Soviet trade with the countries of Eastern Europe, world prices are less relevant. Here trade involves mainly a series of bilateral exchanges—Russia may sell 1,000 3½-ton trucks to Czechoslovakia in exchange for 1,650 6-inch lathes. World prices can be attached to these barter exchanges to determine whether Czechoslovakia and the other Eastern European countries get a better deal than if they had sold their products at world prices.

The Eastern Europeans believe the prices they pay the Soviet Union for their imports are generally higher than what they get for the same goods in the world market. And the prices they receive on their exports are generally below those they might receive in the world market. Paying more for imports and receiving less for exports is what Schachtian policies are all about. And the Rumanians and Bulgarians participate in these policies in the 1960s and 1970s for the same reason they did in the 1930s.

The Ruble Is a Heavy Currency

The Russian currency—the ruble—and the currencies of other Eastern European countries are not included in the world hit parade of currencies, since individuals are not free to sell rubles and zlotys against dollars, Swiss francs, or marks. Transactions in Western currencies by residents of Eastern countries are strictly controlled. Individuals do not buy or sell rubles because they expect that the ruble may be devalued or revalued in terms of the dollar or of gold. Comparisons of interest rates on bank deposits in the Soviet Union and the United States are not meaningful, since the interest rates on financial assets in Communist countries are not market prices.

When the Russians and other Eastern Europeans export, they are paid in dollars, marks, or some other major currency; they are apt to deposit these funds in the Moscow Narodny Bank in London or in another Western branch of one of the Russian banks. Similarly, when they import, they write checks against their deposit balances. Trade with the nonplanned economies is conducted in one of the Western currencies, largely because Western firms would not have the incentive to hold the ruble or the means to sell it.

282

Perhaps a better indication of the Russian position in finance are the large grain purchases in 1972 and again in 1975. Bad harvests—and bad management—necessitated large grain imports. The wheat came from the United States as the residual supplier. Whenever harvests have been poor, such wheat deals have been necessary. Part of the imports has been financed by credit, part by sale of gold. In bad crop years (1965 and 1972), Soviet gold sales are unusually large (see Table 18–1); such sales are last-resort financing.

TABLE 18–1

Soviet Gold Production

(in millions of dollars at $35 per ounce)

YEAR	PRODUCTION	DOMESTIC USE	SALES	RESERVES
1965	175	34	556	1,030
1966	183	36	—	1,177
1967	196	36	15	1,322
1968	204	39	12	1,475
1969	209	42	—	1,642
1970	230	45	—	1,827
1971	248	45	23	2,007
1972	285	46	170	2,076
1973	298	47	340	1,987
1974	308	48	114–228	2,019–2,133

SOURCE: U.S. Government.

Nevertheless, the Russians fantasize that the ruble is at the top of the hit parade—this is their money-market counterpart to inventing the sewing machine. The ruble needs a price in terms of the dollar, the mark, sterling, and other Western currencies. Foreign embassies in the Communist countries need the local currencies, and so do foreign tourists. Moreover, a peg is necessary for the ruble; it cannot float in the exchange market because the necessary conditions—that buyers and sellers meet freely to exchange national monies—are not present. Since no Western country has been willing to peg its currency to the ruble, the Russians must peg the ruble to a monetary asset used in the West.

In 1937 the ruble was pegged to the U.S. dollar at 4 rubles to $1. During the cold war, the Russians did not appreciate the implied dependence on the dollar. So in 1950 the ruble was pegged to gold at a rate of 140 rubles per ounce of gold. Actually, the peg might have been 100 or 200 rubles per ounce; in the Soviet Union the gold price has no significance in determining how much gold is produced, what it is used for, or when it is sold abroad. But once the ruble was pegged to gold, a ruble-dollar exchange rate could be readily calculated. Given the U.S. gold parity of $35, the exchange rate was still 4 rubles to the dollar.

In 1961 the Soviet Union underwent a currency reform, largely to tax speculative hoarders of rubles. All outstanding ruble notes were declared worthless and had to be exchanged for new notes at the rate of 1 new ruble for 10 old rubles. At the same time, the Russians set a gold parity for the new ruble at 32 rubles per ounce. Then the exchange rate between the new ruble and the U.S. dollar could be readily calculated as the ratio of the price of 1 ounce of gold in terms of each currency. And so the new rate was $1.11 U.S. = 1 ruble.

Now the ruble was worth more than the dollar—or at least so it seemed. Since the ruble price of gold has no economic significance, the Russians in effect had first decided on the dollar-ruble exchange rate they wanted, then set the ruble price of gold accordingly. If they had set a gold parity for the new ruble at 7 rubles per ounce, the exchange rate would have been $5 U.S. to 1 ruble; with a gold parity of 1 new ruble to the ounce the exchange rate would have been $35 U.S. to 1 ruble.

The currency reform at the ratio of 10 old rubles for 1 new ruble suggests that all ruble prices should have fallen by a factor of 10; each new ruble would then be 10 times as valuable as each old ruble. Thus, the ruble price of gold should have fallen from 140 rubles per ounce to 14 rubles; the dollar-ruble exchange rate would then have been $2.50 U.S. per ruble. But in terms of purchasing power, the ruble would have been grossly overvalued. So the Russians used the commotion of the currency reform as a smoke screen to devalue the ruble in terms of the dollar from 1 ruble = $2.50 U.S. to 1 ruble = $1.11 U.S., an increase in the ruble price of the dollar of 125 percent.

This dollar-ruble exchange rate was largely symbolic: no private holder of rubles could buy dollars at this price, and it was unlikely that many holders of dollars would buy rubles. Since Soviet trade with the West consists largely of swapping bundles of exports for bundles of imports, the exchange rate was irrelevant for balancing Soviet payments and receipts with other countries.

When the dollar price of gold was increased in 1971 and 1973, the ruble got heavier relative to the dollar, since the public price of gold was unchanged. Moscow gloated. But the Russians had an exchange rate problem; they had to decide whether to peg to the dollar, thereby allowing their currency to float in terms of the mark, the Swiss franc, and sterling, or to join the snake, allowing their currency to float in terms of the dollar and sterling. One thing was clear. They could not rely on market forces to bail them out; the planners had to make a decision. So they tended to stick with gold and continued to revalue the ruble in terms of the dollar, first by 8 percent at the end of 1971, then by nearly 10 percent in early 1973. The ruble was getting respectable.

The Zloty Is Not a Heavy Currency

In Western terms, the ruble and other Eastern European currencies are greatly overvalued; their purchasing power is much less, at the official exchange rates, than that of Western currencies. Because the exchange rates in the Soviet Union and other Eastern European countries are so out of line with market reality, their governments have set up a special exchange market for tourist transactions where the rates are half or less than half the official rate. Because of exchange controls, a black market has developed in U.S. dollars. The premium in the black markets—the percentage spread between the black market rates and the official rates—varies from 200 to 400 percent. Thus, the official rate for the Bulgarian lev is $1 = 1.2 leva, the tourist rate is $1 = 2 leva, and the black market rate is about $1 = 4 leva. The official rate for the Albanian lek is 5 leks = $1, the tourist rate is 12.5 leks = $1. The black market rates suggest how unreal the official rates are (see Table 18–1). That the exchange rates for tourists from capitalist countries may be 150 to 250 percent higher than those for tourists from Socialist countries is one indication that each Eastern European country recognizes how grossly overvalued are the currencies of its neighbors.

Table 18–2

Exchange Rates of Eastern European Currencies
(currency units per U.S. dollar in 1974)

COUNTRY	CURRENCY	BASIC RATE	TOURIST RATES		BLACK MARKET RATE
			SOCIAL-IST	CAPITAL-IST	
Albania	lek	4.14	6.25	10.25	33.00
Bulgaria	lev	1.97	.58	1.65	2.30
Czechoslovakia	koruna	5.97	7.20	9.71	21.25
East Germany	mark	1.842	2.39	2.52	9.15
Hungary	forint	9.148	9.78	23.35	32.15
Poland	zloty	3.32	11.42	33.20	85.85
Rumania	leu	4.97	6.20	14.38	26.15
Soviet Union	ruble	0.746	—	—	2.72

SOURCES: Franz Pick, *Pick's Currency Yearbook* (New York: Pick Publishing Corporation, 1974); *International Currency Review*.

Note: The black market rate is approximate.

The Ruble-Dollar Seesaw

Occasionally, the Eastern European countries make a cautious move toward freer trade relations with the Western countries, a move which may or may not be associated with an increased role for market-determined prices in their economies. Yugoslavia has gone much further in this direction than the others. Thus, Yugoslavia belongs to the International Monetary Fund and has sought to make its currency convertible. The Yugoslav dinar is readily traded, and Yugoslavs can hold foreign currencies and travel abroad. The foreign exchange value for the dinar is set at a level which—together with a variety of import controls—balances Yugoslavia's payments and receipts with the rest of the world. Several extremely large devaluations of the dinar were necessary in the early stages of Yugoslavia's opening to the West. Czechoslovakia was moving in the same direction when the Russians returned to Prague in the summer of 1968. In time, other countries in Eastern Europe may also move toward greater decentralization of decision making, although a substantial easing of restrictions and moves to greater payments freedom will require extensive devaluations of their currencies.

From time to time, the Russians and other Eastern Europeans, stimulated or threatened by the success of the European Economic Community, announce plans for a common market of their own. For planned economies, a common market might mean free trade; stores and factories in each country could import from foreign sources as well as domestic sources. But this approach would require that each factory know the foreign as well as the domestic demand for its product. A common market for planned economies would require integration of the planning systems of the member countries.

The exchange rate relationship between the Soviet Union

and its Eastern bloc neighbors would have little significance once the planning systems were integrated. The currencies of other Eastern European countries—the Polish zloty, the Hungarian forint, the Romanian leu, the Albanian lek—have parities, usually expressed in terms of gold or occasionally in terms of the Russian ruble. Actually, the statement of a parity in terms of gold (like the ruble's parity in terms of gold) is meaningless, since there are no gold transactions. But the exchange rate for the zloty in terms of the ruble might be computed from the parity of each of these currencies in terms of gold. Given the parity of the Polish zloty in terms of the dollar—about 4 zlotys to $1—and the ruble-dollar rate of 1 ruble = $1.11, the price of the ruble in terms of the zloty should be 4.2 zlotys to the ruble. But the Poles peg the zloty at 13.8 zlotys to the ruble.

Zlotys are cheap in terms of rubles, and that's good for the Russians. Nearly all of the Eastern European currencies are cheap in terms of the ruble, which is even better for the Russians. The foreign exchange costs of the Russian diplomatic establishment in Eastern Europe—the thirty-eight divisions of the Russian Army that sit between the Vistula and the Oder—are thus reduced.

Poland collects a large supply of rubles from its sale of zlotys to the Russians. And these rubles are used to settle imbalances in the barter trade—to pay for Russian oil and steel. The exchange rate structure is favorable to the Soviet Union and costly to the smaller Eastern European countries. Capitalism may have gone out with the czars, but imperialism did not.

Barter, Credits, and Détente

Moscow has a Pepsi-Cola franchise, as well as one or two branches of New York banks. Pepsi has arranged a barter deal; it will import a Russian vodka to the United States. The U.S. demand for vodka has been growing more rapidly than that for gin, Scotch, and bourbon; it remains to be seen whether the Russian demand for Pepsi will grow as rapidly.

Pepsi for vodka is only the frosting on a much larger cake: the extensive efforts to facilitate industrial growth in the Eastern bloc. Fiat put up a massive automobile plant, and the Russians have already begun to export the Russian Fiat—not to be confused with the Polish Fiat or the Spanish Fiat or the Fiat Fiat. Mack Trucks is involved in a similar program to build a turn-key truck factory. For numerous other industrial products, Western firms have built the Soviet plants from scratch and trained the local managers.

In a few cases, the Eastern Europeans have paid by exports; in many cases, however, credits available from the West have been the financing mechanism. The Hungarians, the Poles, and other Easterners have been nibbling at the fringes of the Euro-currency market; at the end of 1974, their outstanding borrowings totaled about $32 billion.

Much the largest source of financing has been the Western governments, which have been eager to promote exports—and the employment associated with such exports. While the same credits might have been used to finance investments in the industrial countries, the demand was inadequate; there were enough automobile and steel plants in the West already.

Major questions involve how large these debts might become and whether there is any likelihood of default. The problems that individual lenders have in getting repaid should be distinguished from the problem of repayment of lenders as a group. The Soviet Union and the other Communist economies are almost certain to repay promptly as long as they wish to maintain their credit ratings. So the funds from new loans will be used to repay outstanding loans. At some stage, however, these lenders may decide that the outstanding debts of these countries are too large, or the Communist countries may decide they no longer wish to increase their debts.

If they are to reduce the total volume of their debts to the Western countries, then their exports must increase relative to their imports. Will the Western countries be willing to take these imports? And what incentive will these countries have to repay their debt after they no longer wish to borrow?

PART III

Epilogue

 19

Fitting the Pieces Once Again

Someday, perhaps, the international money problem will disappear. Perhaps the nation-state will be phased out as the basic political unit. Or independent countries may merge their currencies into a common international currency.

Neither event, however, seems imminent. Over the last fifty years the number of countries has increased sharply, as colonial empires have broken up. Nearly all the newly independent countries have opted for their own currency, and some of them have gradually moved to monetary policies directed at their domestic objectives. And many other countries that have long been independent have oriented their monetary policies to domestic objectives.

The nation-state appears unlikely to be phased out in the foreseeable future as the basic unit for organizing political activity—for supplying law and order and deciding on income distribution and economic priorities. Nor is there any indication of a broad-based movement toward the merger of monies. While there are plans for economic and monetary integration in Western Europe, such moves are far from complete. And this plan stands alone. No other group of nations seems close to planning seriously for a common currency.

A merger of national monies makes economic sense only if the economic structures of the participating countries are similar —if their business cycles have similar phasing, if their labor forces grow at a similar rate and are similar in terms of skills, and so forth. Even then, vested interests, both economic and political, would strongly oppose the merger. For the demand for a national money is closely linked with the exercise of sovereignty. Control over the growth of the money supply is one of the most effective measures available to government leaders as they seek increased support from their constituencies.

National monetary policies result from political forces within individual countries. For this reason, prices rise more rapidly in some countries than in others. So payments imbalances are inevitable. Usually the countries with the most rapid increases in prices incur payments deficits. Eventually adjustments are needed to restore the payments balance. Either exchange rates must change, or else some other variable that will balance international payments and receipts must be altered.

Inevitably, the anticipation of changes in the exchange rate leads to conflicts, for profit-oriented business firms, anticipating these changes, seek to achieve profits or at least avoid losses from the realignment. But if these firms as a group earn profits, they impose losses on the central banks. And these shifts of speculative funds sometimes take the initiative away from the authorities; they may be forced to alter their exchange rate, economic controls, or monetary policies earlier than they had planned. Moreover, authorities in the deficit countries and in the surplus countries are frequently at odds with each other about who should take the initiative in reducing the imbalance. And they also disagree about the best policies to use in reducing imbalances and on whether to rely on market forces or on bureaucratic decisions.

The increasing domestic focus on national monetary policies led to the breakdown and collapse of the IMF rules. These rules were a guide to national behavior: they indicated when countries could change their exchange rates and when they couldn't, and when they could use controls on international payments and when they couldn't. The purpose of the rules was to ensure that in attempting to solve its own economic problems, a country would not dump the problems in the laps of its neighbors.

If new rules are not devised, the system will increasingly rely on ad hoc approaches to problems. Then each country will adopt the measures that suit its immediate needs and interests, with minimal regard for the external consequences. The new rules must provide for greater flexibility among national currency areas; they must find a happy balance between enabling countries to follow policies appropriate for their domestic objectives and minimizing the possibility that some will pursue "beggar thy neighbor" policies and complicate the price, employment, or payments problems of other countries.

Designing the arrangement most likely to work requires foreknowledge of the types of economic problems that are likely to be dominant in the next five, ten, and twenty years. Unemployment? Inflation? Unemployment and inflation simultaneously? Will recessions and booms occur at the same time in the United States and Western Europe, or will they occur at different times? Will nationalism continue to become more powerful? And what about national attitudes toward market forces and bureaucratic regulation? The types of rules most likely to be effective vary as the set of answers to these questions varies.

One frequently mentioned alternative to new rules is to rely on authority: to endow those who manage the international monetary institutions—the IMF and its successors—with the power to make the necessary decisions. But this approach seems untimely, for one counterpart to the increased attention to domestic objectives is that most countries are increasingly reluctant to delegate substantial decision-making power to an international institution; they fear constraints on their domestic policies. Almost inevitably, the important decisions are likely to be made in national capitals. The managers of international institutions are going to be responsible to committees of representatives from national capitals; in other words, the managers may police the rules, but they will not set the rules, nor will they determine when the exchange rates must be changed, or by how much.

Crises—especially about changes in exchange rates—are inevitable in a multiple-currency world. While U.S. authorities, German authorities, and many economists favor floating exchange rates, many countries, especially the smaller ones, appear committed to a return to pegged rates. And the more important foreign trade is in a country's economy, the stronger this commitment is. The United States and Germany believe that a return to pegged rates will impose constraints and complicate the attainment of their employment and price level objectives.

The alternative to changes in exchange rates as a way to balance international payments and receipts is direct regulation of international payments. One attraction of this approach to the authorities is that the political costs are smaller. The objection to the controls approach is that it fragments the international economy, especially if relatively few transactions are controlled. The more comprehensive the controls over imports and exports of goods as well as securities, the more nearly this approach is equivalent to a change in the exchange rate. The distinction is that the bureaucrats rather than market forces determine when the controls must be changed. But while academicians can talk about the attractions of controls as long as they are comprehensive, the bureaucrats and politicians are likely to find compelling reasons for numerous exceptions to comprehensive controls. Eventually, the rules must deal with the issue: what are the acceptable forms of controls, when can they be used, and how do they relate to changes in exchange rates?

The greater uncertainties involve the future supply of international money—the monetary role of gold, the international role of the U.S. dollar, and reliance on paper gold. As long as foreign central banks hold more than $150 billion of liquid dollar assets, the U.S. Treasury will remain reluctant to agree to convert the dollar into other international monies.

Either gold will be demonetized or its price will be raised. Gold demonetization could occur passively; the gold parity might remain at $42 without any transactions taking place. Gold transactions among central banks would decline. Central banks in deficit would sell their gold in the commodity markets, rather than at the monetary price. But such sales are likely to be minimal until the conviction spreads that gold will be demonetized.

The gradual demonetization of gold is very likely to require agreement on a comprehensive arrangement to produce a new international money; otherwise the system would be subject to a severe shortage of international money. The paradox is that the decline in credibility resulting from U.S. gold demonetization may make it more difficult to obtain agreement on alternatives. In any negotiations the Europeans would be preoccupied with the concern that if the United States could effectively demonetize gold, it might also "demonetize" the new international money by refusing to buy the money in exchange for dollars.

The alternative to gold demonetization—a worldwide increase in the price of gold—seems less impractical and unlikely than it did several years ago, even though most economists and editorial writers wish to be rid of the barbarous relic. While the continued use of gold as money may be barbarous, the continued demand for gold reflects the fact that some countries lack faith in the commitments of other countries. And so they put more value in a commodity money than in a paper money. Their decision may be wise or unwise—but it *is* their decision. Objections to a higher gold price are varied: the left wants to burn South Africa, and the right wants to burn the Soviet Union. But these criticisms are largely political rather than economic. Relatively little attention is given to the implications of a higher gold price (or of gold demonetization) for the monetary system. And while taking gold out of the mines of South Africa to bury it again in the vaults of central banks is stupid, at least those who want gold pay the costs.

An increase in the gold price means more gold would be available to satisfy the monetary demand. And so, for a few years, much of the annual demand for an increase in the international money could be satisfied from gold production. The increase in the monetary value of existing gold holdings would enable central banks to move toward the preferred combination of gold, dollars, and SDRs in their international money holdings. Obviously, an increase in the gold price will not resolve all international monetary problems in perpetuity. No price can be fixed forever. An increase in the gold price will be necessary as long as there is a gold shortage—and as long as gold remains in the system.

A U.S. initiative to increase the world gold price has some strong arguments in its favor. Many Europeans prefer this solution, and they would bear nearly all the economic costs. There may even be some favorable impacts on the relationship between the dollar and other currencies as a result of gold revaluation, for the ratio of U.S. gold holdings to foreign holdings of dollars would increase.

The European preferences are conditioned by the monetary events of the last decade and especially by their dependence on the United States—and their interpretation of this dependence. The countries in Western Europe want greater control over their own monetary policies. But their attitudes are ambivalent; these countries want to achieve payments surpluses while ensuring that the United States does not have a deficit. Such attitudes are inconsistent. And they want to achieve price stability while maintaining pegged exchange rates, two objectives which are consistent only if the United States achieves price stability. Perhaps the United States will. But U.S. price-level performance will almost certainly be determined by U.S. needs, not by European needs. And the U.S. price-level performance is not likely to be affected by whether gold remains in the monetary system.

Just as no price can be fixed forever, so no currency is likely to be at the top of the hit parade forever. The shift from dollars into gold and to other currencies in 1970 and 1971, a result of U.S. inflation and speculation against the dollar, may suggest that the dollar's tenure as the top currency may be over. Yet the shift from dollars may have been short-term and not long-term, no more than an anticipation of the change in the exchange rate.

Political pressure will certainly develop to diminish the international role of the dollar. Foreign countries do not like the asymmetry of having to revalue or devalue their currency relative to the dollar. In effect, they hope that a revision of the arrangements might protect them from U.S. inflation; they hope either for an external constraint on U.S. policy, perhaps in the form of a limited amount of gold to finance payments deficits, or for a U.S. initiative in reducing its deficits. The move toward a paper gold arrangement is in effect a political device to provide more of an external constraint on the United States—to reduce the impact of U.S. policies on other countries. The political route is taken because economic forces are still likely to keep the dollar in the top spot.

This conflict is not unusual; it is what the international money game is all about. National interests conflict, on both major issues and minor issues, and the bureaucrats and politicians see their own roles as requiring that they achieve gains for their constituents. So each will agree to modify institutional arrangements only if their constituents gain. The conflict is inevitable as long as there are national monies; while changes in the rules and structure may shift the thrust of the conflict, they cannot eliminate it. So the varied solutions—eliminating gold, raising the gold price, relying on paper, letting exchange rates float—do not eliminate the conflict; they merely change its nature and timing.

INDEX

Index

Index

International monetary authority: problems inherent in, 163–65

International Monetary Fund (IMF), 7, 159; exchange crises and rules of, 54; money produced by, 24 (*see also* Special Drawing Rights); national monetary policies and, 294–95; and new international money, 40–41; objectives of rules of, 170; and OPEC, 236; Yugoslavia in, 287

International Monetary Fund Articles of Agreement, *see* Bretton Woods System

International money: central bank needs in, 22, 37, 107–08; end of pound sterling as, 108–12; gold as, 22–24, 77, 88–90; IMF and new, 40–41; problems of adopting, 164–65; proposals for, 162–69; U.S. as producer of, 105; as unlikely prospect, 166

International money supply, 22–28; forcing U.S. deficit, 39, 40; growth of, 30–31, 35–37; in international financial system, 22–28; short (post–World War I), 32; uncertainty over, 296–97

International regulation of external currency market, 124–27

International Settlements, Bank for, 7

Interest rates: borrowing costs and low, 97; capital market and, low, 255–56; on dollar bonds, 254; on Eurodollar deposits (1969, 1970, 1971), 124; export credit arrangements and, 269; on financial assets, 99–101; and growth of Eurodollar market, 122; national money and higher domestic loan, 99; rise in, in national currencies (1960s), 106; taxes and bank, 196

Intervention assets, defined, 22

Investors Overseas Services, Ltd. (IOS), 215–28

Iran, 230, 271, 272

Israel, 20

Italian banks, 210

Italian lira, 5; *see also* Eurodollar market

Italy, 88; corporate tax rate in, 188; dollar holdings of (1960s, 1970s), 42; fall of stock prices in (1961), 223; government holdings in, 139; IOS and, 218; market value of equities in, 220; new international money and, 40; and OPEC, 235, 241; threatened with bankruptcy, 299

Jamaica, 164, 250

Jamaican dollars, 95

Japan: bureaucracy in, 136; dollar holdings of (1960s, 1970s), 42; floating rate used in, 15; foreign banks in, 208; nationalist bias of, 139; and oil price increase (1973), 229–30; and OPEC, 237, 239–41; payment surpluses in, 41; price increases in (1970s), 143

Japan, Bank of, 15–16, 46, 170; approach of, to exchange rate, 66; revaluation losses of, 48

Japanese banks, 210

Japanese firms, 244, 246, 258

Japanese yen, 170; anticipated revaluing of, 27; assets in, 102; crisis in (1972), 5; floated (1973), 46; as international money, 110; new parity for, 44–45; revalued, 3, 42; supply growth in, 152–53, 165, 169; yen price of dollar, 6; *see also* Eurodollar market

Johnson, Lyndon B., 83, 133

Index

Index

Index

Index

United States firms, 247–48, 258; *see also* Multinational firms

United States payment imbalance, *see* Payments imbalance

United States Treasury, 167, 269; holdings in gold (1949–1960), 79–80; interest rates on debt of, 197; and retaining gold in monetary system, 89; and threat of dollar devaluation (1960s), 81

Value: gold as store of, 77

Venezuela, 208, 230, 247, 250

Vietnam war: inflation from, 41–43, 59–60, 105, 133–34, 143

Washington, George, 29

West Germany, 88, 105, 172; currency of, *see* German marks; dollar holdings of (1960s, 1970s), 42; dollar standard and, 106; fall of stock prices in (1961–1969), 233; floating-rate and, 170; foreign subsidiaries in, 250–51; gold purchase and level of U.S. troops in, 39; government intervention in, 136; induced to buy U.S. military equipment, 38; IOS and, 218, 219, 223, 225–26; labor and inflation paranoia in, 134; market value of equities in, 220; monetary policy of, 154; and monetary reform, 131–32; money supply growth in, 153; new international money and, 40; OPEC and, 237, 239–41; payment surpluses in, 41; per capita income in, compared with British, 154; price increases in (1970s), 143–44; raises price of mark (1961, 1969, 1971), 3–4; taxes in, 187–88

Westminster (bank), 210

Wholesale commodity prices: doubling (1940s), 79

Wholesale price index increase, 152; 1914–1970, 79; 1970–1973, 108

Wilson, Harold, 56

Wood, Gen. Leonard, 251

World Bank, 229, 265; international loans and, 269, 270

World War I: financing, 129; gold standard relevance reduced by, 31; inflation and, 31–32; monetary policies during, 20–21

World War II: gold glut and inflation during, 79; monetary policies during, 21

Yom Kippur War, 236

Yugoslav dinars, 287

Yugoslavia, 247, 287

Zambia, 168

312